these are the
ENDANGERED

these are the

drawings by Bob Hines

Distributed by Stackpole Books
Cameron and Kelker Streets
Harrisburg, Pennsylvania 17105

ENDANGERED

text by Charles Cadieux

THE STONE WALL PRESS, INC.
241 30th Street, N.W.
Washington, D.C. 20007

Published June 1981
Second Printing–January 1982

LIBRARY OF CONGRESS CATALOGING IN PUBLICATION DATA

Library of Congress
Catalogue Card No. 80–54448
Cadieux, Charles
  These are the Endangered
Wash., D.C.: Stone Wall Press, Inc.
8105   801117

ISBN 0–913276–35–9

Illustration Credits

Cover—Drawings by Bob Hines

Front Matter—Drawings by Bob Hines

Chapter 1— Drawing by Bob Hines

Chapter 2— Drawing by Bob Hines
>Photo courtesy U.S. Fish & Wildlife Service—Luther C. Goldman

Chapter 3— Drawing by Bob Hines
>Photo courtesy of Michigan Dept. of Natural Resources

Chapter 4— Photos courtesy of Florida Power and Light Company

Chapter 5— Drawing by Bob Hines
>Photo courtesy of U.S. Fish & Wildlife Service—Fred Sibley

Chapter 6— Drawing by Bob Hines
>Photo courtesy of U.S. Fish & Wildlife Service—Steve Hillebrand

Chapter 7— Drawing by Bob Hines
>Photo by Conrad N. Hillman

Chapter 8— Drawing by Bob Hines
>Photo courtesy of U.S. Fish & Wildlife Service—K. Stansell

Chapter 10— Drawing by Bob Hines

Photo of applying tags to a manatee courtesy of U.S. Fish & Wildlife Service—Charles Smith

Chapter 12— Photo courtesy of U.S. Fish & Wildlife Service—William Julian

Chapter 13— Drawing by Bob Hines

Chapter 14— Drawing by Bob Hines

Chapter 16— Drawing by Bob Hines

Chapter 19— Photo courtesy Bureau of Sport Fisheries & Wildlife—Luther C. Goldman

Chapter 20— Drawing by Bob Hines

Chapter 21— Drawings by Bob Hines

Chapter 22— Drawings by Bob Hines
>Photo courtesy of D.H. Ellis

Chapter 24— Photo courtesy of U.S. Fish & Wildlife Service—P.W. Sykes, Jr.

Chapter 25— Photo courtesy of U.S. Fish & Wildlife Service—Sanford Wilbur

Chapter 26— Photo courtesy Bureau of Sport Fisheries & Wildlife—Luther Goldman

Chapter 27— Photo courtesy of U.S. Fish & Wildlife Service—Dr. Robert Thomas

Chapter 28— Drawing by Bob Hines

Chapter 31— Photo courtesy Bureau of Sport Fisheries & Wildlife—Luther Goldman

Chapter 33— Photo courtesy of U.S. Fish & Wildlife Service—Rex Gary Schmidt

Chapter 34— Photo courtesy of U.S. Fish & Wildlife Service—Luther Goldman

Chapter 35— Drawing by Bob Hines

Chapter 40— Drawing by Bob Hines

Chapter 43— Photo courtesy of Bureau of Sport Fisheries & Wildlife—W. H. Julian

Chapter 47— Drawing by Bob Hines

Table of Contents

Preface

None among the world's nations devotes more attention and resources, including money, to fish and wildlife conservation than does the United States. Much good has been and is being accomplished.

Despite this record, however, some species became extinct. In most instances, this occurred before the emergence of natural resource agencies or before they were well enough equipped to respond. Today the agencies are better prepared—legally, financially and technically—to counter endangerment situations.

The endangerment of animals—its causes and corrections—is the subject of this book. Case histories of well-known endangered species illustrate the author's recommendations.

This is a book of hope, not futility. It shows that a determined society, possessed of knowledge, understanding, patience and funding, can ease, at least in the United States, endangerment's threat to interesting, unique and irreplaceable fish and wildlife populations.

Daniel A. Poole, President
Wildlife Management Institute

Montana Grayling

1

These Are The Endangered

A Brontosaurus more than fifty feet long crawled out of the black ooze and sprawled on the sandbar. He was sick unto death. His labored breathing grew weaker as the sun rose in the morning sky. As the heat of full day baked his huge bulk, his skin dried and cracked with splits of more than a foot showing in his swollen sides, yet he showed no sign of movement until well into the afternoon. Suddenly, his huge body thrashed in wild convulsion. He lifted his neck and struggled to regain his feet; then he dropped back to the hot sand. His breathing slowly became weaker—then stopped. The huge animal was dead.

Five hundred yards downstream, my wife and I parked our motor coach beside the Green River in Utah to begin our camping vacation. We were thankful that millions of years had elapsed since the dinosaur's passing. In fact, there was a gap of many million years between the passage of the dinosaurs and the appearance of a humanoid who could be considered as a possible ancestor to the Cadieux human who camped in Utah. I am content that we do not inhabit a world which shelters dinosaurs. It would be very inconvenient to have to dodge *Tyrannosaurus Rex* on my way to work in the morning. Frankly, I'm just as happy that the dinosaurs became extinct.

The extinction of a species, or group of species, is nothing new. It has been going on as long as there has been life on this planet of ours. Species come and go as they always have with the orderly evolution of life forms. Neither good nor bad, this action of species' creation and species' extermination is as much a part of life on our planet as is the rising and setting of the sun, or the changing of the seasons. Such creation and extermination of species is part of the routine of life by which nature rearranges its supply of building blocks: the genes and chromosomes which determine the nature of a species and, to a lesser extent, the actions of a species.

The principles of evolution were sketched by Charles Darwin after his epic voyage in the *Beagle*. As Darwin watched the seagoing iguanas on the Galápagos Islands, he marvelled at the way nature was able to rearrange genes and chromosomes to develop new birds and animals adapted to the situation they faced in their particular environmental niche. The iguana was a seagoing animal in the marine environment of the Galápagos Islands; on the Baja California peninsula, the iguana became a cactus-climbing desert dweller

1

who didn't see water for months at a time. In the tropical rain forest of Mexico, the iguana became arboreal and fond of fresh water in abundance. This was simply a rearranging and shifting of the blocks of life, in infinite variety; for as long as all of the building blocks are available, there are infinite possibilities for their arrangement. When even one building block is gone, however, the mathematical reduction in the number of possible combinations is startling.

It was this rearranging of building blocks which first brought *Homo sapiens* down out of the trees. It was this rearranging which enabled *Homo sapiens* to pick up a rock and cheerfully bash in the skull of his neighbor. By so doing, he became a tool user. In some anthropological systems, the ability to use tools defines the higher anthropoids and becomes a definition of man. The discovery that some birds and lower primates use tools, however, has dimmed the appeal of this "tool users are humans" theory in the past hundred years.

Certainly there were many failures along the path of possible combination and recombination of building blocks which led us up out of the mists of eons past and made us the successful life form we are today.

We have been much too successful.

Whether evolution was the result of trial and error over millennia or the result of an omniscient decision by an omnipotent Creator is really not relevant to our discussion. According to the Bible, there were only eight people on earth after the flood. They were Noah and his three sons, and their four wives. None of the women were named in the Biblical account—Women's Lib had a long way to go in those days. Now it must be apparent that these eight humans were the sole repository of the building blocks by which the process of evolution had to go forward. God said "Go forth and populate the Earth and I will give you dominion over the birds of the air and the fishes of the sea and the animals of the land," (or words to that effect, depending upon which version of the Bible you favor).

Did we obey the Divine command? There are now nearly five billion humans on this planet, so we certainly have "gone forth and populated the earth." How about the second part of the Lord's mandate? How have we succeeded in our dominion over all other species?

We have done very badly. We have failed to recognize that the right of dominion does not carry with it the right to exterminate.

Scientists tell us that life was first created by a lucky combination of an electric spark, proteins and amino acids. In the ages since that spark started, many different life forms have been dominant over other life forms. Surely we cannot believe that other forms of life stood up to the fearsome tooth-studded jaws of *Tyrannosaurus Rex?* Yet he disappeared. Was he unable to cope with cataclysmic changes in climate? Or did some tiny life form, perhaps a parasite, bring him down? We do not know.

Probably there was a time when the trilobite was a dominant form of life on the planet. Its existence without change must have signalled that it was a successful life form, evidenced by the fact that experimentation stopped in its case—stopped for lack of a need to improve.

It is possible that many life forms have taken turns being dominant over other

2

life forms. It is also possible that some of these dominations persisted for longer than man has been on the planet. We cannot know.

We do know that man has been the only life form which has exercised complete dominion over all other life forms, and this is the first time that this terrible responsibility has ever fallen on one species. Today, man holds the power of life or death over every single species of life on this small planet—including his own! Many species have become extinct as a result of man's actions and inactions. If we look at it all from the viewpoint of the ten thousand other life forms, the dominion of man has not been good.

There is nothing we can do about the mistakes of the past, just as there is nothing we can do about the seemingly random experimentation with life's building blocks which nature carried out before we arrived on the scene and will continue to carry out after we have departed. Our purpose here is to take a look at the very short span of time that man has been dominant on the North American continent.

Our activities in this field must be viewed against the magnificent tapestry of 600 million years of natural gene arrangement and rearrangement. Yet that tapestry furnishes only the backdrop—it does not change our responsibility for our actions. Because we cannot alter the past and because we cannot dictate to nature, we will not concern ourselves with the evolutionary loss of species; we will, rather, take a look just at our own record during the past few hundred years.

That record shows a calamitous callousness in our disregard of the needs of other life forms; it also shows an amazing solicitude for these needs.

Our record includes the extirpation of the passenger pigeon. The passage of this numerous species once blocked out the sun. Although there is a claim that the last passenger pigeon died in a Cincinnati zoo in 1914, the passing of this species was unnoticed. But our record also includes the tremendous effort put forth to save the whooping crane from extinction. Between the loss of the passenger pigeon and the beginning of the fight to save the whooper, an amazing reversal of public awareness occurred.

Writing about those passenger pigeons, Aldo Leopold said, "For one species to mourn the death of another is a new thing under the sun. We, who have lost our pigeons, mourn the loss. Had the funeral been ours, the pigeons would hardly have mourned us. In this fact, rather than in nylons and atomic bombs, lies evidence of our superiority over the beasts."

Such mourning is based upon sentimentality, or perhaps upon a feeling of guilt. We can hold ourselves in high esteem because we harbor such feelings, but there is another, much more compelling reason for our concern. Our own survival is surely at stake. Wildlife functions as a Distant Early Warning system for mankind. If the world is dangerous for the Kirtland's warbler, is it safe for humans? If the environment is so full of noxious chemicals that the brown pelican is unable to manufacture a shell for its precious egg, are we not affected by those chemicals? Perhaps we might worry that all life forms are being eliminated, the weak and defenseless first, the stronger to die at a later date. Are we headed inexorably into a day when there will be only carp in our

3

polluted waters, only Norway rats upon our lands, only vultures gliding through the poisonous fumes of a sick planet—and finally, only the planet itself, silent and dead, perhaps to await again the fortuitous spark of electricity on amino acids and proteins, a hundred million years from now?

In the eons past, the only way one species could harm another was by overt action (killing and eating) or by destroying the young of the next generation. Now, however, man is able to destroy entire generations of species without knowing he has destroyed anything. Now the byproducts of man's plastic life, long after they have been cast side, can kill species. PCB's injected into an uncomplaining environment continue to kill fish in rivers hundreds of miles downstream and kill birds in other continents—long after man has ceased using them, and long after it is possible to trace the source of the lethal substance.

Like the caged canary which the miner once carried into the underground shaft in a test for the presence of deadly methane, all life forms on this planet are carried willy-nilly, and without choice, as captives on a finite globe, into a future which only mankind determines.

In the following pages, we will look at what has happened to the species which the Almighty gave mankind dominion over. Perhaps by studying what has happened, we will be able to prevent further catastrophes. Perhaps, by watching the fate of defenseless warblers and of fish which cannot escape their environment, we can learn to control our own actions. Thus, we might escape the final judgement—the extinction of humans on a planet which we fouled past the point of survival. Perhaps we can prevent death by our own carelessness, and the subsequent loss of the important building blocks which might lead to a finer, better race of humans, or suprahumans, as evolution continues to experiment for another hundred million years.

Let us take a look at how North American species have fared under mankind's dominion.

2

The Whooping Crane

In 1941, there were only twenty-one whooping cranes; they were the lone survivors of their species. These birds were headed for extinction. Today there is still a question of whether or not the whooping crane will survive.

These twenty-one cranes were the survivors of a species which nested from Nebraska north into Canada, from the Rockies across to Iowa and on down into Louisiana and Mississippi. Their bones are found in fossil deposits dating to eons before man appeared. We find enough mention of their use as food to know that they were definitely not rare in pioneer days. In fact, I cannot agree with the estimate commonly given today that there were only 1,400 whoopers when Columbus' arrival started the despoliation of this continent's wildlife.

But, even if that minimum figure is accepted, we must bear the responsibility for causing the decline from 1,400 to twenty-one. How did it happen?

The whooper is a classic example of the territorial animal in its nesting habitat. It stakes out its own territory, announces it to the rest of the whooper world with its sonorous trumpeting call, and then bitterly defends its territory against all intrusions. As mankind moved into the central plains, the whooper moved his nesting territory northward, ever northward, constantly searching for a territory to call his own, secure from man's intrusion.

The plow and drainage shovel stole his nesting habitat, and the crane was only seen during migrations when he flew down across Saskatchewan, the Dakotas, Nebraska, Oklahoma and Kansas on his way to an ever shrinking wintering area on the Texas Gulf Coast.

Each year fewer of the big white birds flew north to disappear into the wilds of Canada, to nesting areas whose locations weren't even known to mankind. During the summer months the whooping cranes were a complete mystery. No one knew where they had gone. In the fall they reappeared. Sometimes they had with them the rusty colored young of the year; some years no young birds came south.

The ecological conscience of the people of North America awakened to the plight of the whooper about the same time that the Aransas National Wildlife Refuge was established in 1937. Aransas protected the cranes on their wintering grounds, and the Fish and Wildlife Service began to keep records of their numbers, thus documenting the population decline of this tallest of all North

American wading birds. The Audubon Society sent Robert Allen to watch over the whoopers. His selfless dedication to the task and his outpouring of writings about the cranes awakened the public to the plight of the whooping crane.

When the United States first surveyed the whooper, we found a very unlikely candidate to wage a battle against oblivion. It was more than six feet tall, with black wing tips and a red head contrasting with spotlessly white plumage. The adult whooper was a lover of solitude; a great white bird with a sonorous call on his nesting grounds who was otherwise almost mute.

Slowly at first, and then with increasing effect, efforts to save the whooper began to move. The creation of Aransas National Wildlife Refuge was the most important event; without it the whooper would have long since been found only in museums and photographs. Audubon Society full-time personnel marshalled support and conducted basic research into migration paths. The Air Force was coerced into stopping flash bombing of their gunnery range near the refuge. State and federal enforcement personnel redoubled their efforts to stop illegal shooting of the cranes, and succeeded. An educational program, started by the Audubon people, showed good results. In those pioneer days, the work of Robert Allen, Audubon Society biologist, stood out. Without Allen, it is doubtful that the public and governmental efforts would have even begun, much less succeeded as they did.

Results came very slowly. The crane had the deck stacked against his survival. In 1954, mankind finally discovered the nesting grounds of the whooping cranes in Wood Buffalo National Park in Canada. In this far northern nesting area the growing season is woefully short. The whooping crane young must grow up in a hurry, learn to fly in a hurry, and then undertake a 2,100 mile flight before they are strong enough for the rigors of such a journey.

Whoopers do not breed until they are five or six years old. They lay only two eggs, but the female begins incubation as soon as the first egg is deposited in the ground nest. It is three or four days before the second egg is laid. As a result, the first egg will hatch out two or three days before the second egg. Often the adults will take the first hatched offspring and go away, leaving the second egg to cool and die. Even if both hatch, the older sibling is too big and too strong for the younger to compete with. The younger sibling starves or is killed by being stepped upon.

The approach of winter starts the southbound migration before the whooper chicks have really had enough time to strengthen flight muscles. As a result, they stop more often than safety would dictate on the long flight southward. Intensified law enforcement efforts have greatly reduced human danger to the migrating cranes, but the natural dangers from predators, weather conditions and fences and wires which are obstructions to flight still remain. However, whoopers make good parents and usually position their chick between them as they feed. Their food needs are easily met, as their tastes are catholic, running from frogs, lizards and fish, to grain, berries and roots, as well as crayfish and grasshoppers.

Whooping crane numbers grew slowly, from 21 in 1941 to 48 wild birds in 1968, up to 59 in 1971, and then a disastrous drop to 49 in 1973. From the 1973 drop, the graph took a decided upturn. In the fall of 1979 there were 119 total whooping cranes alive in the world. Today radio and television networks carry stories of the arrival of the new whooper crop each October, and the world anxiously awaits the total count to see if the cranes are going to gain or lose this year. An important development is that the count now comes from two quarters, for we now have two separate populations of whooping cranes. How that came about is a good story in itself.

Biologists theorized that they might be able to sneak in and steal one of the two eggs the whoopers lay each year. This egg could be hatched in an incubator in Patuxent, Maryland. Since whoopers usually come south with only one chick, the other egg would be left to be hatched and reared by its natural parents. In this way, both eggs would have a greater chance of survival.

Six eggs were removed by Canadian and FWS personnel in 1967, ten more were taken from the Wood Buffalo nesting grounds in 1968, and ten again in 1969. Not at all surprisingly, the wild flock brought MORE young birds south when the second egg was stolen than it had averaged before the egg-napping began. The captive flock grew to twenty-two birds in 1970. The wild flock was up to fifty-nine birds in 1971, but it was far from safe, as was demonstrated by the drop back to forty-nine in 1973.

A whooping crane defends his territory. Note the seven foot wing spread.

Attempting to maximize the breeding potential of their captive birds, the FWS installed lights which gave the captive flock twenty-two hours of daylight, the same as they would have enjoyed on the Wood Buffalo Park nesting area. The cranes did their stately courtship dance. The male cranes showed every sign of noticing the girl cranes, but they did not mate.

Artificial insemination provided fertile eggs in 1975 and Patuxent began to learn about the perils of rearing whooper chicks. In 1978 one captive female laid ten fertile eggs and another added nine to the total. However, incubator-hatched cranes showed a frightening tendency toward a weakness of the leg joint, and geneticists shook their heads gravely, afraid that this might be a defect brought on by decades of line inbreeding. However, it was found that the fault lay somewhere in the incubation procedures, for eggs hatched under foster parents didn't have this weakness.

Not wanting to have all of their eggs in one basket, the Fish and Wildlife people decided on a daring addition to their propagation program. They would put whooper eggs under wild sandhill cranes at Grays Lake, Idaho, and let the slightly smaller gray cranes do the incubation for them. It was hoped that the resultant offspring would then follow their foster parents to wintering grounds on the Bosque del Apache National Wildlife Refuge in New Mexico.

To give this cross-fostering a real try, fourteen eggs were collected from whooper nests in Wood Buffalo Park in 1975 and transferred by helicopter and jet aircraft to Grays Lake, Idaho. Three of those eggs were infertile, and predators got two more. Nine hatched! One of the chicks disappeared in a June snowstorm and two more faded out of the picture in July. But five whooping cranes followed their sandhill foster parents down to Bosque del Apache National Wildlife Refuge ninety miles south of my home in Albuquerque, New Mexico.

The transfer of eggs from Wood Buffalo to Grays Lake has continued with a new twist added. Eggs produced by the captive flock at Patuxent, Maryland, have been transferred to the Grays Lake sandhills, successfully hatched and joined with the Bosque del Apache flock.

This last winter, there were fifteen of the tall white birds wintering in the Rio Grande Valley of New Mexico. About ten of them were usually seen on the Bosque del Apache NWR and the other five were seen on private land, and upon state-owned wildlife lands, in the vicinity of the refuge. How interesting to note that the total of fifteen at Bosque and environs is exactly the same number of wild birds in existence in the whole world in 1941.

As the birds went north to the breeding areas in 1980, there were seventy-six birds in the Wood Buffalo-Aransas population; another fifteen in the Grays Lake-Bosque del Apache population; and twenty-eight birds in captivity, most of them at the Patuxent Endangered Species Center.

One goal of the Recovery Team currently overseeing the flight of the whooper against extinction is to have forty nesting pairs in the Wood Buffalo-Aransas flock. It now supports a total of seventy-six birds, but that is a far cry from forty pairs. Whoopers don't mate until they are five or six years old. Mortality is highest among juveniles who seem to have the wandering foot during their first two years away from their parents.

A second objective of the Recovery Team is to have at least two other discrete populations of at least twenty mated pairs per population. It would seem that the objective of twenty mated pairs at the Grays Lake NWR would be very easy to attain, inasmuch as they have put fifteen individuals into that population successfully in just five years. However, it is still too early to know whether or not the "imprinting" of the young whoopers onto the sandhill cranes who reared them is good or not. What if the whoopers think they are sandhills? What if they choose sandhill cranes as mates, resulting in a hybrid? Chances of that occurring in the wild are considered remote, because of the very different courtship calls and courtship dances of the two different species. However, artificial insemination has proved that such a hybridization is possible, even if not probable.

Dr. Rod Drewein, Consultant to the Whooping Crane Recovery Team, feels that we have a very long road to travel to transform the present fifteen immatures at Bosque del Apache into twenty mated pairs of adults. But the entire whooping crane cheering section—a big one—is understandably elated by the results of the Grays Lake cross-fostering experiment. It will be continued.

However, there is another objective—remember? That objective is to start another discrete breeding population and increase it to at least twenty mated pairs. At first glance this would seem very simple. The sandhill crane nests over a tremendous area of Canada, and winters from New Mexico east to Louisiana, with a quarter of a million individuals wintering at Muleshoe, Buffalo Lake and other refuges in Texas, five or six hundred miles away from Aransas NWR.

That sounds great except for one thing. These are **LESSER** sandhill cranes; the good foster parents at Grays Lake are the **GREATER** sandhill cranes. No matter, I thought, for a biologist needs a micrometer measuring mid-toe length to tell the difference between lesser and greater.

The lesser sandhill crane would not make a good foster parent for the whooper because its own chicks mature much more rapidly than do the chicks of the whooper (or the greater sandhill crane). Its growing season, dictated by its far northern nesting habitat, is not long enough to hatch out a whooper and bring it to flight stage before the lesser sandhills would all be gone on their own southward migration.

We cannot use the half million lessers for foster parents for whooping cranes. Cross-fostering has demonstrated itself to be far and away the best system for introducing a whooper into a wild habitat. Either we will have to introduce a greater crane population somewhere, and then use it to foster a whooper population there, or develop some other method of introducing whoopers into the population, giving them some guidance as to how to reach the wintering grounds and find their way back to the desired breeding area. This seems like a formidable task, and it will be. However, as their expertise grows, and the numbers of the captive flock grows, the avian researchers at Patuxent should be able to provide more eggs and more young birds for experimental introductions.

The whooping crane is definitely not out of the woods yet. The ominous pall of extinction still looms over the entire species. But there is now room for cautious optimism.

I cannot explain the attraction so many people feel for the whooping crane. Much sportsmen's money has gone into the effort to save the bird, yet every sportsman knows that the whooper will never be numerous enough to support a hunting season. People from every walk of life have gotten hooked on watching the struggle since 1937. Personally, I find the whooper absolutely fascinating.

One of the low points of my professional life came when we were not allowed to bring charges against a man in a small town near the Canadian border. He had shot, killed and eaten an adult whooper during the southward migration in the fall. We recovered feathers, definitely identifiable as whooper plumage, from the disposal area. We had a detailed description of the bird and the secondhand story of how it was shot, and how it looked when "Daddy carried it in with its head up over his head and its feet still touched the ground." The man's minor-aged daughter provided all of our evidence. Unfortunately, under our laws the evidence was illegally obtained. The miscreant went unpunished.

The whoopers have also given me some happy moments. I remember the day I sat in a photo blind on the Aransas Refuge and watched no less than thirty-four whoopers parade past through a heavy rain. The heavy rain made photos impossible, but the sight of thirty-four whoopers in view at once was a thrill I'll never forget. That thrill was matched when I first spotted a wild whooper wintering on the Bosque del Apache.

I remember standing on the Aransas Refuge with Earl Benham, watching the whoopers take off and spiral upward in widening circles as they usually did when about to start their northward migration. "Wonder how many will come back next fall?" Earl said. I knew what he meant, for a lot of us suffered each time the count went down and rejoiced when it went up.

A mystique has grown up around the whoopers. This was started by the legendary Robert Allen of the Audubon Society and led by a small group of refuge managers who served on the Aransas at one time or another—Jim Stevenson, Julian Howard, Earl Benham, Jim Harmon, Huyson J. Johnson, Dr. Ray Erickson, Fred Stark of the San Antonio Zoo, and a dozen others. These men and others have protected the birds on their long flights to and from the undiscovered breeding grounds. They have protected these birds on their wintering grounds and devised new ways to make more feed available to them. Men such as these who have also worked with the birds in zoos and later the Patuxent Center have so far probably made the difference between survival and extinction for this species.

Today we have a situation where every law enforcement officer, state or federal, will drop everything and hurry to guard a migrating whooper reported to be in his territory. We have the Audubon program of volunteers who monitor migrations and report sightings methodically to provide a factual basis for migration studies. We have great interest in this endangered species, far more interest than could be explained by any intrinsic value the big bird may have. This interest is the most valuable asset the whooper has in his struggle for survival.

We have seen a growth from fifteen birds in the wild in 1941 to ninety-one in the wild in 1980. Surely we are on the way to success. On the way? Yes. Surely? Not yet.

Most of the losses now seem to be occurring in the juvenile population. Whoopers kick the young of the year out of the family group about the time they head back north to nest. The juveniles wander aimlessly for several years, only rejoining the flock for long periods of time on the wintering grounds. This wandering is probably an adaptation designed to make sure that the juvenile can find a mate. But this wandering trait exposes the wanderer to dangers not anticipated, nor even known at this writing. The lost birds have been the wandering juveniles. Where will the wandering youngsters from the Rocky Mountain flock venture? Can we even anticipate that this wandering trait is genetically transmitted in the first place? Could it be that it is learned from the parent and will not be taught by the sandhill foster parents?

Although guarded by two nations, watched over by scientists of many disciplines, worried over by millions of people, and wintering at two separate wildlife refuges, the whooping crane is still a long way from survival as a species. If the total world wild population ever reaches 1,000 we will have reason to cheer, but that figure isn't even dreamed of today.

The choice of the whooping crane as a symbol of man's efforts to save endangered species was a poor one. The odds against its survival have always been very long. They still are. How discouraging to have the very symbol of the endangered species struggle perish! But there is hope that man's concern will enable the whooper to survive. That hope gives us reason for working ever harder to ensure that survival becomes reality.

If the whooping crane can be saved, we can save other species. Perhaps we can even save mankind.

3

Kirtland's Warbler

Perhaps the rarest of all small birds, the Kirtland's warbler now numbers something less than 500 individuals in the entire world. It is the only tail-wagging warbler with a gray back. If you need more identification, you'll have to go to the source: a six county section of northern Lower Michigan. In the counties of Crawford, Oscoda, Iosco, Roscommon, Kalkaska and Ogemaw, the 1979 census found 210 singing males.

Intensive searches in other states and nearby Ontario turned up one bird, a singing male observed in Jackson County, Wisconsin. Evidently he didn't have a mate, although two singing males had been found there the year before. A single singing male had been censused in Renfrew County, Ontario in 1977 and 1978, but did not answer the roll call in 1979. The same is true of a singing male heard in Gatineau County, Quebec, in 1978.

The Kirtland's warbler has **NEVER** been found nesting anywhere other than in northern Lower Michigan.

To further emphasize the "choosy" nature of the bird, the Kirtland's warbler nests only in stands of young jack pines. Furthermore, these pines should be in stands of at least eighty acres. They must be dense stands, or the warbler won't find them attractive. The warblers prefer jack pine stands when the stands are six to thirteen years old and range from five to six feet tall. The trees are no longer attractive to the Kirtland's warbler when they reach the height of sixteen to twenty feet.

This preferred type of forest growth was plentiful in the old days when frequent wildfires destroyed stands of jack pines and, at the same time, created ideal conditions for the regeneration of young jack pines. When there were frequent fires, the Kirtland's could pick and choose. Many dense stands could easily be found.

Enter Smoky the Bear and modern fire prevention practices. Wildfire was no longer frequent, and fire was looked upon, not as a creator of habitat for warblers, but as the greatest tragedy that could befall the profits of the timber manager. As tremendous areas of forest were protected from fire, they matured into even-age stands of tall pines, completely unacceptable to the picky Kirtland's warbler.

When the first nest was discovered in northern Lower Michigan in 1903, the

13

population had undoubtedly already taken quite a drop. We have no accurate estimate of what pre-Columbian populations might have been, nor do we know why the species did not scatter out and inhabit young jack pine stands in other states. Since 1903 bird watchers have reported the tiny singer from fifteen counties in Michigan and in widely scattered locations in Minnesota, Wisconsin and Ontario. But let me repeat: The Kirtland's warbler has never been known to nest anywhere except in northern Lower Michigan.

The exact "home" territory of the Kirtland's warbler must vary from year to year, as jackpine stands reach varying stages of maturity. However, the bird moves only a short distance, selecting a new home territory within a mile or so of the place where his grandmother nested.

Harold Mayfield was one of the first to get interested in the Kirtland's warbler, and in 1953 he and a group of thirty other bird lovers attempted a census—a count of all the breeding males singing during the early part of the nesting season. Logically enough, they assumed that the male had a female to sing to, or he wouldn't have anything to sing about. In that first attempt, probably the first time that a census of the entire world population of any species of bird had been attempted, they recorded 432 singing males.

A similar census in 1961 gave a total of 502 singing males, which would indicate that the species was holding its own. However, ten years later the 1971 count turned up only 201 males! The situation was obviously desperate and action was needed. But what do you do to help a species which has put itself in jeopardy by being so very choosy? Surely the diminutive bird could learn to find nesting habitat in different environments? Perhaps it could, but the question is really unimportant, for the Kirtland's warbler does not choose to live in other habitats.

The bird is reported to winter in the Bahamas, but we don't know if it is in danger there. The warbler is almost never sighted during migration; so we do not know whether it requires protection during the twice a year voyage over land and sea from northern Lower Michigan to the islands in the sunny Atlantic. How remarkable indeed, if the bird was noticed during migration, considering the pitifully low population and the secretive bush-to-bush flitting path followed in migration.

Under terms of the Endangered Species Act of 1973, the Kirtland's warbler was listed as an endangered species and a Recovery Team was named to recommend courses of action which could arrest the decline of the population of the warbler. John Byelich of the Michigan Department of Natural Resources was named to lead the Recovery Team.

The Recovery Team took swift action. They continued the annual census and widened its scope to take in other possible areas to be sure that they were not missing populations of warblers which might have shifted their nesting location *en masse.* No such luck. The warbler has never been known to nest outside of the young jack pine stands of northern Lower Michigan.

Knowing where these dense stands were, the Recovery Team posted the areas against entry from May 1 through August 15 of each year. This was necessary to minimize human intrusion during the critical nesting period. They

didn't want to have a case where the species was exterminated by those who were most interested in its surivival—the dedicated bird watchers who annually flock to the Michigan area, hoping for a glimpse of the Kirtland's warbler, the twenty-second most-wanted bird on most birders' lists.

They began operating cowbird traps adjacent to all of the known nesting colonies, because the cowbird's parasitic habit of depositing its eggs in the nests of smaller birds could be very detrimental to the Kirtland's warbler. The larger cowbird progeny crowd out, and starve out, the legitimate youngsters. Often the warbler rears only the unwanted cowbird, allowing her own young to starve.

Probably of most importance in the long pull is the action by the Recovery Team to dedicate 135,000 acres of jack pines, owned by the state and federal government (and within the known nesting range) to the type of management which will annually produce at least 35,000 acres of the jack pine habitat which the choosy Kirtland's warbler requires to survive. The Recovery Team is not just planning on holding its own. The short term goal is to provide habitat for a minimum of 1,000 nesting pairs. Timber management and timber harvest will be scheduled to coincide with the needs of the birds, which will, perforce, lower profits for the timber managers.

The Recovery Team is also thinking about the eight to nine months of the year when the Kirtland's warbler is absent from Michigan. No one has actually pinpointed the wintering sites of the warblers, although they are known to be in the Bahamas. Until the actual wintering area is delineated, there is no way in which studies can determine whether or not the Kirtland's warbler needs protection on the wintering grounds.

The tiny Kirtland's warbler and the large whooping crane have much in common. Both are so reduced in numbers that a single natural catastrophe could wipe out a major part of the world's population. Both species have attracted a devoted group of human friends, people who are willing to devote their time and efforts far beyond the requirements of a nine to five job to assure that they'll be around in years to come.

But they are also very different. The crane is long lived, while the life span of a warbler is measured more often in months than in years. The crane is safe on its southern wintering area, and until recently its northern breeding area wasn't even known. The warbler seems to be safe now on its northern breeding area. Nothing is really known about its southern wintering area.

It would be difficult to demonstrate a monetary value for the crane, and almost impossible to show that the passing of the Kirtland's warbler would cause anyone loss of money. Yet surely we humans are advanced enough to know that when we cause the demise of a species by our actions—no matter how well meaning our forest fire protection is—the last individual of that species takes a lot of things with him when he goes across the threshold of extinction.

That last individual going into the shadows takes along a priceless set of genes which cannot be duplicated, cannot be copied, cannot be the basis for any further evolutionary development. When that last individual passes into the beyond, we should know that there is less time than there was before for us to make sure that we do not follow the same path.

Surely we must know that if we cannot save Kirtland's warblers and whooping cranes, we cannot save our planet, and we cannot save ourselves.

4

The American Crocodile

You can easily see why mankind would rally around such species as the whooping crane and the Kirtland's warbler in their fights for survival. The crane is a majestic bird and the warbler a lovable little bit of feathered song. But how do you arouse interest in saving the American crocodile? When the word "crocodile" comes up, the average American is apt to have mixed emotions—perhaps a shudder of revulsion at the thought of the big lizard with the tooth-studded jaws, perhaps a bit of atavistic antagonism for a species which eats humans, perhaps the reaction, "I hope they all are killed off so that it will be safe to go swimming."

There obviously won't be much of a cheerleading section for the survival of the American crocodile. Although our croc, *Crocodylus acutus*, doesn't grow to the gargantuan size of the Asiatic and African versions, and although our croc is not known as a man eater, public support will be based on the broad principle that the crocodile is a native species, deserving of a chance to exist.

The American crocodile population was in serious condition. Allies were badly needed. Once fairly numerous in the lakes and estuaries of both Atlantic and Pacific Coasts of the tropical portions of both Americas, the crocodile became greatly reduced in numbers and a candidate for the "extinct" label. At the time that the U.S. Fish and Wildlife Service listed the American crocodile as "endangered" it was thought to be in serious trouble only in the United States portion of its range. Later, the International Union for Conservation of Nature and Natural Resources listed it as endangered all across its range, which extends from Cuba, Hispaniola, Puerto Rico and both coasts of Mexico from Sinola and Tamaulipas down to all the Central American countries and Colombia and Ecuador.

The listing by the IUCN is largely symbolic and educational, and will have little effect in countries which so far cannot afford the luxury of worrying about other species when their own worries are paramount. The only population that will directly be affected to any great extent is the Florida population—the only wild American crocodiles in the United States.

The National Park Service has been an ally of the unloved saurian for many years, because of longstanding NPS policy to preserve, unchanged, native flora and fauna. Although Everglades National Park is prime crocodile habitat, the Park Service has records dating back at least to the early 1950's which show that the croc was decreasing in numbers. When it attained the "endangered" listing, there were probably less than 300 existing in Florida.

Normally shy and intolerant of human intrusion into its environment, crocs are creatures of shallow bays and rivers where brackish or fresh water serves as their escape cover, and where their customary diet of fish and crabs is easily available. The massive environmental changes wrought on the coasts of Florida have almost eliminated the preferred habitat of the croc, with the obvious exception of the Everglades National Park. Biologists studying the status of the crocodile in Florida waters estimate that there were probably no more than two thousand crocodiles, at the most, in the 1890's. This was after they had been hunted for their hides for many years.

The Recovery Team for the American crocodile describes the range and distribution of the animal in the 1970's as: Everglades National Park along the mainland shoreline of Florida Bay from Terrapin Bay east to Long Sound and on adjacent islands in the northeastern bay, and less frequently west to the Cape Sable peninsula; also, on the upper Florida Keys from lower Plantation Key north to the upper end of Key Largo, and along Cross Key to the mainland shoreline of Barnes Sound, Card Sound and southern Biscayne Bay north to Black Point. A second group of crocodiles exists in the lower Keys, within the boundaries of the Key Deer and the Great White Herons National Wildlife Refuges, on Big Pine, Little Pine, Howe, Johnston and upper Sugarloaf Keys. In all of this 1970 range, the total number of crocodiles was estimated at between 100 and 400 animals, including no more than 20 breeding females.

We have already identified two allies for the American crocodile: the National Park Service, and the Fish and Wildlife Service, which had afforded incidental protection to the crocs in several refuges which had been established particularly for other species. Other small populations remained in the very few areas of its historic range which had not felt the impact of dragline and bulldozer.

How can you restore habitat for the crocodile after its original home has been usurped by housing developments? Not even the federal government can afford to buy back those billions of dollars worth of waterfront and give them to the crocodiles. That habitat is obviously gone for good, making it doubly imperative that we must preserve some of the habitat which remains, or the croc will not survive. We had better find more allies for the crocodile. We cannot go to the waterfront home builders and ask them to help us save the American crocodile. It wouldn't help to sell homes if the advertisement stated, "A crocodile guaranteed in your front yard." But when the Recovery Team got to work, it found an ally in a strange place. Public utilities had long been considered enemies of any nature conservation effort, because they were structured to seek profit as the *sine qua non* of their existence. They had to make a profit, first, last, and always, and they seldom thought of anything other than the efficient pursuit of profit.

Enter a public utility that decided to cast its lot with the environmentalists instead of railing against the costs of protecting the environment. Enter Florida

Power and Light, which not only saw the handwriting on the wall, but read it. FPL became one of the allies that the American crocodile so badly needed. The Turkey Point Plant, operted by FPL, is the scene of an intensive study of American crocodile population dynamics, financed by the utility company. There are two other studies, one by the National Park Service in the Florida Bay area of the Everglades National Park, another in the Basin Hills area of northern Key Largo by the Florida Game and Freshwater Fish Commission. Both are adding to our knowledge of the crocodile.

Florida Power and Light has also demonstrated its environmental concern in the struggle of the Florida manatee to escape extinction. Warm water outflows from the power plants are part of the requirements placed upon utilities by various legislative provisions designed to safeguard the environment. When we provide an area in which heated outflows can cool before being discharged into natural waters, we create a situation which is very attractive to the cold blooded saurians, even as it is attractive to the manatee which has not evolved with the ability to react to marked changes in water temperatures.

Florida Power and Light, allied with the National Park Service, the Fish and Wildlife Service and the Florida Department of Natural Resources, protected the American crocodile from human disturbance, studied its territorial needs, and intensified its study of crocodile movements and requisites. The highlight of the FPL-funded study was the application of radio transmitters to the necks of several adult crocs and the use of radio telemetry to map their movements accurately.

Results of the first few years of investigation have given us cause for some optimism for the survival of the Florida population of the American crocodile. Whereas the previous commonly held belief was that almost no juveniles had survived, due mainly to raccoon predation and to intolerance for salt waters, study has now shown that quite a few of the newly hatched crocodiles survive through their first year. In a personal communication to me, Paul E. Moler, Recovery Team leader, reported that 1980 shows that we are recruiting adults into the breeding population, with the study at Turkey Point pointing to the survival of significant numbers of subadult animals in the four to seven foot class.

Today the most pressing problem facing the American Crocodile Recovery Team seems to be the problem of protecting suitable habitat—the little that still exists—outside of the Everglades National Park. These areas are not sufficiently protected, and crocodiles are still occasionally killed by vandals or run over by automobiles on U.S. Highway #1, or on Card Sound Road.

Although we must keep in mind that American crocodile numbers have declined rather steadily over the last thirty years, there is now room for cautious optimism that the croc can be saved.

Hopeful signs include the increase in the number of known nests, which went up from twelve (all in Everglades National Park) in 1977, to more than twenty now. Some of the newly found nests were on the Turkey Point project of Florida Power and Light. Perhaps these nests were always there, but their existence wasn't known until after the increased survey work studied these areas.

Another hopeful sign emerges from the studies of nest predation. We had thought that this was a great source of mortality to the crocodile population; however, research shows that only about 15 percent of the nests are destroyed by predation. This is certainly an allowable figure, for few species can claim much more than that as a survival rate in their reproductive attempts.

The Recovery Team had planned to rear juvenile American crocodiles in protected environments until they were about eighteen inches long, at which size they become more often the predator than the prey. The prevailing thinking was that this artificial coddling of the juveniles was necessary to ensure sufficient recruitment into the subadult and adult populations. Research has shown that this step will not be necessary, for the crocodile can handle its own needs when its critical habitat is protected from human intrusion.

Because the crocodile does seem to have a great potential for reproducing its own species, the Fish and Wildlife proposal to establish a 6,000 acre refuge on Key Largo has great significance. This area contained at least seven known crocodile nests in 1978. Protection from intrusion is important because the female usually opens the nest to allow the newly hatched young to escape into the water. During this period the female is most vulnerable as she makes repeated trips to the nest site.

There is little apparent likelihood that we will lose this species in the immediate future. This is due to the splendid cooperation between Florida Power and Light Company, the Florida Game and Fresh Water Fish Commission, the National Park Service and the U.S. Fish and Wildlife Service. Because a public utility learned that protection of endangered species is excellent public relations, an ally has been found for the unloved reptile.

Perhaps the biggest question to face the Recovery Team in the next decade will be, "How many crocodiles are enough?"

5

The California Condor

His wings span three yards of the California mountain air. All of that aerodynamic lift is needed, for his body may weigh as much as twenty-two pounds. The California condor is the largest of all soaring land birds on the North American continent. Sitting on a rocky shelf in the Sespe area, his skinless head seems repulsively naked. He is awkward and clumsy, a carrion eater with little to recommend him to the beauty lover.

Soaring on an afternoon thermal high above these same mountains, he is one of the most beautiful fliers in the world. Gone is the awkward appearance; gone is our memory of the scavenger's beak and the naked head. We see only the great wings which effortlessly manage a river of wind and allow him to soar without moving more than a primary wing feather. He is a master aviator riding the wind, a bird of beauty soaring wild and free.

The condor has been riding the thermals ever since the Pleistocene, gliding along the airwaves while his watchful eyes search for food far below. He doesn't have to catch or kill his prey, for the condor eats only carrion. If an automobile kills a rabbit on the road, the condor makes his dinner from that rabbit—if he can beat the crows, ravens, magpies and his smaller cousins, the vultures—to the kill.

Whether you consider him an ugly scavenger or one of the most graceful of all flying creatures, the hard fact remains that the California condor is the rarest bird in America, and perhaps the rarest bird in all the world. There are now approximately twenty-eight in the wild, and one in captivity.

The condors have the cards stacked aginst them. It is doubtful that they may even answer the roll call in the next century. What happened?

Their normal breeding grounds have been invaded by man, and the condor is very intolerant of human intrusion. However, there is more than ample breeding habitat in this world, and the condor certainly hasn't occupied even one-one hundredth of it. Condors have been shot by men ever since the first firearm-carrying individual arrived in California. But shooting has not been an important cause of their troubles over the last three decades.

Many of the big birds have been killed by speeding automobiles, for they are slow to get airborne from flat land. If they come down to eat a road kill (and they have been known to alight for even the few bites that a road-killed gopher provides), they cannot take evasive action fast enough if an automobile comes their way.

Their biggest problem, however, is their slowness to reproduce their own kind. They do not mate until they are five or six years old. If they can find a mate, they set up housekeeping by depositing only one egg on a protected shelf in the mountains. This egg is incubated for forty-two days before it hatches. Then a period of about seven more months follows in which the parents must feed the fledgling. This means that the project begun in February is still occupying the parents full-time in late September.

Evidently that long period of dependency is enough to discourage the birds from repeating the process next February, for they usually nest only every other year.

This low reproductive potential makes the California condor even more vulnerable to the insidious effects of DDE and other chemicals which are ingested with their food—the condor being at the top of a food chain—and make it difficult for the female to lay an egg with enough shell material to carry the embryonic condor through the forty-two days of incubation.

Whether or not DDT, and its metabolite DDE, is guilty as charged will probably never be ascertained. One immature bird found dead in 1974 was carrying enough DDE in its tissues to put it in the class with other birds whose reproduction failed because of egg shell thinning. However, very few condor eggs or other body parts ever become available for analysis. Circumstantial evidence shows that spraying with DDT was widespread within the condor range in the years of 1964 to 1969, and DDE has been detected in the membranes of condor egg shells over the last decade.

Whatever the evidence shows, the condor population is at such a low state that the loss of even one egg can mean the difference between survival and extinction of the species.

Why is one egg so important? In today's wild population there are twenty-five to thirty individuals. That means that we probably have only eight breeding pairs (at the most optimistic guess), and we may have only three breeding pairs (at the most pessimistic guess). Eight nesting pairs will lay only four eggs per year. If all eggs hatch, and all young survive to the sub-adult age, we have only added four young per year.

If there are five nesting pairs, we can hope for the year's reproduction to be 2.5 birds on the average year. But today's census data strongly argues that annual production is less than two condors per year! There was only one young bird confirmed in 1979. This will not sustain the population, and neither will the 2.5 birds per year nor the optimistic four young birds per year which could conceivably be produced by eight mated pairs in the wild. When a population continues to record more deaths than births per year, that population is doomed to extinction.

At what rate is the condor sliding into oblivion? When extensive study began after the passage of the Endangered Species Act in 1973, experts estimated a population of fifty birds. Today, these same experts estimate a population of twenty-eight birds. That means we have lost half of the world's population in about five years!

California condors at roost.

We are not postulating a situation wherein the other half of the wild population will be gone in another five years. The situation is not that bad. The California condor is long-lived. Some individuals have been known to live as many as forty years. We can always use the rose-colored glasses to see this prospect: a pair mates when they are six years and lives to be thirty, enjoying twenty-four years of production. In that twenty-four years, they produce twelve young condors. Unfortunately this has not been happening. We must assume that the current trend toward extinction will continue.

Without the rose-colored glasses, the realist looks at the wild population and comes to the only logical conclusion: The wild population will disappear, to all intents and purposes, in another four or five years unless something is done.

We said "to all intents and purposes" because we know that two or three or even seven of the birds may linger on for forty years more. Unmated individuals in the wild would mock us for our failure in our fight to preserve their species, but they would be without the ability to increase their own numbers. History might record that the last unmated condor lived into the 2000's, but the biologist would know that the species was no longer viable, long ere the last bird breathed its last.

We said "unless something is done," and we did have something definite in mind. The California condor may be perpetuated through artificial propagation in captivity.

When the Recovery Team had its first sessions, they planned a contingency project: the artifical propagation of California condors. The proposal met with loud opposition from those who still felt that the wild population of fifty could perpetuate itself. To be ready for artificial propagation, should the decision be made, the Patuxent Research Station secured Andean condors—not the same as the California, but very similar—and began a crash program of learning how to rear them in captivity. They succeeded and now have the artificial propagation of Andean condors down to a science. But while they were learning how to propagate condors artificially, the wild population dropped down to less than half of what they started with.

The Fish and Wildlife Service and the California state people are working closely with the Audubon Society which has a very great interest in the case of the condors. Because these groups, and most of the others with an interest in endangered species, are composed of reasoning people, a consensus of opinion was reached that "something must be done." The Recovery Team announced that a program of trapping unmated pairs out of the wild population would begin in January of 1980. The threat of legal action to stop the wild trapping forced the postponement of that plan.

Obviously, there is an emotional opposition to the captive propagation idea. There is a great difference between saving a species in the wild and saving the same species in captivity. This emotional reaction to the captive propagation idea was most eloquently expressed in the June 1979 issue of the *Yodeler*, the publication of the San Francisco Bay Chapter of the Sierra Club:

"If we resort to captive breeding of condors, we are not saving the bird. We are only saving the genes and feathers...a condor raised in captivity is different from a wild condor in ways we may never learn to measure, but we will know the difference in our hearts."

It seems to this observer that there is a choice between saving the "genes and feathers" and saving nothing. A policy of watching and waiting inevitably dooms the species. The California condor is a good candidate for propagation. A captive condor in the Washington Zoo laid thirteen eggs in eleven years, showing that it might even be possible to recycle the female to produce more than one egg per year.

Artificial insemination, double clutching, recycling, cross-fostering—techniques which have worked with captive populations of whooping cranes, peregrine falcons and other species—may work with California condors. But they cannot work if they are not tried. Friends of the Earth has been the motivating force behind the litigation threats which have postponed the livetrapping of condors from the wild flock for at least the 1980 breeding season. This David Brower-led group still threatens to stop the last ditch effort to save the condor by court action. However, the Recovery Team feels that they will be able to go ahead with the trapping of juvenile birds in the winter of 1980-81. Nevertheless, the obstructionist tactics of Friends of the Earth carry with them a fearful responsbility. A one year delay in putting the propagation plan into action might spell the difference between extinction and successful propagation and return to the wild of captive-reared birds.

In the face of the total absence of an alternative plan, captive propagation is surely needed at once. This has worked with two of the wildest of bird species: the peregrine falcon and the whooping crane. The peregrine falcon, which will establish a new nesting eyrie in Maryland this year, couldn't care less that its grandparents were reared in captivity at Cornell University. If the falcon were to consider the situation at all, it would probably have enough sense to be glad that it was allowed to exist as a species.

Without captive propagation, the California condor seems doomed to extinction in the next decade.

6

The Peregrine Falcon

During the fall of 1979, we got a great deal of pleasure watching a game being played by two families of immature birds in the grove of trees surrounding our rented home on the Outer Banks of North Carolina. A family of young bluejays, impudent representatives of their clan, took great delight in tempting a pair of immature Cooper's hawks. With their greater precocity, the jays were able to outmaneuver the young raptors with ease. A jay would stir up a noisy ruckus and hop from branch to branch, always getting nearer to the young hawks. When the hawks were tempted almost beyond endurance, the jay would impudently take flight. The hawks would go hurtling after it. The jay would then land on a branch where his greater agility afoot would render him safe from the fast-flying but slow-hopping hawk.

On several occasions I was amazed at how narrowly the insolent jays escaped the claws of the hawks. Time after time the jays tempted, and time after time the hawks took the dare—trying their best, which was never quite good enough. The game always ended with the young hawks sitting disconsolate on a high branch while the blue jays shrieked a few final insults at them from less than a yard away. I often wondered where the adult Cooper's hawks were; why they didn't put an end to the unequal game. Perhaps they would have had more agility afoot, or more speed on the wing. Then the jays would have found that their game had a tragic ending.

One particular morning we had been prevented from filming our movie on surf fishing by the heavy cloud cover and high surf which muddied the waters. About ten o'clock the wind died down and I began to be hopeful that we would be able to film in the afternoon. Taking a cup of coffee, I went outside to check on the weather. I was just in time to hear the raucous screeches of the jays as they set about their game of baiting the hawks. I sat down to watch the show.

Twice the jay teased the young hawk into a rage. Twice he flew across the open space between the southern pine and the yaupon thicket, and twice the hawk floundered after him. The hawk didn't come within a yard of sinking talons into the blue-backed daredevil.

The third time the bluejay flew across the open space, the discouraged young hawk simply glared at him, watched intently, but showed no sign of leaving his perch in pursuit. Disappointed at winning the game so easily, the jay grew bolder. He hopped from branch to branch, his impudent tail flipping up and down to balance his moves, coming ever closer to the young hawk. He made several feinting motions, as if he would launch himself toward the safety of the yaupon, but the hawk watched without even raising his wings in readiness to pursue. He had no intention of making a fool of himself this morning.

With a couple of sarcastic remarks, the jay took flight, bound for the familiar yaupon and safety. A hurtling shadow entered the picture and a hawk hit the jay in mid air, fully ten feet from the shelter of the yaupon. A small puff of blue feathers danced in the light breeze as the hawk did a tight Immelman turn and lit on a dead branch of the pine. A very dead bluejay was clutched in its talons. There was a silence in the woods. The other bluejays sat motionless, making not a sound. The ravens that had been dancing on the wind near the edge of the canal were strangely silent, and even the ducks on the canal were swimming slowly away from our home.

It took only one look to solve the mystery. This was no bumbling young Cooper's hawk; this was a full grown peregrine falcon. As he began pulling feathers from the breast of his dinner, I tried to remember how long it had been since I had seen a peregrine in the wild. They were completely gone from my part of the nation and were only to be seen in migration.

Later that afternoon, I rode with Pete Anastasi on a trip to Pea Island National Wildlife Refuge. We hoped to ask the refuge personnel if they, too, had sighted the peregrine. Our questions were all answered long before we got to the refuge. Enroute we saw no fewer than six peregrines, all busily doing what they do best—catching and killing birds in flight. The refuge log confirmed what our eyes had told us. The peregrine falcon was present in numbers, migrating southward along the eastern edge of our nation. Did this mean a return of the rare and endangered aerial assassin to the eastern United States from which it had disappeared?

Not really, for the nesting population of peregrines in the eastern half of the United States was extinct. You cannot restore a population considered exterminated. But it was only the U.S. part of this eastern North American block of peregrines that was extinct. The Canadian and Arctic portions of this same population were still there.

Never numerous, peregrines showed no measurable decline throughout the early part of mankind's occupation of the eastern states. In 1942, Dr. Joseph Hickey found that there were 275 known nesting sites of peregrines in the eastern United States. He knew that 210 of these eyries were active in 1942, and he felt that there were probably 350 nesting pairs in the area, inasmuch as they had not located all of the eyries in the study. At this same time, there were some 133 known nesting eyries in Canada and Greenland, which might contribute migrating birds to the area each fall and spring.

In 1964, growing concern over the decline in peregrine populations led to a further study. Investigators compiled a list of 209 known peregrine eyries and found that none of them was in nesting use! It seemed ridiculous to blame the drastic decline on such natural enemies as great horned owls, or egg collecting, or indiscriminate shooting. These losses had been present for a century,

Cecil D. Andrus with peregrine falcons. When Andrus was Secretary of the Interior, falcon eggs were actually hatched atop the Interior Building.

and the natural enemies had been present as long as the peregrine flew the skies. Why the terrible loss in a matter of twenty years?

A third major survey was launched in 1975. The inescapable conclusion was reached that the peregrine falcon was extinct as far as breeding pairs in the eastern United States were concerned. The breeding population of peregrines, which had remained remarkably stable during the period when mankind was eliminating the passenger pigeon, the great auk, the Heath hen and (almost) the American bison, was suddenly disappearing. Before we knew the real answer, the breeding population had disappeared in the eastern United States.

To put the reason for this in simplest terms, the peregrine had lost the ability to make egg shells within the female falcon's body! Researchers found the reason, although they found it too late to help our eastern U.S. peregrine. DDT, and its metabolite DDE, were convicted of the crime. DDT was a great boon to mankind, or so we thought, because of the part it played in the elimination of insect-borne diseases. But these chlorinated hydrocarbons simply did not go away after they had killed the pest we wanted killed. They seemed to last forever in the food chain. Birds ate the insects whose bodies carried the residue of DDE, and the birds kept the chemical in their tissues, concentrating it as they continued to feed on insects which carried new supplies of DDE. Being at the top of a food chain, the peregrine was one of the greatest accumulators of chlorinated hydrocarbons in its body.

The most visible result of this accumulation of DDE was the failure to make an eggshell thick enough to serve as the holder of the embryonic young peregrine while it developed. Researchers documented a 20% to 26% decrease in egg shell thickness of the peregrine in the eastern United States at the same time that the crash in peregrine populations occurred, and noted that this was shortly after the chlorinated hydrocarbons became available for public use.

The peregrine was not the only bird to accumulate too much DDE and lose its reproductive ability. Other birds showed the same disastrous result; yet only the peregrine seemed to be completely extirpated from half of the nation by this unseen killer.

The use of chlorinated hydrocarbons in the United States has been greatly restricted since the loss of the peregrines, but it is still being used in the Latin American countries which are the southern termination of the peregrines' migration. Although we have no evidence to bear this out, we may still be losing peregrines on these wintering grounds.

At first glance it appears unlikely that anything can be done to assist the comeback fight of such a bird. Fiercely independent and proud, the peregrine nests in the most inaccessible spots. It is a very unlikely candidate for a human-aided comeback. However, the bird had been a favorite of falconers for centuries and much was already known about its needs. At Cornell University and at several other places, researchers found the ability to propagate the peregrine in captivity. Cornell refined the technique to the point where they could rear as many as 200 young peregrines per year. Pioneer work was done by Dr. Heinz Meng, who raised seven young from one captive pair.

A Recovery Plan was formulated and immediately implemented. The plan called for a complete inventory of suitable reintroduction sites throughout the eastern states and a ranking of these sites for priority in reintroductions; for immediate stepping up of captive propagation from wild stock; for a program of law enforcement protection for the endangered birds; and for a program of public information to gain public support for the recovery project.

Based on known nesting sites of the past, eleven areas were selected for reintroduction. The first area to receive artificially propagated birds was the Chesapeake Bay, with the Delaware-New Jersey-Virginia Coastal area second, and the Hudson River Valley-Catskill Mountain area third.

Selecting the brood stock for the Cornell Peregrine Factory posed a problem for geneticists. Although no scientist can arbitrarily assign an individual peregrine to a particular subspecies without knowing the area from which he comes, there was concern that the extinct species had been mostly non-migratory. If this non-migratory behavior was genetically determined, then there was a chance that the particular genes had perished with the subspecies. No matter where the scientists obtained brood stock, the resulting young peregrines would migrate. This migration would greatly increase their chances of picking up metabolites of chlorinated hydrocarbons on the wintering grounds. The bird might even migrate to northern climes in search of its genetic ancestors, thus abandoning its eastern states reintroduction home.

After much soul-searching, peregrines were chosen from the Arctic tundra of North America, from the Aleutians and Queen Charlotte Island on the western coast, and from both Scotland and the Mediterranean regions in Europe. Given the ability to produce peregrines in captivity, there was still much to be learned about the process of returning them to the wild state, equipped to make their way in a world where food was not going to be handed to them on a platter.

"Hacking" is the process of gradually releasing captive young falcons—giving them semiliberty while still feeding them as they become accustomed to life in the wild. This allows the birds to learn how to feed themselves. Gradually they become less and less dependent upon mankind until finally they are freed. Hacking has the added advantage of starting the "imprinting" process. As the bird becomes accustomed to the area where it is hacked, it is more apt to return to this site. This process resembles the natural way in which an adult returns to its nesting site.

Cornell University began the hacking method of releasing the propagated peregrines to the wild in 1974 and has continued the program with marked success. Of the first 152 young falcons released in this manner, 112 survived to the stage of independent existence. They were truly returned to the wild.

In the spring of 1979, peregrine falcons paired, nested, and laid eggs at eyries in the United States for the first time in twenty years! One of the most fascinating stories to come out of the 1979 resurgence in peregrines is the story of Scarlett, a female who took up permanent residence on the 33rd floor level of the U.S. Fidelity and Guaranty building in downtown Baltimore. Although she seemed to have all of the requisites for falcon paradise, especially a never ending stream of city pigeons available to her, Scarlett lacked a mate. In the spring of 1979 she was obviously trying to get along without a mate as she went about nest building on the ledge of the skyscraper, even without a male on the horizon. Cornell University tried a daring experiment. They enlisted the cooperation of Chesapeake and Potomac Telephone Company, and put a captive male in a big cage atop the company's nearby building. Blue Meanie was his name and his presence was immediately noted with great excitement by Scarlett! She flew down to his cage and took the pigeons and quail offered her on the ledge outside of his cage.

On April 4, 1979, Scarlett laid the first egg to be seen in the outdoors east of the Mississippi River in more than twenty years. Obviously that egg had to be infertile, since Blue Meanie was still confined to his cage. He was falconry trained and eleven years old, but the Cornell people decided to risk him before Scarlett had laid her complete clutch and begun incubation, in the hopes that the two birds would mate immediately. Released, Blue Meanie took off and flew up to the 33rd floor level. Scarlett joined him in ecstatic joy, and they flew off wing tip to wing tip. But they flew off into the sunset, and Scarlett returned alone! Blue Meanie might have been too old for Scarlett; we don't know. Perhaps her maternal instincts brought her back to the two eggs she had laid, while the tiercel wanted a honeymoon fling before settling down to serious housekeeping. Maybe he remembered that male peregrines do all of the hunting while their mate is incubating, and he didn't feel up to being the provider.

Scarlett, however, laid her third infertile egg and began incubation. When the full period of incubation was completed, Cornell removed her eggs and substituted downy young falcons from the incubators. Scarlett was a good mother, and she fledged two males and two females. Just think what she might have done if she had a real mate!

At the same time, Interior Secretary Cecil D. Andrus approved a project to release peregrines in downtown Washington, D.C., using the roof of the Interior Building as a release site. The Fish and Wildlife Service set up a closed circuit television arrangement to allow visitors to the lobby of Interior a view of the young birds.

Why encourage peregrines to nest on skyscrapers? First of all, this environment is familiar to the birds. They have often chosen such sites on their own initiative. The food supply furnished by urban pigeons is one attraction, but the skyscraper also closely approximates the mountain ledges which are the birds' favorite wild nesting site. Although the birds are exceptionally fast flyers, they have difficulty catching and striking their prey in normal level flight. We have often watched mourning doves escape the pursuing peregrine in level flight. But if the bird follows its normal falconry instincts, it gets above its prey and hovers while waiting for the opportune moment. Then, with half closed wings, it "stoops," dropping like a feathered bullet to strike its prey. Although the element of surprise in the "stoop" is a great help, the added speed of the free fall makes the peregrine's attack almost impossible to avoid.

In addition, once the falcon has struck its prey and tries to carry the heavy load back up to the eyrie, updrafts against the side of the building enable the bird to sail majestically to its hungry young, without even flapping its wings. However, Interior's scant seven floors—and artist Bob Hines penthouse eighth-floor—hardly qualifies as a skyscraper, or as an eyrie site for a falcon.

While the eastern peregrine falcon was benefitting from a carefully thought out, beautifully implemented Recovery Plan—budgeted at more than half a million dollars a year through 1984—the other falcon populations in Alaska and on the west coast were in a different situation entirely. Never extirpated, but merely reduced in numbers, they posed a less dramatic challenge. Yet some of the same requirements were there: the need to survey nesting sites, to provide protection for the existing wild population, to enhance breeding habitat, and to educate the general public to the needs of the rare birds.

The earliest educated guess as to numbers of the remnant population in the Pacific Coast States (and Nevada) was made by Bond in 1946. He compiled a list of 136 known nesting sites and made "a gloriously wild guess" that there might be twice that number. The records show that nesting was successful, and that breeding populations were stable until 1950; a serious decline was documented in California in the early 1960's. By 1969, only ten known nesting sites were in use in California. As DDT spread its doubtful blessing by conquering mankind's ancient scourges of malaria and other insect-vectored diseases, similar fates befell peregrines in the other western states as well as in the eastern states, in Europe, and in most of the world.

Eggshell thinning is still a danger to Pacific coast peregrines, more so than to the eastern birds. To offset this danger, western recovery teams have introduced healthy birds into failing nests to keep eyries active. Interior populations of peregrines have had better reproductive success than the coastal birds. That has helped to maintain the remnant population. Programs developed in the much more ambitious eastern program will be used in the west as additional "pen-reared" birds become available. The west coast Recovery Plan aims at preserving breeding habitat for 165 breeding pairs, while the eastern U.S. plans call for establishing 350 breeding pairs.

Californian attempts at increasing the wild population include double clutching, cross-fostering and hacking back young birds that are captive and incubated from wild eggs. Need a road map for that sentence?

Double clutching refers to the proven technique of removing the first clutch of eggs laid to induce the female to produce another clutch. It works.

Cross-fostering is the practice of putting peregrine falcon eggs in the nests of other species of hawks to be incubated, hatched and reared. This works quite well, as almost all hawks are very tolerant of such practices, seemingly hatching and raising anything that is put in their nest. One hawk even hatched and attempted to mother chicken eggs placed in her nest. She never could understand why the chicks refused field mice for dinner. Cross-fostering has the added advantage of having a mother there to protect the young birds when they are most defenseless. Scientists have not yet determined whether or not imprinting to the foster mother will have a bad effect upon the young peregrines.

Hacking back refers to the practice of slowly releasing into the wild young peregrines which have been hatched in an incubator from wild eggs secured by double clutching. Got that?

Being of an optimistic turn, I can foresee a rosy future for this graceful falcon. I can even foresee the day when there will be a pair of peregrines for every suitable habitat niche—a number far higher than the 350 nesting pairs in the east and 165 breeding pairs in the west, which is the early goal of the recovery efforts now underway.

The peregrine falcon nearly disappeared from the earth as a result of widespread use of chlorinated hydrocarbons known as DDT. Because the trend was reversed in time, and because mankind has demonstrated that we care for this beautiful, free-soaring bird over which God has given mankind dominion, we still have the peregrine. The world is that much richer!

7

The Black-footed Ferret and Prairie Dogs

We have all heard the adage that "a specialist is one who knows more and more about less and less, until he knows absolutely everything about absolutely nothing."

Specialization, either of physical characteristics, or of adaptation to a particular environmental niche, has always been a facet of the evolutionary process. To fill a specialized need, beavers developed a split claw to groom their fur better. To balance himself while airborne on his long leaps, the kangaroo evolved a heavy tail. To warn of approaching danger, the pronghorn antelope developed a specialized patch of erectile white hairs on its hindquarters to heliograph warnings of approaching danger. To fill the need for guidance systems in the absence of light, bats developed an airborne sonar to reflect their own sounds back to them as they bounce off of objects which could be dangerous.

Specialization has helped many species to survive in the face of dangers to the entire species. On the other hand, too much specialization can sometimes doom the specialist.

Long before the first human animal set foot on North America, the black-footed ferret discovered prairie dogs. This mink-sized, light tan member of the weasel family found that he could kill a prairie dog any time he wanted dinner. He could easily travel down the prairie dog burrow; the sod poodle was no match for the killing ability of the ferret's sharp teeth. The burrow failed to protect the prairie dog, but it provided security for the ferret against larger predators.

In pre-European days, prairie dogs were everywhere on the open prairie in a huge area stretching from the state of Chihuahua in Old Mexico to northern Saskatchewan, and from the Rocky Mountains to the plains of Illinois. The prairie dogs lived in "towns"—great collections of burrows, some of them as big as ten by thirty miles in area!

There were billions of prairie dogs and only an estimated few black-footed ferrets. No one has any real clue as to how numerous the ferrets might have been when their population was at its height. Almost strictly nocturnal, the ferret spends the daylight hours underground and is seldom seen except by the biologist armed with a spotlight. Even then, it is very difficult to be in exactly the right place at exactly the right time to spot a ferret.

We can assume that the ferret was not numerous. It certainly was never numerous enough to reduce the numbers of its prey population, the prairie dog. These rodents were lovers, not fighters. They boasted a reproductive potential that led one Texas rancher to tell me, "All you need to start a prairie dog town is one female dog and the prairie."

The prairie dogs killed by the ferrets were quickly replaced by more of the same fast-breeding dogs. The ferret knew a good thing when he saw it. He moved into the prairie dog town and settled down to enjoy the soft life. Because he lived among his food supply, he had no reason to go hunting. He ate a prairie dog when he was hungry.

When the female ferret was about to bear her young, she chose a safe, dry burrow freshly made for her by the constantly digging prairie dogs. She brought forth her young there, and she fed them on prairie dogs as soon as they were weaned. The prairie dogs moved away from the ferret's burrow, but they never moved more than twenty or thirty yards and never seemed to make an effort to escape the slim killer. They realistically accepted their fate, for they had no means of escaping the ferret.

Straight prairie dog might have been a monotonous diet, but it was easy and healthy. The ferret began to specialize in prairie dogs, and specilization became greater. The ferret reached the point where it ate only prairie dogs. Conrad N. Hillman, of the South Dakota State University Cooperative Wildlife Unit, wrote:

"Field observations indicated that ferrets fed entirely on prairie dogs, but thirteen-lined ground squirrels, pocket gophers, deer mice, and cottontail rabbits, as well as upland plovers, horned larks and western meadowlarks were potential prey for ferrets. Ferret scats were found infrequently and it is assumed the animals defecate underground. Two scats found were composed of only prairie dog hair and bones. Ferrets were never observed to prey on animals other than prairie dogs except those made available for experimental studies."

While the population of black-footed ferrets and the population of prairie dogs was obviously in some kind of dynamic balance (as opposed to a static balance where both populations remain constant), we do not know whether or not the ferret became part of the complicated society in the prairie dog town. Burrowing owls moved into the dog towns, usually choosing unoccupied burrows for their own nests. The western diamondback and other snakes, poisonous and non-poisonous, also sought shelter in the burrows. Sometimes the rattler dined on young prairie dogs. I am sure of this, for I have removed the remains of young prairie dogs from the stomachs of freshly killed rattlesnakes in South Dakota. Upon occasion, the snake undoubtedly also dined on young owlets or on the eggs of the burrowing owl. All three species seemed to thrive in their cooperative housing project. The prairie dogs did all of the cooperating; the others enjoyed the fruits of the dogs' labors, sometimes enjoying the dogs themselves.

We suppose that the black-footed ferret simply avoided the rattlesnake and bypassed the burrowing owl as he went about his business of daily dining on a never ending supply of prairie dogs.

Never ending supply? So it must have seemed for millennia.

Enter mankind as the villain. Prairie dogs ate grass which man wanted to feed to his ever-increasing hordes of cattle and sheep. Even as man's herds overgrazed the available food supply, the destructiveness of the prairie dogs was emphasized.

Mankind waged war on the prairie dogs, using poison grain baits to kill them. The first try was oats treated with strychnine, but some of the dogs noticed the bitter taste of the poison before ingesting a lethal dose. Those dogs got very sick, but they recovered. The job of eradication had to begin again. Then man came up with *Compound 1080*, sodium monofluoracetate, which has no odor, no taste, and seemingly gave no advance warning to the animal which ate the treated grain. *Compound 1080* spelled the end of the prairie dog metropolis. The decline in numbers was sudden, swift, catastrophic. In less than two decades, the prairie dog became a rare sight over most of its historic range. Texas, which once sported prairie dog towns stretching more than one hundred miles in one direction, now preserves a special park in Lubbock so that the tourists can see a prairie dog or two.

The effectiveness of *Compound 1080* can hardly be exaggerated. Two expert riflemen used a big dog town north of Onida, South Dakota, as a rifle range. The prairie dogs were self-erecting rifle targets for the high powered rifles which were capable of executing the dog at ranges up to 250 yards with utmost certainty. These two riflemen shot 500 rounds apiece per day for two weeks. That's 14,000 rounds fired, and these men seldom missed. They must have killed, conservatively, at least ten thousand dogs in that two week period. Yet they could find no difference in the numbers of dogs available to their guns the next week; rifles had no effect against the really big dog town.

Registered Herefords needed the grass which those dogs consumed, so a rancher made the decision to poison them. *Compound 1080* oats were used and in one week the entire dog town was eliminated. I came through there one week later and searched in vain for a live prairie dog.

Similar elimination programs occurred all over the range. In two decades, the yipping millions were reduced to a few scattered dog towns, most of them far back in the foothills where some sentimental rancher had decided to maintain a remnant of the old west.

Mankind called this reduction **Progress.** Based on material standards it was progress; with the prairie dog gone, there was more grass for the steer. But the free-lunch counter for the black-footed ferret was almost gone.

The United States Fish and Wildlife Service, which now leads the fight to save rare and endangered species, directed the "control" program which led to the catastrophic drop in prairie dog numbers. Based on man's needs, this was a model program. Based on the needs of the black-footed ferret, it was a catastrophe. The model program for control of prairie dog numbers almost caused the eradication of another species.

By the time it was obvious that we had inadvertently almost eliminated another species when we "reduced" the prairie dog, we learned another fact of life—or maybe "fact of death." The prairie dog has a great reproductive potential and is able to rebound quickly in numbers. The ferret does not. When conditions were perfect for the ferrets, with limitless prairie dog populations at their disposal, the black-foot did not experience a population increase.

Conrad Hillman, reporting to a symposium in Rapid City, in 1974, said that prairie dogs were now far more numerous in Mellette County, South Dakota than they had been six years earlier, but that the numbers of black-footed ferrets had not responded accordingly. James W. Carpenter, a research veterinarian for the Endangered Wildlife Research Program at Patuxent, Maryland, postulated that the wild population of breeding age ferrets was so low that inbreeding with resulting genetic defects was the result. If his hypothesis is true, there is small chance for a natural rebound in the wild population.

A few ferrets remain in South Dakota, where they are being studied by state and federal researchers. Latest reports were that some 3200 acres of prairie dog town in Mellette County were maintaining a ferret population. Ferrets have been observed there every year from 1964 through 1974. The ferrets were successfully reproducing—at least one litter per year was sighted from 1966 through 1969.

But outside of South Dakota? I saw the last black-footed ferret I have ever seen in the wild in 1970 in southern Utah. For half an hour I watched as it hunted through an ancient and unoccupied prairie dog town, entering burrow after burrow in a methodical search for the prairie dog which was no longer available.

Remnant populations may exist outside of South Dakota, for we must remember that it is difficult to see this nocturnal animal even when you are looking for him. Since 1971, ferret sightings have been reported from North Dakota, Nebraska, Kansas, Oklahoma, Colorado and Wyoming. Older reports have been documented from Montana, New Mexico and Utah. Although all of the evidence indicates that South Dakota is the last range of the black-footed ferret, we must remember that only in South Dakota is that intensive search continuing.

Perhaps there are other places where a black-footed ferret comes to the surface after the sun has gone down, sniffs the air and then goes trotting, unseen, from burrow to burrow till he finds the aroma of live prairie dog. Perhaps there are other areas where the black-footed ferrets feed on prairie dogs, unseen by humankind. Perhaps...

Perhaps we can raise the black-footed ferret in captivity? Perhaps we can teach it to eat other things? Perhaps we could then reintroduce captive-reared ferrets into prairie dog towns where there would be no danger of poison programs removing the prairie dogs?

No, it doesn't seem that we will succeed in this attempt. Two pairs of black-footed ferrets, live-trapped in South Dakota, were taken to the Patuxent laboratories of the Fish and Wildlife Service for possible propagation in captivity. One pair was too old to put much faith in its efforts. Two years later the older female gave birth to five young. But four of the five were dead when born and the fifth one was so weak that it only lived a few days. The younger male suffered from cancer, and the older male was a poor candidate for semen collection. Tersely, the Patuxent report summed up as follows:

> "Although two black-footed ferret litters were produced, eight of the young were stillborn and the two remaining kits died within two days. This, in addition to other breeding difficulties and pathological processes encountered in the black-foots, may be a reflection of conditions occuring in the wild population. These conditions may also be responsible for the recent decrease in the numbers of black-footed ferrets in the wild. However, we are optimistic that captive propagation of this species using the techniques developed at Patuxent may still be a reality if, and when, additional young, genetically heterozygous animals can be found and taken into captivity."

Despite the professional optimism of the propagation experts at Patuxent, and despite all of the newest advances in storing semen for years in a frozen condition and then inseminating young females with the semen, the best chance—a not very good chance—for the black-footed ferret's survival is in the wild.

A single black-footed ferret was sighted on the Badlands Gunnery Range in South Dakota in 1969. In 1970, the Department of Defense, the Department of Interior and the State of South Dakota entered into an agreement for the preservation and protection of prairie dogs and ferrets on more than forty-two thousand acres of ferret habitat! Wonderful cooperation, to be sure, but was it in time?

With a very low wild population, the chance of male encountering female during the brief breeding season becomes remote. A hereditary trait of young males when they come to breeding age is to travel far afield in search of other ferrets. When there were greater populations of ferrets in the wild, this was beneficial in preventing inbreeding. Today, it almost precludes the young ferret male's chances of finding a mate. His overland search is dangerous, as it takes him away from his safe prairie dog burrows. His chances of even finding another prairie dog town are slim, much less his chances of finding a prairie dog town which supports a population of ferrets.

The black-foot is probably the rarest species of mammal in North America. The prognosis for survival is not good. Extreme specialization has not helped the ferret adapt to changing environment.

Between the time when this chapter on black-footed ferrets was first written and today, when the book must go to the publishers, things have happend in the world of the ferret. All of the news is bad. There has only been one confirmed sighting of a black-foot in the wild since 1974. That would indicate that the ferret is either extinct or approaching extinction.

That sighting was in the spring of 1979. In a telephone conversation with Dr. Raymond L. Linder of the South Dakota Cooperative Wildlife Research Unit at Brookings, I asked, "Can anyone tell me that there definitely is a black-footed ferret alive today?"

"No one can make that statement, to the best of my knowledge," replied Dr. Linder.

"Can we say that the ferret is now extinct?" I asked.

"No, we cannot make that statement for the simple reason that we haven't tried hard enough to find one," said Dr. Linder.

I asked the research leader if he "thought" there was still a black-footed ferret alive in the world. He said that it was his "feeling," not based on any evidence, that there were still black-footed ferrets somewhere.

Other researchers are not that optimistic; most of them say that the ferrets are gone—either extinct, or so low in numbers that extinction could not be staved off, even if we could find a pair of breeding age.

Did the black-footed ferret become extinct while I was writing this book?

8

Wolves

One of the more interesting cases of a species finding its way onto the list of the endangered is that of the red wolf. Halfway between coyote and lobo wolf in size, it looks very much like an oversized coyote, but it isn't.

In the year of 1959, I was making the rounds of government trappers in northeast Texas with John White, who was the supervisor of Predator and Rodent Control activities in that area. I was pestering John with questions about how you could tell a red wolf from a coyote. John got sick and tired of trying to convince me how different they were—"Hells bells, Chuck, they ain't nothing alike. A dummy can tell 'em apart from fifty feet." About that time we saw that the next trap had been disturbed, and we started to follow the drag marks to find the trapped animal.

"There," said John, pointing about two hundred yards ahead, "is your red wolf. Any fool can see that it isn't a coyote!"

I had to agree with him. The trapped animal looked bigger, was longer legged, and had a different shaped head than a coyote. The skull was sent to the taxonomists of the Smithsonian. I was convinced that it is easy to tell a coyote from a red wolf. These experts came back with their decision after making the cranial measurements of the skull we furnished them. Their decision? Part coyote, part domestic dog!

For a long time we went by a rule of thumb that said that if the animal weighed over so many pounds, it was a red wolf. If it weighed less than the arbitrarily chosen weight, it was a coyote. Then we found an entire family of coyotes in Archer County, Texas which weighed between forty-two and forty-five pounds. There was no room for error. They were coyotes—whoppers!

Obviously there was a true race of red wolves in the southeastern and south central part of this nation in earlier days. Perhaps, at one time, these red wolves were the only canines occupying a tremendous area of land ranging from central Texas through Arkansas all the way to the Carolinas. Perhaps there were no coyotes in that area, for the coyote seems to favor drier, more open country. Perhaps there were no timber wolves in that area for the same reason.

But from the earliest days of which we have records, there has always been hybridization among wolves, red wolves, coyotes and domestic dogs. This hybridization has given the taxonomists a lot of trouble in correctly labeling specimens even when they are in the hand. However, Curtis J. Carley, who has worked with the Red Wolf Recovery Team Effort in Texas and Louisiana for many years, feels that there is a simple, fool-proof method of deciding between coyote and red wolf. According to Carley, adult male red wolves seldom weigh less than fifty pounds, while adult male coyotes seldom go over thirty-five pounds. Adult male red wolves measure at least twenty-seven inches at the shoulder, adult male coyotes almost never stand more than twenty-five inches at the shoulder. To oversimplify, if it is big, it is a red wolf; smaller, it is a coyote.

Color is not a useful tool in identifying any of the *canidae* because they seem to display an amazing difference in colors even as littermates. Any color from dark black to almost white has been recorded at some time or another through some part of the overlapping ranges of the coyote, the red wolf, and the timber wolf.

Because all canids seem to follow the dictum, "When I'm not near the one I love, I love the one I'm near," hybridization has diluted the gene pool of the red wolf. There may no longer be a true red wolf; that is a red wolf with no taint of coyote blood in his ancestry.

However, the Red Wolf Recovery Team has succeeded in live-trapping many specimens from known red wolf territory. These specimens have been tranquilized and carefully examined, even having x-rays taken of their bone structure. The specimens exhibiting most nearly the qualifications to be called red wolves were shipped to the rearing station in Tacoma, Washington. Note that most of the red wolves trapped were in poor condition—not due to the trapping trauma, but due to parasites which infected them. Heartworms were common and played a large part in diminishing the vigor of the animals. Even hookworms were found in the animals trapped in the wild. Infestations of the sarcoptic mange mite were difficult to cure as the infestations were so much worse than any encountered in domestic pets, and formulations were not available to handle extreme infestation cases.

The future of the red wolf depended largely upon the success of captive breeding programs which were based on breeding populations of known red wolf strains. Success was also dependent upon a relocation program which would reintroduce the large predator into parts of its historic range which would be more hospitable than the range from which they were being live-trapped—namely southeastern Texas and Louisiana.

Using a pair of wolves from the Tacoma breeding station, Buddie and Margie, an attempt was made to study the experimental release and reintroduction problems on Bulls Island, South Carolina. That particular area was chosen for several good reasons. The State of South Carolina had a good endangered species program. Bulls Island was part of a National Wildlife Refuge, so there were no problems with getting landowners' permissions. There was a good deer herd on the island, with no known predators, and an excellent crop of rodents and other small animals which would form most of the normal diet of the red wolves. Bulls Island was just that, an island, which gave a bit more control of the movements of the pair after release.

Wildlife Biologist Curtis Carley holding a tranquilized male red wolf, "Buddy," shortly after his recapture during a wolf translocation experiment on Bulls Island.

With full television coverage, Buddie and Margie were released on December 13th, 1976, after being equipped with radio telemetry equipment to track their movements. After a short period of time, Margie moved to the mainland. This disrupted the experiment, so she was tranquilized by a dart fired from a helicopter and recaptured. Because there was no chance of a lone male becoming a naturalized citizen of South Carolina, Buddie was recaptured.

Although the plan was to release the same pair again, using slightly different techniques, Margie died of an uterine infection, seemingly unrelated to the capture—just one of those things that happen. A second pair of mated wolves was being readied in the Tacoma breeding complex, when the female of the pair took a few easy laps around the holding pen and dropped dead. Heart-worms!

There was a mated pair of red wolves being held in captivity on the Anahuac National Wildlife Refuge in Texas after their capture in Louisiana. This pair was chosen for another Bulls Island experiment. John and Judy were airlifted to South Carolina, kept in the acclimation pen for six months, and then released.

John and Judy remained together, splitting their time between Bulls Island and nearby Capers Island. The evidence is that they produced a litter of pups in April although no trace of the pups was ever found. We have to assume that the young were victims of hookworm or other parasites which infect so many of the pups of the red wolf.

Remember that this Bulls Island project was an experiment to learn how to release and reintroduce the red wolf. It was not an attempt to start a viable population. So, after it was certain that they had no pups to take care of, the helicopter was used to recapture John, after live-trapping Judy. Both of the animals had gained weight while in the wild. They were returned to the captive breeding program. The Recovery Team is now searching for suitable mainland sites for reintroduction of a viable wild population. They have not yet selected an area.

During the 1976-1978 period, considerable work was done with the identification of wild populations which might contain red wolf strains. This work was done under the supervision of Howard McCarley of the Austin College Biology Department and Curtis J. Carley, of the U.S. Fish and Wildlife Service. They used tape recorded red wolf howls to elicit responses from the red wolves and/or coyotes within hearing range. They came to the conclusion that the pure strain of red wolf was gone from Texas and occupied a very limited range in Louisiana. The future of the red wolf depended upon the captive breeding program, which still contained fewer than thirty wild-caught red wolves.

Why did the red wolf lose out and allow his range to be taken over by coyotes? Some researchers have reported that man's efforts to stop depredation by the larger wolf resulted in a vacuum which the smaller coyote rushed in to reclaim. Others feel that the red wolf crossbred with the smaller coyote so regularly that the gene pool labeled "red wolf" was drowned in the larger gene pool labeled "coyote." Every conceivable gradation of red wolf, coyote, timber wolf and domestic dog that can be imagined has already been documented as having occurred in the wild. The great variety of sizes exhibited by the coyote tribe—with adult males weighing as little as twelve pounds and as much as forty-five—is indicative of the widespread infusion of larger animal genes in the smaller animal population. Or, conceivably, the other way around.

In any event, the only red wolves now thought to be "all" red wolf are in captivity. Outside of the certified stock at the Tacoma Breeding Center, it would be a very wise red wolf, indeed, who knew his own father. It would seem that we are too late to save an interesting species. Or was it ever a real species? Perhaps the red wolf was an intergradation between the little "prairie wolf" which we know is a coyote, and the large timber (or lobo, or gray) wolf which we know is a wolf. We will never know, because we didn't start soon enough to save this species. Its fate was sealed through hybridization before we knew it was in trouble.

A very different situation exists with the small remnant populations of timber wolf still found in the lower forty-eight states and with the much larger population found in Alaska.

The eastern timber wolf was found at one time throughout most of the eastern United States and southeastern Canada. At the present time, however, that same wolf occupies only about 3% of the historic range, represented by small populations in Minnesota, Michigan and Wisconsin. The Interior Department listed the wolf as "endangered" in 1967. The Superior National Forest in Minnesota was closed to the taking of any wolves in 1970. Wolves have been protected by the state laws of Michigan since 1965, and by the laws of Wisconsin since 1957.

Eastern timber wolves are big animals, running from fifty to just over one hundred pounds for the males, slightly less for females. They exist in family packs, numbering from two to eight animals. When conditions are favorable, each pack occupies a territory of 50 to 120 square miles or more, and there is much evidence that the species is definitely territorial. Wolf litters, averaging five pups, appear in April or May. Like coyotes, the wolf has a tendency to produce larger litters when there is heavy pressure against the species. No one knows how this "larger litter" syndrome is triggered, but statisticians have proved that it happens.

Normally the prey of the timber wolf is the deer, moose or beaver that occupies his terrain. Abnormally (when surrounded by man and his agriculture), the list of prey promptly enlarges to include dogs, sheep, cattle, turkeys and all other farm animals.

During the period of awakened ecological conscience since 1960, there has been a tendency to "pooh-pooh" claims of wolves causing livestock damage. The trend has been to glamorize the wolf, to point out his lifelong pair-bonding, to glorify him as an excellent parent and to derogate all of his meat eating to the role of "culling out the old, the sick and the infirm" from prey herds.

This new tendency to excuse everything the wolf does is one extreme; the other extreme is the old fashioned fear of the wolf which describes him as the greatest danger to man and man's animals. This extreme holds the view that man and wolf cannot coexist on the same earth. Both extremes are wrong, of course. Reality is found in the middle ground.

Friends of the wolf often fail to realize the fact that the wolf is a danger to the farmer. In 1976, Mr. Leroy Rutzke of the Minnesota Department of Natural Resources wrote to the Eastern Timber Wolf Recovery Team Leader the following warning paragraphs:

"To an individual farmer attempting to make a living for himself and his family, the timber wolf can be, in effect, a very bad animal. It matters not that 99% of the contiguous United States has no wolves nor that the loss of livestock to wolves is an extremely minute fraction of the country's total livestock production. What matters is that the wolf can destroy the difference between success and failure for that farmer. The timber wolf has received a bad name because he hurts the livestock raiser in the same way that a holdup man hurts you."

And again from the same source:

"The wolf is an integral part of our wilderness environment. It is necessary to a natural balance in wilderness ecology. However, in our current fascination with this animal, we must not forget that outside of the wilderness the view of large wolf populations as a menace to livestock raising is NOT folklore or misconception."

Please remember that these prophetic words of warning come from a member of the Recovery Team, devoted to perpetuating the eastern timber wolf.

As Rutzke says, there is reason for the farmer to oppose the existence of timber wolves in his livestock pastures. In addition to this reasonable opposition, there is a large body of unreasoning fear of the wolf—a fear carried down from pioneer days when entire herds were lost to wolves, and when every tale of an encounter with a wolf was embroidered into a life or death struggle.

As a result of three centuries of being persecuted by livestock raisers, the eastern timber wolf is now restricted to that area contiguous to the Canadian border in Minnesota, where Canadian wolves spill over into our country. Northern Minnesota, having the largest border area touching Canada of all the states, has the most wolves. Isle Royale National Park in Lake Superior has harbored a resident pack of about forty wolves in its roughly 210 square miles at least since 1975. Interesting studies have been conducted there concerning the relationship between wolves and moose on the island.

Probably fewer than two dozen wolves exist in all of Michigan. Wisconsin has only scattered reports and very few reliable sightings over the recent past. If the eastern timber wolf is to be saved in the United States, we must start with Minnesota.

Wolves breed well in captivity, so artificial propagation can be used to provide a population—but a cage-reared population is not a viable wild population. Just as pen-reared red wolves are unable to make a living in the wild, the pen-reared timber wolf probably can't feed himself on wild deer.

However, there is no problem acquiring live, wild-trapped timber wolves from Ontario and Quebec where they are plentiful and relatively unloved. If the price is right, many wolves can be purchased. The problem is finding a place to release the newcomers without arousing a storm of protest. Note that the first transplant attempt was aimed at the relatively unpopulated regions of the upper peninsula of Michigan. In 1974, four transplanted wolves were released there. Biologically and ecologically, the transplant was well planned and should have succeeded. All four wolves died at the hands of humans. Ecologically acceptable doesn't mean socially acceptable.

Despite most people's first reaction—immediate and vociferous opposition to the transplants—a concerted public education program could gain public acceptance of the plans to reintroduce the timber wolf into carefully selected areas.

Transplant efforts are currently under investigation in such widely separated places as: Maine; the White Mountain National Forest; the Adirondack Forest Preserve area of northern New York; an area of the southern Appalachians in Virginia and West Virginia (most of it in the George Washington and Monogahela National Forest area); and another area of the southern Appalachians which includes parts of North Carolina, Tennessee and north Georgia; western South Carolina and southwestern Virginia; the upper peninsula of Michigan; and an area of northern Wisconsin.

In addition to plans for reintroducing the wolf into many parts of its former range, the Recovery Team also asks for improvement of deer habitat. This provides more and better food for the wolves. If expansion of wolf numbers is permitted, the team also anticipates management of some prey species populations to increase their numbers, such as reducing the hunter kill of white-tailed deer. Obviously, this rouses instant reaction from the hunting fraternity who fear that we are "closing the deer season to feed the wolves." Because sport hunters have always been in the vanguard of all conservation moves, and because these same sport hunters willingly tax themselves through the Pittman-Robertson Act and Dingell-Johnson Act in order to provide more federal funds to finance wildlife restoration programs, an educational program hopefully will be able to secure grudging acceptance of such management practices. There's a long row to hoe to accomplish this hoped-for acceptance of the timber wolf comeback. With the opposition of both the livestock operator and hunter, the program is doomed to failure.

Having heard the howl of a wild wolf in the night, I hope that this sound will always be part of America's legacy to generations of sportsmen and outdoorsmen yet unborn. We must remember that the increase in man's numbers crowded out the wolf. Without a decrease in man's numbers (an almost impossible achievement), there is scant chance of the wolf returning to most of the area he once inhabited.

The wolf in Alaska and Canada is in lesser danger of extermination for the same reasons. Where human population density is low, the wolf has fewer problems. Where there are many of us, there are few of him. Nevertheless, shooting wolves from helicopters has made a recent impact on the population. Additional pressure comes from the Alaska Fish and Game Department which cites the wolf for causing periodic crashes in the caribou population.

The western Rocky Mountains of the contiguous forty-eight states have recently shown a marked increase in numbers of timber wolves, although we are talking about very low numbers to start with. Again, we have a situation in which the wolves seem to be immigrants from Canada and are in goodly supply, with perhaps a few small pockets of wolves which have existed through the years. We thought that all wolves were exterminated during the major predator control era between 1870 and 1940. The western timber wolf is slowly reoccupying parts of its former range, especially in Montana. The Wolf Ecology Project begun by the University of Montana has been collecting data on the wolf in a range which extends into Canada on the north, western Montana, the northern half of Idaho, and that corner of Wyoming occupied by Yellowstone National Park.

A systematic program of exterminating wolves was even carried on in Yellowstone National Park during the years 1914 to 1926, and the remnant population in that park is, even today, insufficient to project a significant recovery in numbers without the introduction of animals from outside. Surely an increase in timber wolf numbers would be preferred to the ghastly spectacle of Park Rangers shooting wintering herds of elk to reduce their numbers.

Wolves were almost unknown in the west from 1940 through 1960. In 1973, the northern Rocky Mountain wolf was listed as endangered in the United States.

The very large areas of national forest land, national park land and national wildlife refuge land in the Rocky Mountain west surely make the possibility of reintroduction of wolves seem much easier than in the densely populated east. The people of the United States can have as many timber wolves roaming suitable habitats as those habitats can support, if people are willing to host the wolf. But to a very important segment of the population, those people who own the land and/or run livestock upon it, the wolf is an added business expense which they cannot tolerate.

The wolf is in no danger of extermination as a species. Can we return the wolf to the lower forty-eight states?

9

The Brown Pelican

A wonderful bird is the pelican.
His bill holds more than his belly can.
He can carry enough in his beak
To last him a week,
I don't know how the hell he can.

Most of us learned this nonsensical poem when we were kids. Most of us were fortunate enough to see the pelican, for the white pelican was a common visitor and nested over much of the inland United States. The brown pelican was found along almost all of our ocean shores. Happily, we are not worried about the white pelican today, but we have reason to fear for the endangered brown pelican.

A large bird which may weigh more than eight pounds, the brown pelican has a wingspread of seven feet. His grotesquely large beak, short tail and waddling walk make him appear clumsy on land, and he is no great beauty sitting on the water. But as a flier, he ranks among the world's best. Flying in a staggered line, pelicans patrol the coasts, flying effortlessly just above the tops of the waves, hunting for signs of fish in the waters below. When he travels longer distances, he rises to great heights and seems to glide most of the time, with only an occasional flap of those great wings propelling him along.

As he hunts for fish, the pelican is the embodiment of grace. Once he finds them, however, all grace and beauty are forgotten. He flops awkwardly but accurately down at his prey, his long bill stabbing expertly. The first time I remember watching brown pelicans diving into the water to catch menhaden driven to the surface by bluefish below, I thought that they would surely break wings and necks as they hit the water with a great splash. But they are tough birds. Not only did they survive the crash, but almost always came up with fish crosswise in their beaks. Those unlucky fish were quickly flipped back into the huge pouch for storage while the pelican went after a second, third and fourth.

The brown pelican seldom flies very far inland, and seldom ranges more than fifteen to twenty miles out to sea in search of food. Because this bird is such a creature of the coast, its fortunes must rise and fall with the biological health of our coastlines, estuaries and small islands.

A colony nester, the brown pelican deposits its eggs, usually three, in a nest built of dead vegetation; sometimes they are deposited directly on the ground. The young look like fuzzy footballs at first and are dependent upon the parents for food for a long period of time after hatching. There may be something poetic about a hawk bringing mice to its young, even something appealing about a robin flying to the nest with a beak full of worms. But there's little beauty in the way a pelican feeds its young. The young waddle to the parent, shrieking and clamoring and flapping their wings, begging to be fed. The parent bird opens its huge mouth and the young bird almost climbs inside, frantically grabbing for food being regurgitated by the adult. It isn't beautiful, but it works. The young grow rapidly.

Because brown pelican numbers have always shown remarkable rises and declines, the disappearance of the bird from Louisiana and most of Texas almost went unnoticed. In the 1960's the damage was done. The fact that the Louisiana population disappeared entirely within the four years 1957 to 1961, shows us that an extremely lethal agent caused the decline. **Which** lethal agent is still being debated. We cannot accuse DDE because that chemical is not lethal to adult birds; it only inhibits reproduction. Yet the adult birds disappeared.

At approximately the same time, or maybe a bit later, the brown pelican in California suffered a catastrophic decline. There the lethal agent was easily identified. Egg shell thinning caused by DDE, a metabolite of DDT, was obviously the culprit. Brown pelican populations in California were on the brink of extinction until 1973, when the trend was reversed. DDE residues were less common in California after the cessation of its use as a pesticide, and the pelicans quickly responded.

DDT was to blame in California. This was proven by finding concentrations greater than 1,000 parts per million of DDT (and/or DDE) in body tissues. No such clear-cut evidence was found in Louisiana, yet there the brown pelican was suddenly and dramatically eliminated.

South Carolina had a small nesting population which showed signs of declining in the early 1960's. These numbers have been relatively steady since. The salvation of the brown pelican was found in Florida, for the bird's numbers there remained at or near historic population levels during the crises in other parts of its range.

Very little is known about the status of brown pelican populations in other parts of the Caribbean or in Mexico's Pacific Coast waters. From the unreliable evidence of a windshield survey, I feel that the brown pelican population in the Sea of Cortez has gone down about 70% during the score of years that I have been visiting that great fishing ground. The Midriff Islands which formerly held big populations of nesting brown pelicans were totally without nesting birds in the last years of the sixties and early years of the seventies. The pelicans now seem to be making a comeback there, based on the same unreliable survey.

Bear in mind that DDE was carried into the upper reaches of the Sea of Cortez by the Colorado River, which is used for irrigation across a huge part of Colorado, New Mexico, Utah, and Arizona, and picks up its lethal load as it travels through these lands which are sprayed with many agricultural chemicals. The sheer immensity of the Sea of Cortez undoubtedly was diluted enough to allow the few remaining pelicans to persist through the DDT years, and to stage a comeback after the chemical was removed from the market in the U.S.

Fish are excellent bio-accumulators and will collect such chemicals as DDT or Endrin in their body tissues to a far greater degree than what is found in the surrounding water. Because his diet is almost entirely fish, the pelican is at the top of this particular food chain—a dangerous place to be when we are dealing with pesticides.

Unlike most of the endangered species which are described in this book, the brown pelican was being helped long before the Endangered Species Act was passed. In 1968, biologists from various states, the federal government and the National Audubon Society met at Rockefeller Wildlife Refuge in Louisiana to chart a course of action to save this endangered bird.

Immediately thereafter, they began publication of the *Brown Pelican Newsletter*, to keep each other informed about any developments in the bird's fight for survival. Each concerned state agreed to conduct an annual census, a great step forward. Without factual information as to actual populations, a state could lose all of its nesting colony and never know it. Officials of the Southeastern Section of the Wildlife Society and the Southeastern Association of Game and Fish Commissioners jointly formed the Brown Pelican Committee.

Public interest in trying to save a species seems to be one of the *sine qua non* prerequisites for a successful fight against extinction. Here the Brown Pelican Committee seems to have done a good job.

But the brown pelican is still in a precarious position. Even without knowing how many birds we once had, we do not know why their numbers crash-dived so abruptly in 1957 in Louisiana. Which factor or combination of factors caused them to decrease in numbers in Texas? We also don't know whether or not there are healthy populations of the brown pelican elsewhere in the Caribbean. Because we cannot quantify the loss of brown pelicans, we can hardly set goals for their re-establishment. We can only protect their nesting areas and continue to arouse public interest in the plight of the pelican. and, perhaps most important of all, we can continue to gather the necessary baseline data which will tell us, eventually, how our colonies of brown pelicans are doing.

Stable populations of brown pelicans in Florida have provided stock for reintroduction into Louisiana waters. The results seem to be promising. Populations of captive and permanently crippled Florida birds are furnishing the basis for reintroduction into parts of their former range in Texas.

The Recovery Team, recognizing its position in stepping into the middle of the campaign to save the brown pelican, has come up with rather ill-defined goals for recovery of the species. However, it is totally unrealistic to recommend goals without data upon which to base those goals. Rather than set numerical goals, the Recovery Team has wisely decided to continue what seems to be working, and to continue trying to gather the facts so that we can achieve realistic goals in the future.

As this book goes to press, we are optimistic about the future of the brown pelican. Except for Florida, this bird almost left us during the DDT/DDE days, but we are not sure even now that DDT/DDE was the culprit. The brown pelican is coming back, after the decrease in DDT use. The Recovery Team sees some success in establishing nesting colonies. That project will continue.

Cautiously, the Recovery Team also recommends captive breeding for three purposes. First, to maintain a gene pool in case some catastrophe eliminates the wild populations all over the range, as these birds disappeared from Louisiana in 1957 to 1961. Second, captive breeding will allow for more necessary basic research. Third, the existence of a captive flock creates many good opportunities for public education as to what the pelican looks like, why it should be protected and where its enemies can be found.

Today, it seems that "whatever we are doing, we are doing right." The brown pelican is regaining some lost ground from the 1957 to 1971 period. But, as almost every biologist says, "Further study is needed." The pelican is not out of danger yet.

10

The Manatee

A sailor on one of the first European vessels to venture into the shallow waters of the Caribbean saw his first manatee. As the big seacow turned to swim away, something about that ungainly animal reminded the sailor of a woman. He called it a mermaid, hinting at a resemblance to the legendary half woman-half fish figure which had lured sailors to their death throughout many mythological stories. The same creature was immortalized in the stories of the lorelei.

Anyone who could imagine that this ten foot long, two thousand pounds of shapeless blubber, with its rubbery face full of stiff bristly whiskers looked like a lovely woman had to be considered a candidate for the psychiatric ward. Surely the sailor had been away from home too long.

Generically speaking, the manatee is a relative of the elephant, but an elephant which evolved in a watery environment. The biologist describes this mammal as a "massive, fusiform, thick-skinned, nearly hairless animal with paddlelike forelimbs, no hindlimbs and a spatulate, horizontally flattened tail."

Perhaps that early observer was misled by the somewhat elephantine grace with which the sea cow moves through the water. Misled or not, the "siren" appellation has lasted. The manatee was given the scientific name of *Trichechus manatus*, of the order *Sirenia*. That early observer didn't get a look at the fat face with the whiskery chin, or he would never have considered it feminine.

The manatee has a placid temperament. Some biologists claim that this is the only mammal which cannot be goaded into fighting. It will not fight to defend either itself or its calf, although there is obviously a strong bond of affection between cow and calf. The manatee never had to learn to "fight back" because it never had an enemy in all of its evolutionary history.

The manatee has an enemy now. That enemy is us!

Ever since the Spaniards first came to Florida, the manatee has been killed for its meat, oil and thick skin. Surely its numbers declined drastically during the period between the coming of Ponce de Leon and the action of the Florida Legislature in 1893, which gave complete legal protection to the manatee. The law was not enforced, and the manatee continued to decline in numbers.

Then came a new enemy—the outboard motor. With the tremendous increase in recreational boating in the beautiful waters of Florida, the manatee

faced a danger with which it could not cope. By grazing on underwater vegetation in shallow waters, the manatee spends a great part of life just under the surface. When a motor boat approaches, the manatee tries to get away from danger by diving. Its reflexes are slow and top speed through the water is probably about thirteen miles per hour. A speeding boat travels at several times that speed. The sea cow can't get out of the way, and the whirling propeller opens great gashes in its blubbery hide. Often the speeding motorboat carves up the manatee. The boat operator doesn't even know he hit anything live. All he feels is a gentle bump as the skeg flips up and over the dying animal.

Man's water control structures are also death traps for the gentle manatee. When a control gate is opened, the sudden outrush of water pins the manatee against the intake structure and holds it long enough for the animal to drown. The cooling water coming out of power generating plants in Florida is quite a few degrees warmer than the surrounding waters. Because these artificially created "winter resorts" are available, the manatee has stopped moving back south with the advent of cooling weather. He and his family congregate in the outflow of the plant to laze away the winter days.

There had always been some warm water refuges occurring naturally, such as the warm springs at Crystal River, where the appearance of the manatees each November had been taken as a sign that winter was almost there. However, by 1977, there were twenty-three warm water refuges used by the manatee, and only six of them were natural warm spots. The other seventeen were power plants or other industrial facilities which discharged warm water. Florida Power and Light owned five of the largest plants in terms of manatee use during the winter months. This utility has been very good at recognizing its responsibility to the animals, which are attracted to the warm water winter resorts, and has granted the Florida Audubon Society more than a hundred thousand dollars to study the situation. In addition, Florida Power and Light has spent more than a quarter of a million dollars in an educational program requesting people to leave the manatee strictly alone in its restricted winter home.

Why leave them strictly alone? After all, the peaceful, slow-moving manatee is no danger to humans. The humans mean no harm. They only want to get close enough for a picture, or close enough to touch one of them, or just close enough to get a better look.

But this attempt to get closer is often misinterpreted as an attack by the shy manatee. The manatee tries to escape such close contact with humanity by leaving the warm waters of the spa and fleeing into the colder waters. This often proves fatal, for the manatee has never learned how to tolerate great changes in the temperature of the watery environment where all of its life is spent. A variation of only a few degrees can lead to bronchopneumonia. Leaving the warm water for a couple of hours can be fatal for a manatee!

The full shutdown of a complete warm water discharge for a day or two could cause the loss of the entire herd wintering there! Of course a shut down is the last thing that any power company wants, because profits disappear when the

Mr. John C. Oberheu, Recovery Team Leader for the Manatee Recovery Effort

plant is shut down. Nevertheless, all plants have down time, and the danger of a real catastrophe for the manatee is ever present.

Unable to adapt to cold weather, sliced and gouged by whirling propellers and drowned in water intake structures, the manatee faces a very real danger of extermination, despite the cooperation of Florida industry, the Florida Department of Natural Resources, the Florida Audubon Society and, very importantly, the full cooperation of Sea World of Miami, which has the facilities and the knowhow to nurse wounded manatees back to health.

The Florida population is estimated at somewhere between 800 and 1,000 manatees. Seventy-two manatees wintered in the Crystal River headwaters in the winter of 1977-78, which shows how vulnerable the population is, with large numbers of animals concentrated in one place, subject to danger from one occurrence. Their numbers probably are declining drastically. We do not know that, however; we can only assume that the greatly increased **known** mortality which has been observed in the last five years indicates a loss in manatee numbers. Other observers have claimed that the increased mortality is due to increased numbers, placing more individuals in jeopardy. No one now claims that the manatee is increasing in numbers in Florida.

How about in other countries? Puerto Rico has a remnant population of probably less than 100 manatees. They were extirpated from the Virgin Islands

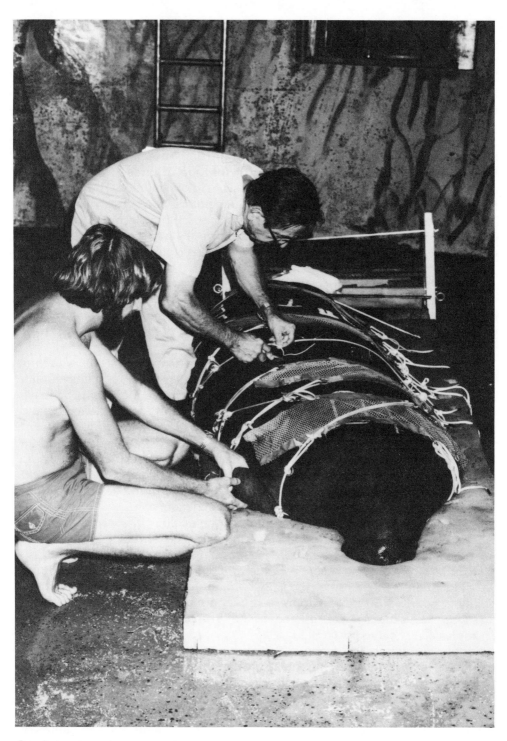

Applying tags to a manatee

long, long ago. Historically, the manatee was found along the Central and South American coastlines all the way down to southern Brazil, also Jamaica, the Dominican Republic and many other island countries of the Caribbean Sea. Their status today is poorly known, but it is doubtful if any nation, other than the United States of America, is concerning itself with the fate of the sea cows in their waters. Lack of funds and the slow development of an ecological conscience in developing nations prevent much needed help for the manatee outside the waters of Florida and Puerto Rico.

The manatee is completely herbivorous, grazing on marine vegetation entirely. Newborn calves begin to graze at the age of three weeks, but they continue to suckle their mother for as long as eighteen months. The calf is over three feet long when born and weighs in the neighborhood of sixty-six pounds. Single births are the rule, although there is a hint that twin births may result at the end of the 385-day gestation period. Cows seem to give birth only about every three to five years, which gives the species a mighty low reproductive potential to recover from any population disaster.

Although they do congregate in the available warm water spots in the wintertime, manatees are not normally gregarious. In fact, the only natural congregating observed is the pairing of male and female for a brief mating period, and the only natural long-term association of manatees seems to be that of cow and calf.

We know that the adult manatee will consume as much as 100 pounds of vegetation per day. With their reduced numbers this statistic has little significance. Obviously the manatee is not going to overgraze the very productive underwater pastures of its homes in Florida. Conversely, any benefit accruing to mankind as a result of manatees clearing obstructed waterways of "water weeds" will be too small to be significant.

The manatee neither helps nor harms mankind. Does this mean that we do not have a duty to allow it to continue living? Does its economic "unimportance" justify its extinction? Or does our "dominion" over the manatee species carry the responsibility to save the manatee from extinction?

My opinion is that we are duty bound, by an ecological conscience which differentiates us from the beasts, to give the manatee a chance to succeed or fail as a species, without being killed by man and his machines.

Floridians have begun a very well thought out campaign to save the manatee. Education of the boating public to the manatee's existence and its vulnerability to whirling propellers is stressed. Certain concentration areas of Florida's waterways are closed to all boat traffic in an attempt to reduce the danger of "manatee meets motorboat."

Serious study is being given to the matter of the artificial concentration of manatees in warm water effluents in winter time. The industrial entities concerned seem to be giving excellent cooperation, partly as a matter of good public relations, and partly as a matter of good business. Perhaps it will be necessary to screen the manatee away from hot water effluents, which will be extravagantly expensive. Perhaps these hot water effluents must be diluted or dispersed as they come into contact with naturally cooler waters. This would also be very expensive. Perhaps there are ways which can be discovered to make the warm water less attractive, such as the introduction of a chemical deterrent into the water—something that is very distasteful to the sea cows.

The whirling propeller is the greatest danger to the manatee. The reduction of this mortality element is the greatest hope for the manatee's future.

One of the most distressing aspects about any struggle to save a species from extinction is the fact that it takes a great reduction in species numbers to gain the attention of the public. The lower the total population becomes, the greater the unit value of each individual. Support for measures designed to save the last ones can easily be drummed up. How unfortunate that we become emotionally involved in the struggle for survival only when that struggle seems to be lost—as with the whooping crane.

A reduction in numbers down to the thousand mark was necessary before we became deeply involved in the struggle to save the manatee. It is definitely not too late to save this animal now, and there is reason for cautious optimism.

11

The Pennsylvania Rattlesnake

There is a lighter side to the struggle for survival of species, although the individuals in these dramas might not see the humor of their plight. The rattlesnake, as a species, is not threatened with extinction. It holds its own in numbers across a wide area of the west and southwest, despite almost total persecution by mankind. Mankind's enmity toward the rattlesnake can be more easily understood if we recall that a bite from a rattlesnake can be fatal. We know it is always painful. The rattlesnake has few friends; therefore his numbers are not legion.

The rattlesnake had at least one friend during the first week of October in 1979. That friend was Doctor C.K. Dodd, Jr., a staff herpetologist with the Office of Endangered Species in Washington, D.C., a part of the Fish and Wildlife Service. An evening television news show in Baghdad-on-the-Potomac chronicled the fact that Dominique's, a very swank and expensive restaurant, was serving rattlesnake sautéed in red wine. The news story reported that the restauranteur purchased the rattlesnake meat from a supplier in Pennsylvania. Dr. Dodd was a specialist in such matters, and he knew that the Pennsylvania population of rattlesnakes was in a very precarious position. In fact, he used the wording "was rapidly approaching extinction" in a letter to the proprietor of Dominique's that was written on official Department of the Interior stationery.

Dodd's letter continued, "How can you promote the sale of a population which is approaching extinction according to biologists who have studied it within the state? Only by education and prohibition of the exploitation of this species can it be maintained as a viable part of northeastern ecosystems. I respectfully request that it be removed from your menu." Dominique D'Ermo, the restaurant's owner, immediately took rattlesnake off the menu and wrote Dodd to thank him for the information.

So far, so good. Here we have a case of a concerned scientist, who also happens to be a gentleman, writing a letter to a concerned restaurateur, who also happens to be a gentleman, and the exchange of polite correspondence achieving the desired end. Right?

Wrong! Things seldom go that simply in official Washington. Cabinet Official Cecil D. Andrus, who has a better than average scorecard with the environmental community on the national scene, dines at Dominique's and is friendly

67

with Monsieur D'Ermo. When Andrus heard of the letter exchange, he apologized to Dominique D'Ermo in person for his subordinate who had overstepped his authority to use Interior stationery to express his concern for the rattlesnake.

Andrus fired Dr. C.K. Dodd! The legalistic reason was the unauthorized use of official stationery which admittedly was a "no-no." The firing surely contravened the advice given in the Mikado, wherein it is urged that the "punishment fit the crime." The firing also enraged the environmental community, and brought many of the big names in conservation rallying to the defense of the herpetologist. Congressman Dingell called on Andrus to rescind his hasty dismissal of the snake man. Andrus, who stated his belief that befriending rattlesnakes was ridiculous, also stated that the brouhaha over his dismissal of Dodd would "blow over in four or five days." Not by a long shot.

Congresswoman Pat Schroeder of Colorado is Chairwoman of the House Subcommittee on Civil Service. She rather tartly informed the Secretary that "insulting the owner of a cabinet secretary's favorite restaurant is not proper grounds for dismissal of a career civil servant." Promising to hold committee hearings to air the mess if Andrus didn't back off, Mrs. Schroeder averred, "I'm overwhelmed that he thinks he can get away with this."

With the news media having a holiday reporting his discomfiture caused by his own high-handedness, Secretary Andrus obviously required a way out of his dilemma. Although it was common knowledge that he, Andrus, had fired Dr. Dodd, the actual three page letter of dismissal was signed by Fish and Wildlife Service Director, Lynn Greenwalt, because Dodd worked under the Fish and Wildlife banner in Interior. So, there was a way for the Secretary to save face, although it involved "losing face" for Director Greenwalt, a career wildlifer with a long record of integrity and intelligence.

Assistant Secretary for Fish and Wildlife and Parks, Robert Herbst, announced that he was going to review Greenwalt's decision to fire Dodd. He reviewed it, then ordered Greenwalt to rescind the firing and give Dodd a letter of admonition instead. Having been a friend of Greenwalt's for sixteen or seventeen years, and having spent six years in the Byzantine halls of Interior, I can make a couple of fairly well-educated guesses with regard to this tempest in a teapot: Guess Number One is that Greenwalt hated the necessity of signing a "dismissal" letter to Dodd, but acted upon direct orders from Andrus; Guess Number Two is that Andrus ordered Herbst to find a way around the dilemma and to rescind the dismissal because he didn't like the adverse publicity he was getting.

For the person truly concerned with the principles behind our efforts to prevent extinction of species, there are some object lessons in this tempest in a bureaucratic teapot. We must be consistent. If we intend to protect one endangered species, we must be ready to protect another endangered species, even if we have no particular love for rattlesnakes, either on the menu or on the ground we walk upon. Even the lowly rattlesnake, the peril of so many "B" movies and pulp fiction, can summon up some pretty high-ranking support when the chips are down.

We also have a very good form of Civil Service protection for concerned scientists: The Civil Service Subcommittee in the House of Representatives was prepared to rub Andrus' nose in this case if he did not rescind what one Washington publication called his attack of "bigshotitis."

Two more things please me about this whole ridiculous incident. First of all, I'm pleased that a civil servant (Dodd) was incensed enough about the attack on the endangered Pennsylvania population of the unloved rattlesnake to take pen in hand and go to the defense of the rattler (even though I decry his choice of stationery).

Secondly, I'm pleased that congresspersons evidently believe that the language of the Endangered Species Act means exactly what it says. I hope they will be that concerned in defending the Act from other much more serious and much more well-planned attacks (as opposed to Andrus' action which was obviously not preceded by any thought of the consequences).

There will be literally thousands of attempts to weaken the provisions of the Act. They will not be as easily repulsed as was the case of Andrus vs. Dodd.

12

The Delmarva Fox Squirrel

This large, handsome squirrel gets its name from the DELaware, MARyland and VirginiA peninsula which forms the eastern shore of the most valuable estuary in the United States, the Chesapeake Bay.

In almost all of its present range, the Delmarva fox squirrel shares its habitat with the common gray squirrel, which is much more numerous and more widely distributed than the fox squirrel. However, the two squirrels do not seem to inhabit exactly the same environmental niche. The Delmarva likes parklike areas, with large expanses of cleared land which are free of understory. He seems to need very large food-producing trees, such as the white oaks so much desired for shipbuilding since colonial times. These mature trees provide a reliable supply of food, without which the Delmarva doesn't seem to do well. On the other hand, the gray squirrel seems to manage better where there is a lot of understory and less cleared (parklike) ground below its trees. The gray is much more arboreal, while the Delmarva is terrestrial by choice.

Much of the different needs and habits of the two species can be easily explained by their comparative size. The gray is a nimble, quick, small squirrel which climbs easily and prefers to take to the treetops to escape danger. The Delmarva is one of our largest squirrels, reaching weights of as much as two pounds. Such a large squirrel requires a lot of food. The small gray is beset by many enemies, and seldom ventures far from the trees where he can escape. The big Delmarva is safe from all but the largest predators, hence he dares to venture far from trees.

Housing developments in the Delmarva peninsula have greatly reduced the habitat available to the Delmarva fox squirrel. The cutting of almost all mature forests removed the reliable source of mast (acorns), the preferred "storable" winter food. As these cut-over areas were reforested, they became second growth, or scrub timber, with a dense understory. This change from open parklands under mature trees to dense understory was definitely not to the Delmarva's liking.

In colonial times, the Delmarva fox squirrel was found over the entire Delmarva peninsula, as well as parts of mainland Maryland, a large part of Pennsylvania and probably parts of southern New Jersey.

The current range of the Delmarva fox squirrel is very small, restricted to parts of four counties in Maryland and to the Chincoteague National Wildlife Refuge in Virginia. The Chincoteague Refuge in Virginia is in that southern part of the Delmarva Peninsula which is part of Virginia, yet really seems to belong to Maryland. The population at Chincoteague is a reintroduced one, with animals trapped from National Wildlife Refuges in Maryland.

The Delmarva fox squirrel has shown itself to be adaptable to some changes in agricultural practices and very intolerant to others. It adapts readily to farm crops, using corn and even soybeans as fast as they are planted in its habitat. It does not tolerate the elimination of its mast-supplying trees. This is easy to understand. If the "squirrel carrying" capacity of the land is 200 squirrels per square mile for 360 days of the year, but drops down to zero squirrels per square mile for five days of the year, we can be very sure that there will be no squirrels there the next summer. The species will have been extirpated from that area.

The adaptability of the Delmarva fox squirrel has been demonstrated by actually forcing out the competing gray squirrel on lands of the Eastern Neck Wildlife Refuge, and by the fact that it has taken readily to its new home at Chincoteague. Knowing such adaptability, the Recovery Team has high hopes for re-establishment of the Delmarva over large parts of its former range, from which it has been driven by intensive lumbering and by the encroachment of man with his cities and his farms.

The goals of the Recovery Team depend upon preventing further contraction of the fox squirrel's present home range. This seems to be an attainable objective because so much of the land is in state and federal refuge status, and because the people of the peninsula have been alerted to the danger of losing the big squirrel and have reacted favorably to appeals for help. If the present range can be maintained, the Recovery Team will aim for the establishment of ten new colonies outside of that range. Three of these new colonies would be in Delaware and three in Virginia. The Recovery Team feels that it will be necessary for a new colony to be in existence for at least five years and to have demonstrated its ability to increase in numbers before it can be considered successful. The Team feels that attainment of this objective of ten new sustaining colonies would permit changing the status of the Delmarva fox squirrel from endangered to threatened. Twenty more additional prospering colonies, in addition to the first ten, would have to be established before the squirrel's status could be called secure.

Blackwater and Eastern Neck National Wildlife Refuges are seen as sources of seed stock with which to restock former habitats of the Delmarva fox squirrel. These areas are valuable to all wildlife, not merely to the waterfowl and migrating birds for which most of the refuges were originally established.

Trapping and transplanting of Delmarva fox squirrels has been successfully accomplished in several instances, but there are problems. A good-sized group of squirrels must be transplanted at one time. If there are only a few individuals in the restocking attempt, there is too much danger that they will scatter upon the original release and never come together again. Obviously, if male and female don't meet, there will not be a prospering colony.

Much has been learned about release methods also. Squirrels should be kept in captivity in their new home for several weeks so that they may become acclimated to the new surroundings. If this is not done, their initial reaction will be to "get out of here" and head for home as soon as they are released. Acclimated squirrels, gently released at a time of their own choosing, are more apt to stay in the release area.

Two points must be made to place the recovery effort in proper perspective. First of all, an entire species of fox squirrel is not in danger. It is a subspecies. Secondly, the Delmarva fox squirrel has demonstrated tremendous ups and downs in population as the face of the eastern shore has changed, yet it has demonstrated excellent reproductive potential and the ability to adapt. Both are prerequisites for survival.

Unlike the black-footed ferret which seemed unable to change its diet from prairie dogs when that food became scarce, the Delmarva fox squirrel can adapt to soy beans and corn as they become available. Unlike the California condor which produces only one young per two years per mated pair, the Delmarva fox squirrel produces litters of young through most of the year. Furthermore, the young breed during their first full year of life.

The potential for recovery is excellent.

Devil's Hole Pupfish

13

Fish of the Desert

Ages of glaciation formed huge lakes across the northern part of what is now the United States of America. Millenia later these lakes have all but disappeared, and the southwestern part of our nation continues to dry up. Entire species of fish have disappeared, and extreme subspeciation has occurred. As drainages have been cut off, migration between "families" has ceased and further specialization has been induced. Because the struggle for survival has become more straitened, subspecies have evolved differently in order to solve the different problems of their reduced and changed habitats.

One example of this, on a huge scale, concerns the glacial Lake Lahontan, which probably occupied as much as 8,000 square miles of Nevada and California at its heigth. As receding glaciers reduced its water supply, Lake Lahontan began to shrink. The drainage systems flowing from its various parts became more and more discrete, and migration between those drainages came to an end. Some fish populations had to combat increasing alkalinity as their total water supply diminished while the total dissolved solids remained the same. Some subspecies made the change toward greater alkali tolerance. Other species failed to adapt and have disappeared. As total water volumes became less and less, maximum temperatures continued to rise. Some subspecies failed to adapt to the higher water temperatures. Those subspecies, too, are gone.

One of the drainages of Lake Lahontan dwindled down to the Pyramid Lake–Lake Winnemucca–Truckee River complex which early European settlers found as they worked their way west. The Paiute Indians, who were well adapted to gathering a living from these arid lands, inhabited this Great Basin country. The Paiute's tribal name translates to "sucker eaters" according to some students of the Indian languages. Well they might be, for in the years before the white man came, the Paiutes gathered on the shores of Pyramid Lake to feast on the spawning fish that gathered at the mouths of rivers preparing for their upstream spawning run.

According to tribal tradition, the Paiutes ate Pyramid Lake cutthroat and a sucker-like fish which they called the *cui-ui*. Both species of fish were eaten fresh, as well as being smoked and packed away for future rations, and both were dried and used as trade goods with other tribes who did not come to Pyramid Lake.

A geologic moment in this great "drying up cycle" might last for hundreds of years. During one of these moments the white man came to the shores of Pyramid Lake. He, like the Paiutes, found the Pyramid cutthroat trout to be one of the largest (in individual size) of all the cutthroat families. He also found the *cui-ui* present in astronomical numbers, especially when massing for the spawning run upriver. Seemingly, the desiccation of former Lake Lahontan had reached a plateau which offered sufficient permanence for the fishes to have established an equilibrium with their environment. Cutthroat and *cui-ui* were obviously dominant fish species and very successful life forms—at least at that particular plateau in the downward cycle of desertification which was taking place across the great southwest.

Within a small geologic "moment," mankind used up the water supply of the Truckee River. He spread the river out and irrigated his crops. Mankind so reduced the inflow to those lakes that Lake Winnemucca dried up entirely! Pyramid Lake was so reduced in volume—perhaps eighty feet in maximum depth—that the Pyramid cutthroat trout is now extinct. Nothing anyone can do will bring it back.

The *cui-ui* is so reduced in numbers that there are serious fears for its survival. Both Federal and State of Nevada fish culturists have succeeded in hatching the *cui-ui* in numbers. In fact, during the period 1973-1976, the U.S. Fish and Wildlife Service was able to dump more than seven and a half million fry into the lower Truckee River and the lake. Please do not be over-awed by the seven and a half million figure. The survival rate for fry is very, very small—even under optimum conditions. For purposes of comparison, a large carp in spawning condition may contain half a million eggs. Fifteen such fish would produce seven and a half million fry.

Nevada biologists have succeeded in rearing *cui-ui* to provide a brood stock and to allow experimentation to see if *cui-ui* can be successfully fostered in waters other than the Pyramid Lake drainage.

The damage, however, has been done. Decreased stream flows into once-magnificent Pyramid Lake can be blamed on geologic evolution of the Great Basin, with a tremendous "kick in the pants" also added by the white man's irrigation canals which stole so much water from Lakes Winnemucca and Pyramid. Decreased stream flows brought increased dissolved solids readings, increased siltation of spawning beds, and formation of impassable deltas at the mouths of streams formerly used for spawning by these fish who remembered an ancestral anadromous urge from eons past.

Now the water has dried up.

The tragedy of the extinct Pyramid cutthroat, and the *cui-ui*, which benefits from the activities of an aroused civilization determined not to go on losing life forms at such a rapid rate, is a large drama. Yet this large drama is being acted out in microcosms all across the arid lands of the American southwest.

The Devils Hole pupfish is perhaps the best known troubled species. Let's talk about some of the other pupfish species which face similar problems to that of the Pyramid Lake desiccation.

There was the Tecopa pupfish. That's right—"was." This tiny fish, less than an inch and a half long, was first described in 1948 by the peripatetic Robert

R. Miller. It lived in thermal pools and thermal springs located in the drainage of the Amargosa River in southern California. During the 1950's someone built a bathhouse above one of the thermal springs, which changed the channels and disrupted the world of the Tecopa pupfish. At the same time, introduced bluegills began to feed on the tiny Tecopa pupfish. In 1970, the Tecopa pupfish was declared endangered, but it was already too late. A survey in 1972 failed to locate even one Tecopa pupfish. Fisheries biologists hunted for the fish until 1977. The Tecopa pupfish was gone; the bluegills are doing just fine.

As this manuscript is being completed, the final action to declare this subspecies legally dead is still going through the various required legal steps. Its approval is certain, for there are no more Tecopa pupfish. This is the first time that an animal has been removed from the list of endangered species because it is extinct. It will not be the last time.

A related subspecies, the Shoshone pupfish, was also declared extinct by the U.S. Fish and Wildlife Service. This one had never even been listed; so it did not need to be de-listed. Who mourned the passing of these two subspecies? Who should have mourned their passing?

In order to prevent another subspecies from passing into oblivion before it can be listed as endangered, the Rare and Endangered Species arms of the Fish and Wildlife Service has now given the emergency designation of "endangered" to the Borax Lake chub. The fish is found only in one ten acre lake fed by a thermal spring in Oregon's Alvord Basin. Minerals precipitating from the cooling thermal outflows have built up a dam around the lake, which has effectively prevented any migration in or out of the waters of Borax Lake.

Geothermal exploration leases have been granted (through the Bureau of Land Management) for this area. When drilling starts, water may be pulled out from under the Borax Lake chub. At least the chub will have been listed as endangered before it becomes extinct!

The Tecopa and Shoshone pupfish were two subspecies of the Nevada family of pupfishes. The smallest member of this species is the Warm Springs pupfish. The entire known world's population of this tiny pupfish is located in Ash Meadows, Nevada. Their tenuous lease on life is severely threatened by excessive pumping to irrigate crops. This pumping is effectively mining the underground water supply of the basin and lowering the water table drastically. Here is another case of pulling water out from under the pupfish. At the last report, the Warm Springs pupfish's habitat was the area, less than one square kilometer in size, near the School Springs locality.

Icthyologists studying this fish are moving gingerly, for we have proved that man can sometimes kill with kindness. For example, we fenced livestock away from a stream which supported a kindred population of pupfish. As a result of the cattle removal, emergent vegetation grew tall and lush. The lush vegetation had a greater evapotranspiration rate than formerly, and literally dried up the stream we were trying to protect!

Mankind's manipulation of the water table could wipe out the world's population of the Warm Springs pupfish. Can we not spare one square kilometer—out of all the desert southwest—for this tiny fish?

Gray Whale

14

The Great Whales

Strictly speaking, the matter of endangered cetaceans should fall outside the purview of this book. I have tried to limit myself to discussing the birds, mammals, reptiles and amphibians which come ashore, or live ashore in North America and Hawaii. Whales spend all of their lives in the oceans, and thus should be considered outside of our discussion. But no one sincerely interested in the welfare of living species can talk about endangered species without mentioning the great whales.

Today, no species of whale can be considered to be in immediate danger of extermination. The reasons are not found in man's ecological awakening, as in the case of the whooping crane, but rather are found in the laws of economics. When the whale species becomes so scarce that it is not economically profitable to try to take individual whales, whale pursuit stops. Many nations have gone out of the whaling business. Coupled with this economic motivation may be a feeling of shame associated with killing the large whales.

Today there cannot be any justification for the killing of a whale, except for subsistence by Eskimos. Even the subsistence excuse wears increasingly thin as snowmobiles and the other trappings of civilization bring the Eskimo into the twentieth century. For the ancient ways of the Eskimo, well suited to survival in his hostile Arctic *Lebensraum,* seem somehow irrelevant in a society of motorized transport, helicopters, radio and television. In my opinion, within the span of the next two generations there will be no one on this earth who *needs* to kill a whale! Perhaps no one **needs** to kill a whale today.

Whaling in centuries past was a dangerous and difficult task for daring men who sought the big whales in sailing vessels; then rowed to within throwing distance with their harpoons in hand. Many a man failed to return to New Bedford and other whaling ports.

Factory ships now cruise to the whaling grounds, where helicopters are used to locate the whales. Then fast "killer" boats close in on the whale. The gunner aims his cannon. An explosive bomb is then driven deep inside the whale where it explodes. Using compressed air forced inside the whale through hose and pipe, the killer ship makes sure that the carcass will float until it can be hauled aboard the factory ship. Their flensing knives still do some of the work, but machinery does most of the job as the whale is separated into its various components—whale meat to be sold in Japan and other countries as "whale beef," ambergris for use in perfume making, whalebone for the few remaining uses left over from whalebone corset days, and whale oil. But the great bulk of the whale carcasses processed today goes to make dog and cat food!

There is no need to kill whales to provide red meat, for there is no shortage of red meat protein in the coutries able to afford to buy it. No whale meat is offered for sale in those countries which cannot afford domestic meats. Whale oil is unnecessary, for synthetic oils can do everything that whale oil once did—better and more cheaply. Furthermore, a whale certainly shouldn't be killed to provide cat and dog food for our pampered house pets. No dog or cat in the world today is as ecologically valuable as a whale. There is no shortage of pet food from domestic livestock sources. Certainly a whale need never be killed.

While fishing in the Gulf of Lower California, more properly called the Sea of Cortez, I have had grey whales surface so close alongside my twenty-one foot boat that the spray from their blow hole has drifted down on our faces. I have taken motion pictures of whales so close that their tail flukes towered above us and shaded us from the sun as we exposed the film. The misnamed "killer" whales, or orcas, have followed alongside my boat, swimming on their sides, one curious eye turned up to watch us in the boat. I have never felt threatened by any whale, although assuredly I am too much of a coward to swim in the same water with orcas. An orca might mistake me for a seal or sea lion and make a meal of me before he realized his mistake.

While driving along the coastal highway south of Monterey, California, I have watched the magnificent parade of big whales down the coast in their annual migration to Scammons Lagoon on the west coast of the Baja Peninsula. There is now an entire industry devoted to taking nature lovers on whale-watching trips out of west coast ports. The dollar value of this industry each year surely exceeds the dollar value of the few whale carcasses that might still be taken from this population of whales.

The international "take" of whales is supposedly regulated by the International Whaling Commission, which sets national quotas for the various species each year. The quota system is not rigidly adhered to. In fact, the few remaining whaling nations—primarily, the Soviet Union and Japan—simply ignore quotas to their own benefit.

Smaller and smaller species of whale are now being sought by the remaining whalers. No longer able to take the great sperm whale, nor the bowhead, nor the gray—they have sunk to the level of existing on kills of the smaller sei and minke whales. It is quite possible that the only reason the IWC sets quotas on the smaller whales is that they have no information on which to base a closure of the "hunting season" for these smaller whales.

You will surely be awed by the huge blue whale recreated in the Museum of Natural History in Washington, D.C. This might well be the largest animal that ever lived; it dwarfs even the dinosaurs. The unbelievable size of this animal may be the only memory you carry away from a visit to the Museum.

Quite another feeling about whales can be gotten in maneuvering your small boat slowly alongside a forty-ton gray whale swimming with its calf in the rich waters of the Sea of Cortez. As the huge barnacle-encrusted head breaks the placid surface of the sea, and the explosive snorting release of its pent up breath sends spray for forty feet, you unconsciously veer off a little. The great beast then rolls gently over on one side to protect its five ton calf, and the surprisingly small eye looks right at you—in curiosity and not in fear. That is something else. You watch the tremendous bulk slide smoothly under the water and watch the great horizontal tail flukes rise twenty feet out of the water as the whale starts its descent to where the squid are so thick that it can simply scoop up half a ton in one great bite. Experience the excitement of a close encounter of this kind and you can understand the emotion which surrounds the nasty business of whaling.

The most radical of the "whale saving" organizations have actually put their own bodies in front of the whalers' harpoon cannon, having raced their inflatable boats to get to the position of greatest danger. Some of these zealots have actually rammed whaling ships with their own vessels, sometimes on the high seas, more often in ports in Spain or Portugal. One can admire their courage and devotion to their cause, while wondering about their sanity.

Just as the killing of the American bison stopped when their numbers had shrunk to a pitiful few; so will whaling fade away, as the low numbers of these intelligent creatures make it a losing economic game to pursue them. International hypocrisy has been the greatest end product of the International Whaling Commission, but their deliberations have provided a forum for the expression of the world's distaste for this nasty business. In the same way, the "confrontation" tactics of the save-the-whale groups have served to dramatize the plight of the whale. No aspect of whaling today can withstand the pitiless glare of honest publicity about its nefarious work. What a sad commentary on humanity that economics, not compassion and logic, will bring an end to the slaughter of this largest of all intelligent life forms on this planet.

As whales become so few that whalers stop hunting them, perhaps we can work to find a way to prevent the re-emergence of whaling when the whale numbers do begin to come back. They can come back. Today's parade of the leviathans along the California coast is proof that they will come back, if we can stop the ridiculous killing of sixty-ton, intelligent, warm-blooded mammals for the purpose of feeding someone's lap dog.

15

The Apache Trout

The Apache trout is a deep-bodied fish, yellowish or yellow-olive in color, with purple and pink tints. Round spots mark its body, but they are not the spots which are found on brown trout. The fins have conspicuous cream or yellowish tips. There is no red or pink lateral band as is commonly found on the rainbow trout. This very specialized trout is found in only one place.

Specialized subspecies of trout developed in the higher elevations of southwestern mountains. These species evolved in isolation because it was seldom possible for the species to migrate any distance. The limiting factor was that the streams were only cold enough for trout in their higher reaches. As the streams meandered into the hot lowlands of Arizona and/or New Mexico, the waters became much too hot for trout to exist.

This is the reason why *Salmo apache* (the Apache trout) and *Salmo gilae* (the Gila trout) evolved as separate subspecies, although they are very close together geographically. The Apache trout is found in the high country of the White and Black River drainages on the Apache Indian Reservations in eastern Arizona. The Gila trout evolved in the headwaters of the Gila, on the western edge of New Mexico, and on the headwaters of the Verde River, south and west of Flagstaff, Arizona.

When the white man brought the hatchery truck to Apache country, he sought suitable waters in which to stock the adaptable, fast growing, easily handled rainbow trout. The rainbow immediately hybridized with the local trout species and cannot be distinguished from them now.

The fact that the Apache trout and the Gila trout were drowning their distinctive genes in the much larger gene pool of rainbow trout did not go unnoticed on the White Mountain Indian Reservation, which occupies some of the most beautiful high country in Arizona. I am sure that the Apache trout had been studied and written about by taxonomists long before my time, but the real conservation action started when there was a fortuitous combination of personnel interested in the fisheries of the White Mountain Reservation.

Jack Hemphill had been a fisheries biologist for the State of Arizona before he became Fisheries Services Regional Supervisor stationed in Albuquerque. He was well-known and trusted by the tribe. The small colorful trout of the reservation had interested him for a long time. Fisheries' biologists such as

Andy Anderson, stationed in Arizona for the Fish and Wildlife Service, reflected their supervisor's interest in the Apache trout.

At the same time, an enlightened tribal chairman of the White Mountain Apaches, Ronnie Lupe, became interested in preserving this native species. His father had been tribal chairman before him. The tribe acted on recommendations made by Andy Anderson, Jack Hemphill and the cooperating Arizona Game and Fish Department personnel. They closed sections of some of the highest creeks to fishing, to make sure that the relict populations of Apache trout were not going to be eaten by humans.

The tribe provided land for the Alchesay National Fish Hatchery, which was named for a great chief of their people. This new hatchery and others which had stocked these high Arizona waters for far longer were probably the biggest enemy of the native Apache trout. They provided an endless supply of rainbows for all the waters of the reservation. These introduced rainbows overwhelmed the native species in most waters, simply by sheer weight of numbers.

I made a tourism promotion movie for the White Mountain tribe, under terms of a contract signed by the tribal council. At that time, the sincerity with which the Apache leaders sought to protect the remnant population of Apache trout impressed me. I was impressed but not surprised. After all, the Apaches felt themselves to be survivors of a bygone day, just as the trout. It was named after them; it was their fish! Their efforts on its behalf earned them the Conservation Award from the Department of the Interior—an award given for the protection of endangered species long before the Endangered Species Act made conservation fashionable.

I wanted to film one of the sportfishing sequences in the closed high country, because it was such a beautiful spot. The tribe turned me down. I wasn't allowed to carry a rainbow trout up there to take pictures. It was also unthinkable to let me fake fishing sequences in an area which was closed to fishermen—even tribal members.

Although the fish had been known for one hundred years, and had a "recovery program" of its own before recovery plans were talked of, it was not formally "described" until 1972 by Bob Miller, the acme of fish taxonomy from Michigan University at Ann Arbor. Bob Miller named this the Arizona trout, rather than the familiar name of the Apache trout. He then turned around in an epic of inconsistency and gave it the scientific name of *Salmo apache*, which means Apache trout if you read classical Latin. In English, the term changes from the meaningful, specific, descriptive term of Apache trout to the meaningless name of Arizona trout. The White Mountain Apache Indian tribe now has the priviledge of preserving their own "Arizona" trout.

As we write this, the native range of the Apache trout—sorry about that, Mr. Miller—is limited to the headwaters of the best streams forming the upper drainage of the White and Black Rivers in Arizona. Bonita Creek probably carries several thousand Apache trout during part of the year, but its numbers may drop as low as a few hundred after wintering and before spawning replenishes its numbers. According to the Recovery Team Report, the present

83

range of genetically pure Apache trout populations is less than thirty miles of small streams, which is a reduction from approximately 600 miles of streams before the hatchery truck moved into the area.

These biologists feel that there are pure natural populations in four streams on the reservation: Boggy Creek, Crooked Creek, the South Fork of Diamond Creek and the East Fork of the White River. Two creeks, Centerfire and Soldier, hold pure populations of Apache trout on both the reservation and the Sitgreaves National Forest. Populations which show MOST of the criteria for purity of genetic strain are found in six other places on the reservation, and two other locations shared by the reservation and the national forest. Hybridized populations are located in Deep Creek, the North Fork of Diamond Creek and in Paradise Creek on the reservation.

During the years since interest was first raised in the case of the Apache trout, seemingly pure strains of this fish have been introduced into non-historic lakes and streams where no salmonid populations existed. Safe from hybridization, the Apache trout hopefully will increase its numbers in these non-historic areas and thereby provide sources of pure strain, wild-reared Apache trout for reintroduction to water in the historic range.

However, the Recovery Team has turned thumbs down on such introductions into waters in which the Apache is not native. After all, this would be saying that the ends justify the means, and we would be introducing the native fish into waters where it would be an exotic. That is the sin we accuse the hatchery people of commiting. They introduced the rainbow trout into areas where it was not native. This action endangered the colorful little trout of the Apache's land.

The goal of the Recovery Team is to establish and/or maintain thirty discrete populations of pure Apache trout, all within its historic range. When this goal has been realized, according to the Recovery Team, the species should be delisted.

Enhancement of existing populations can proceed if there exists a physical barrier against migration upstream by those lusty lovers, the rainbow trout. When the Forest Service provided barrier dams on Lee Valley and Bear Wallow Creek, they faced problems. Bear Wallow was so isolated that all materials and labor had to be flown in to the construction site. At Lee Valley, members of the Arizona Flycasters Club donated their labor to construct the necessary barrier, designed by Forest Service engineer Lloyd Dille.

If rainbow hybridization can be prevented, the wild stocks of Apache trout have a good chance of perpetuating their populations as they have done for thousands of years prior to the arrival of the hatchery truck. In case they do not perpetuate their numbers, or in case some catastrophe wipes out wild populations, the Arizona State Game and Fish Department has been propagating the pure strain at their Sterling Springs Hatchery near Flagstaff. These fish are from Apache trout collected in 1962 from Ord Creek, one of the better waters which no longer holds any Apache trout. In addition to rainbow hybridization, competition with brook trout for food probably also contributed to the loss of the Apache strain in Ord Creek. Today the Apache Tribe is renovating Ord Creek, carefully eliminating all brookies above the migration barriers, and is preparing to reintroduce Apache trout.

There will be no gain for the fisherman if the Apache trout is removed from the danger list. True to the maxim that small cold streams produce small fish, the average Apache trout is too small for the creel. Perhaps he will grow much larger in reservoirs, but a large Apache trout will only replace a large rainbow trout which is equally attractive to the angler. Will there be a loss to the world if the Apache trout gene pool is submerged in the rainbow trout gene pool? We do not know. Because we do not know, we should fight to preserve the Apache trout—the Apache trout, not the Arizona trout.

16

The American Alligator

In the year 1967, the American alligator was declared by the Secretary of the Interior to be endangered. This brought a huge guffaw from folks down Louisiana way, for they were up to their proverbial hips in alligators. You still cannot find many folks in Louisiana who would agree with the Secretary that the big sun lizard is, was, or ever will be endangered.

Originally the alligator occupied most of the wet country in the coastal region of the southeastern United States from central North Carolina to Texas and into extreme southeastern Oklahoma and southern Arkansas. The northern limit of the alligator's range was roughly the isotherm of 15°C. Where it got colder than that, the alligator did not prosper.

Even at its low population point the 'gator still occupied the same historic range, but in much fewer numbers. Overhunting to provide alligator skins for shoes and handbags was the cause of the decline. Some states tried to protect their gator populations by unilateral action, but found it impossible to regulate the taking of alligators as long as they could be sold legally anywhere else. An experienced man can remove the hide from a fair-sized gator in minutes. Once rolled up and out of sight, the hide makes its way to a legal state where it is sold into interstate commerce for the manufacture of belts, wallets, shoes and purses.

It would be nice to attribute the resurgence in alligator numbers to the passage of the Endangered Species Act of 1973, and assuredly that landmark legislation did help. However, there were plenty of gators in 1973. In response to a questionnaire in that year, the southeastern states reported estimated populations as follows:

North Carolina	1,314	Mississippi	4,700
South Carolina	48,700	Oklahoma	10
Florida	407,585	Arkansas	1,900
Georgia	29,954	Louisiana	200,682
Alabama	12,715	Texas	26,784

Obviously, the alligator didn't seem to be endangered in Florida or Louisiana. However, if you lived in Oklahoma or North Carolina (on the outer edge of the historic range), you might think otherwise.

Faced with the evidence that there were plenty of alligators in some areas, the federal government removed the alligator from the endangered list in Cameron, Calcasieu and Vermilion Parishes in Louisiana. Almost all of the remaining range of the alligator was changed from endangered to "threatened." Alabama and Louisiana remained on the "endangered" list, according to the Secretary of the Interior's action in January of 1977.

The American alligator grows about thirteen feet and attains weights above seven hundred pounds. The female deposits eggs—from twenty to sixty—in a mound nest of decaying vegetation. She often stays nearby to protect the eggs from intruders. Black bears and raccoons are the biggest nest predators, but the list of creatures that eat baby alligators is about as long as your arm. This habit of the female's—to lie in ambush near the nest—was the undoing of a friend of mine one day on a Texas coastal marsh.

Perry was a surveyor for the Fish and Wildlife Service. As he walked across the marsh to survey the boundary of some new refuge land acquisition, he came close to the nest of a big female. As he was spreading the legs of his tripod, the female suddenly let out a hiss that would have done justice to the biggest steam engine in the world, and ran towards Perry—and towards water and her escape route—with surprising speed and agility.

As Perry described it, "Me and that gator was locked in mortal combat right then." He waited till the laughter died away and added, "I ran for three quarters of a mile before I stopped to see which way the gator was running."

Baby gators eat insects, crayfish, and other small aquatic life. As they get older they turn to wading birds, snakes, turtles, small mammals and fish. The really big ones have been known to take deer, pigs, cows and even—upon rare occasion—man himself! Attacks on humans were unheard of until the last couple of decades, but now reports come with increasing frequency, mainly from Florida. I don't know what there is about Florida that incites otherwise peaceful species to go berserk, but I remember that it was unheard of for bluefish to attack swimming humans, until a few years ago on a Florida beach. Since that first attempt, there have been six other reports of bluefish deliberately biting humans. But only in Florida.

For many years game managers have preached that it was the destruction of gator habitat which reduced gator numbers. However, when the gator is given protection from human predators, his population starts to go up immediately, regardless of the quality of the habitat. Hide hunters killed at least two and a half million gators in Florida alone in the years 1880 to 1891. With that big a chunk being taken out of the population, no wonder the total number went down.

This unrestricted killing would have undoubtedly proceeded to the point where it became economically unprofitable to hunt gators, if it had not been for the passage of the Lacey Act in 1969. Only Louisiana had any luck protecting the gator before that time, and the Cajuns' state had done a good job of restoring gator numbers before 1969. With the Lacey Act to back them up, state and federal agents could stop the interstate shipment of gator hides and control the kill to a great degree. When that happened, the gators started back. Today we are up to our hips in gators in the better parts of their range.

The biggest problem facing the Recovery Team for the American alligator is that of gaining tolerance for the existence of big alligators. Most people think that the young gators are kind of cute, and have no objection to living near them. However, as the gator grows to the size where he might conceivably endanger children or pets, humanity becomes intolerant of him. But it isn't possible to have only small gators. The species does not become sexually mature until it is about six feet long. The bigger the female, the larger her egg production. If we tolerate only little ones and kill all the big ones because of the potential danger they might pose, we will soon be out of alligators.

Clearly, the American alligator is not endangered as a species. It never was endangered as a species across its range. Discrete populations of alligators have been endangered and will continue to be endangered unless we can develop a human tolerance for alligators which live in "our" lake or "our" river. Controlling the kill of alligators is imperative even where they are plentiful. Such control is necessary to protect the much rarer American crocodile and some of the similar foreign species which are definitely endangered in their own habitat.

Perhaps an educational program offers the best hope for developing the tolerance that is needed to make life possible for gators. What can we say that is good about the gator? Plenty!

Alligators dig deep holes in their swampy homes. When water levels drop, these deep holes sometimes provide the only water for miles. This saves the lives of countless fish and water-dwelling amphibians and reptiles.

Alligator meat is good to eat.

Alligator hides make distinctive and unusual accessories for male and female humans who wish to appear well-dressed.

Alligators may be a help in controlling undesired species of wildlife in their watery environment, although much research remains to be done before we can say that the gator eats enough to make a difference.

And one final argument—he was here before we were and therefore has a right to exist.

17

Darters

The little snail darter measures less than eighty-eight millimeters in length. This tiny fish stopped the construction of a big dam and impoundment, the Tellico Dam, which is part of the Tennessee Valley Authority.

Congress appropriated funds for construction of TVA's Tellico Project in 1942, but a world war intervened. Funds were again appropriated in 1966, and construction actually started on May 7, 1967. There seemed to be no obstacles in the way of scheduled completion of the dam. On the 28th of December, 1973, the Endangered Species Act of 1973 became law. These dates were duly noted in the history of the project.

Probably no one really noticed that a professor of zoology from the University of Tennessee went swimming in August of 1973. Dr. David Etnier went snorkeling in the lower reaches of the Tennessee River that month and spotted a little fish which looked different enough to arouse his curiosity. He caught the fish in his hands and realized that this was a species that he had never seen before. After going through all of the taxonomic preliminaries, Dr. Etnier named the fish *Percina tanasi,* of the subgenus, *Imostoma.* In our language, he called it the snail darter.

The discovery of this new species of tiny fish was a sad day for the advocates of dams on the Tennessee River and its tributaries. No one had even known that the snail darter existed when the dam was planned and construction begun. But scientists petitioned for endangered listing of the snail darter, pointing out that its critical habitat would be eliminated by completion of the Tellico Dam as planned.

In 1975, the Secretary of the Interior determined that the construction of the dam would result in total destruction of the snail darters' habitat. A suit was filed against TVA in federal court in Knoxville. That court ruled that the Endangered Species Act was not intended to stop construction of a dam which had been authorized long before the Endangered Species Act was passed. The case was appealed to the Sixth Circuit Court which reversed the decision, stating simply that Congress had not excluded the Tellico project from the terms of the act.

The case then went to the United States Supreme Court, which on June 15, 1978, upheld the Sixth Circuit decision. The snail darter had stopped construction of a big dam. But not for long . . .

A Snail Darter

On September 25, 1979, the Congress passed and the President signed into law a bill exempting the Tellico Project from the Endangered Species Act, which made sure that the environmentalists could not again stop construction of that particular dam. Although the delays in construction were very expensive to the construction agency, the delay bought time for scientists to study this new species of fish. The snail darter was found to exist in a few spots other than the shallow riffles where it was first identified.

Before closure of the Tellico Dam doomed the Tellico River population of snail darters, TVA biologists transplanted a total of 710 snail darters from that population to the Hiawassee River in southeastern Tennessee. In a personal communication to me, Harold Hurst of the Recovery Team claimed that this population was reproducing. By the spring of 1980 the propulation was estimated to be at least 2,500.

This Hiawassee transplant population has been so successful that 104 snail darters were transported to a new plant on the Holston River below Cherokee Reservoir. A total of 534 darters went to this second release site. In addition to the 104 from Hiawassee, 434 fish were rescued from above and below Tellico Dam after the river was impounded. It is too early to tell if the transplant to Holston will be successful. The Recovery Team selected a third site just before we went to press. This tiny but mighty fish stopped the entire Tennessee Valley Authority cold in its tracks. The court cases leading up to enactment of the special legislation to exempt Tellico from provisions of the Endangered Species Act were landmark cases—they provided that the law meant what it said—even if it dealt with retroactive cases.

The Recovery Team wants to try artificial propagation, to have it ready in case it is needed. But according to Harold Hurst, "If the Hiawassee River population continues to do well, and the Holston River and another transplant are succesful, we will feel good about the survival of the snail darter."

Was the uproar over the snail darter justified? Was this the pitiful remnant of a species which once occupied a far greater environmental range? It would seem not. During 1974 and 1975 intensive effort went into searching for other populations of the snail darter. A total of 120 separate sites on 43 different watersheds were all thoroughly investigated without finding a single snail darter. Was he ever there?

Was it possible that the snail darter evolved only in this one tributary of one river in order to fit a particular niche? Then why did it not evolve in similar habitats? As part of its life cycle the tiny darter moves downstream from gravel bars; at this stage it is very small and hard to see. It spends a long time in deeper waters before returning to its gravel bar where life began. With this type of travel in its life cycle, why did the snail darter not encounter other sand bars on the way, and other habitats that would be suited to its particular needs?

Why didn't the snail darter colonize other suitable habitats? It adapted soon enough when mankind introduced it to other suitable habitats on the Hiawassee and Holston, yet never made the big step on its own. Was this failure to make the big step a fatal weakness which would have doomed the snail darter, even without the Tellico Dam?

91

Crew collecting snail darters in the Little Tennessee River. Included are four members of the Snail Darter Recovery Team—Price Wilkins (Tennessee Wildlife Resources Agency), Dick Fritz (Tennessee Valley Authority), Hal Boles (U.S. Fish & Wildlife Service) and Gary Hickman (Tennessee Valley Authority)

The Watercress Darter

Not too far from the Tennessee habitat of the snail darter, another small fish, the watercress darter, had been known for much longer. Drs. Donald Brandon and Ronald Altig collected a watercress darter in 1964. Despite efforts to locate other populations, the fish was never found away from Glenn Springs, at Bessemer, Jefferson County, Alabama.

Because it was thought to exist in only that one watershed, the watercress darter was given status as Endangered in 1970. The entire known population of the species was believed to be about 400 individuals, residing in one spring outflow in an area where spring flows are variable and dependent upon recharge by local rains.

To further complicate the picture, Glenn Springs was becoming badly contaminated with coliform bacteria which probably came from septic tanks in the immediate vicinity. Attempts were made to transplant the watercress darter to Prince Spring, which seemed to have the same environmental conditions. That transplant failed entirely.

The newly named Watercress Darter Recovery Team began the work of gathering data on the watercress darter. They found two new populations of the fish, one at Thomas' Spring and the other at Roebuck Springs. Introduction of grass carp into the waters of Thomas' Spring resulted in the virtual elimination of all aquatic vegetation right up to the shore line and of all the watercress darter population. In the case of the Roebuck Springs population, abnormally high levels of nitrogen in the water and the increase in population evidenced by high coliform bacterial counts threaten this population as well.

The Recovery Team plans to save this darter by preserving and enhancing favorable habitat for the species. It thrives in deep, slow moving backwater of springs which are choked with watercress. The heavy vegetation furnishes a steady supply of insects which the watercress darter feeds upon. The team has asked the Fish and Wildlife Service to acquire the Glenn Springs property, to construct low level dams, and to fence off the area from human intrusion. Similar requests are made for the Thomas Spring population. The Roebuck Spring is already owned by the state; so it should be manageable under some sort of cooperation agreement.

The problem of transplanting darters to other waters is currently under study. How sad to note that the biggest dangers to the watercress darter are mankind's filth—coliform bacteria from our sewage, and the introduced grass carp—which is yet another blight that man has inflicted on native species.

The Okaloosa Darter

Still a third darter has joined the list of endangered species. Remnant populations of the Okaloosa darter are found in watersheds approximating 113,000 acres of land. About one tenth of this land is privately owned, but nine tenths is located within the confines of Eglin Air Force Base in Florida. This is the same airbase which has often served as a refugee camp for displaced humans—the boat people from Southeast Asia and the thousands of *Cubanos* fleeing the Communist Paradise which Fidel Castro created in the Caribbean.

The little Okaloosa darter prefers areas of very heavy vegetation in areas of fast stream flow, using the vegetation for protection against predators. The Okaloosa darter seems to be more adaptable than the snail or watercress darter. It will get along just fine in other types of habitat besides its preferred habitat. However, it will not adapt to impoundment life where moving water is replaced by stagnant or very slow-moving waters.

Because very little is known about the requirements of the Okaloosa darter, the work of the Recovery Team is aimed at accumulating the necessary information on which to form a recovery plan. What waters are best suited? Is competition with other small species a limiting factor? Is the population more widely dispersed than previously thought? What is the limiting factor which stops it from spreading out in suitable streams?

When all of this data has been accumulated, the Recovery Team will formulate whatever program is needed to remove the Okaloosa darter from the endangered list, place it on the threatened list, and then ultimately delist it entirely.

Was it only a coincidence that three species of very small fish were discovered to be endangered in this one corner of the United States? Or is it possible that myriads of such small fish species are in existence all over the country, without ever having been identified and studied? Perhaps many species have become extinct even before we know that they existed? That certainly has happened all throughout that awesome span of time during which life has existed on this planet. I believe it is still happening. What should cause us concern is that species are being eliminated—becoming extinct—because of actions or lack of actions by mankind.

Should a small fish of absolutely no economic value to man be allowed to stop or delay a big water impoundment project? Is the prevention—or delaying —of extinction that important? My answer is an unqualified "yes." There is no crime greater than **causing** the extermination of a species; conversely, there is nothing more foolish than trying to prevent the inexorable disappearance of a species which has failed to make the grade—due to its own inherent weaknesses, not to any action by mankind.

The dilemma facing us, as managers of the planet's wildlife, is that we do not know, and cannot know whether we are valiantly trying to save a worthwhile species or foolishly trying to delay the inevitable disappearance of an unsuccessful mutation in the evolutionary development of a species. Because we cannot know, we must always try to preserve the species.

18

The Red-cockaded Woodpecker

Several woodpecker species, including the majestic ivory-bill, have been in danger of extermination for decades. To illustrate their plight, we have chosen the red-cockaded, because there are so many interesting facets to its situation. Each has a bearing on other forest-dwelling life forms.

Once common across most of the southeastern part of our country, the red-cockaded was found from Maryland to Texas and from Missouri to Florida. It disappeared from most of its Missouri haunts by the end of the twenties and from Tennessee and Mississippi in the late 1950's. This woodpecker was lost in southern Florida in the 1940's. Why?

The answer to its decline can be found in the radical change in forest practices which swept across the American southland. The red-cockaded requires mature pine trees for its nests. The nest is excavated into the interior of the living pine tree (this is the only known woodpecker which makes a nest in a **living** pine). All others excavate their characteristic nest in a dead tree. More specifically, the redcock must find a particular tree whose diameter suits its rigid requirements.

Heartwood of mature pines is very hard and difficult to tunnel into. However, when pines reach the age of sixty years or more, a big percentage of them suffer from heart rot, commonly called "redheart." Only the outer layer of the tree trunk carries the life-bearing sap; the heartwood is relatively dry. After redheart sets in, the inner portion of the trunk is softened, weakened, and relatively easy to excavate.

Consider now the tree which is suited to a redcock nest. It must be at least sixty years old, for pines do not attain sufficient bole diameter at younger ages as there would not be room enough for the nest. The tree should be afflicted with redheart, a fungus. Nests have been discovered in trees which did not have redheart, but the clear preference is for the fungus-affected tree.

What happened when man began silviculture in the south? Pines were now harvested in a process called "even age forestry" at the age of forty or less. Trees were not allowed to mature to the sixty-plus age which makes them receptive to redheart and suitable to redcocks' nest efforts.

This woodpecker is small, slightly larger than a bluebird, and certainly has no monetary value for man. Yet it has suffered at man's hands far more than has a species such as the sharptailed grouse which is hunted as a source of sport and food for man. Certainly man's economic interest has not been to cultivate aging pine plantations, for the monetary return from even age culture is far more profitable.

There are probably somewhere between 3,000 and 10,000 red-cockaded woodpeckers in existence today. This sounds like a safe number when compared with the situation of the whooping crane and the California condor, or even the Kirtland's warbler. But consider the strange and intricate clan society of the redcock.

They live in colonies, numbering between seven and fifteen individual birds. Yet the colony only contains **one** breeding pair. One dominant male does the breeding and the receptive female lays her eggs in his roosting nest site, a tunnel which he has excavated into the red heart of a mature pine. The other individuals in the colony may take turns feeding the young or may even take a turn at incubating the eggs, but they do not establish a second nest and raise another brood. The dominant male incubates the eggs at night—alone.

The most feared predator of this species is the gray rat snake, which is perhaps the most arboreal of all American snakes. This snake can easily climb any tree and loves to eat the eggs and young of the red-cockaded woodpecker. Nevertheless, Mother Nature has evened the scales a bit by teaching the redcock, over millennia of evolutionary development, that the gray rat snake fears the resin which oozes from the cut in a living pine tree. The redcock has learned to cut new holes in the living pine, below his nesting cavity, to provide "resin wells"—places where the fresh pine resin oozes out to form a barrier against the snake's upward travel. In some of the older nesting cavity trees this band of resin wells may be as much as a yard in width.

Professor Jerome Jackson of Mississippi State University, perhaps the best informed of all our sources, has proved that the snake will avoid smears of pine resin. In fact, when he smeared pine resin on the underbelly of a snake, he found that this caused extreme discomfort and even resulted in the death of one snake.

As even age forestry replaces the unmanaged wood lot across most of the south, colonies of nesting redcocks may become separated one from the other. This obviously results in a stoppage of the gene flow from one locale to another. As this becomes more and more serious, changes will occur in the evolutionary process attributable to inbreeding. The effect of this change in the "clan society" exhibited by the redcock is not known, but it cannot be beneficial.

Intensive management of the pine forests in the south caused the decline of this bird. A different management of pine forests is necessary to restore these birds. Professor Jackson and others have proposed management of highway and utility rights-of-way to provide corridors of mature pines which will serve as travel lanes for the bids as they range widely in their feeding activity. In addition to being travel lanes for feeding birds, in a larger sense these same aged tree corridors would serve as travel lanes for the species genes; thus insuring their survival unchanged.

Obviously man is torn between two separate pressures where the red-cockaded woodpecker is concerned. Our newly awakened ecological conscience tells us that we must preserve this species, logically and for our own good, because we are the keeper of the other life forms over which we have attained dominion. At the same time, we try to profit from wood production in our forests. That profit motive dictates cropping pines before they are of maximum use to the redcock. In a tug of war such as this, the dollar viewpoint always seems to triumph, and this bodes poorly for the little redcock.

However, we have seen ample evidence of a willingness to cooperate on the part of the big timber companies. Over the last two decades larger timber companies have learned well the public relations value of managing the wildlife on their lands. In this case, we can hope that their public relations awareness will dictate the setting aside of aged pine stands to serve the needs of the redcock. Of perhaps more importance, these companies are the best sources of funds to finance the research that is clearly needed—research to discover why the redcock only raises one or two fledglings in a normal nesting effort, although the female lays as many as seven eggs in one nest cavity. Research is also needed to find out why only one male does the breeding per colony. Furthermore, we must find out why the colony needs such a large foraging area to successfully feed the young.

If one looks only at present census figures, the red-cockaded woodpecker does not appear in immediate danger of extinction. If one looks at the decline in numbers and the obvious causes of that decline, that danger becomes very real. Can the profitable management of forest lands include management to benefit this endangered species?

19

The Everglades Kite

There used to be a small gourmet restaurant in the old city of Quebec, Canada, which served the most delicious *escargot* that I have ever eaten. A stone baking vessel contained a dozen inch-wide holes bored in its surface. The snails were placed in those holes on top of a half teaspoon of good cognac. The snails were removed from their shells, of course. Then the cooking vessel was covered with a half inch deep layer of creamy white cheese sauce. Undoubtedly there were other ingredients, for the French have a way with the snail.

The snails simmered in the boiling cognac, while that tangy flavor permeated every centimeter of their tasty molluscan bodies. The delectable cheese sauce melted down into the *escargot*, making the search for the *pièce de résistance* a gourmet's delight. If I could eat that dish of *escargot* at every meal, I would never order anything else. But that might be dangerous. I might get so attached to my "dish of dishes" that I would not be able to eat other foods if my restaurant were to close its doors, or be replaced by a Burger King.

This is exactly what happened to the Everglades kite.

The Everglades kite is a small hawk about eighteen inches in length, sporting a wingspread of nearly four feet. This bird loves snails. In fact, only one kind of large snail will do for its tastes: the apple snail.

Over millennia of evolutionary development, the Everglades kite stuck with its choice—*escargot* or nothing. As a result, it became beautifully adapted to feeding upon the delectable morsels of the wetlands. An excellent flier, this hawk could hover effortlessly while its sharp red eyes searched the waters below for signs of snail. Sharp-taloned feet were beautifully adapted to grasp the almost round snail in its shell; a recurved, slender beak was perfect for extracting the morsels of snail from the shell. They come out easier after they've been cooked in cognac and cheese, but the Everglades kite never learned that refinement.

The Everglades variety is only one of the many snail kites which flourished in the wet areas stretching from northern Florida down through all of the Caribbean and Central American countries and across more than half of South America. In the unbelievable bird wealth of South America, scant attention has been paid to snail kites—until we in the United States learned that our Everglades kite was in big trouble. Big trouble indeed!

As the decade of the eighties opens, there are only about 165 Everglades kites left in the United States of America. Their range, which once covered all of the Florida peninsula, is now restricted to several impoundments on the headwaters of the St. Johns River; to the west side of Lake Okeechobee; to the Lake Park Reservoir in the Loxahatchee Slough area; to the eastern and southern portions of Conservation Area 1 (Loxahatchee Refuge), Conservation Areas 2A, 3A; the southern part of Conservation Area CA2B; the southwestern corner of Conservation Area CA3B; the pocket between Conservation Areas CA3A and CA3B; and the northern part of Everglades National Park.

Although we do not have records of actual counts, the Everglades kite was once present in far greater numbers than we can now tally. What happened?

Basically, mankind moved in and changed the habitat. The kite could not adapt to the changes. Man drained huge areas of what was once an ocean of shallow water and grassy sloughs to plant crops. The drained fields lost their apple snails. When the snail was gone, the epicurean diner was out of luck. Without snails to eat, the Everglades kite disappeared from large parts of its historic range.

Man introduced the water hyacinth, and its lush green growth covered snail habitat, making it impossible for the kites to hunt snails in that jungle. The man-introduced punktree, from Australia, is also moving into freshwater wetlands and forms dense stands of trees which preclude snail hunting on the part of the kites.

Exotic plants were bad enough, but drainage was the major enemy of the Everglades kite. Drainage removed its snail dinner; and without its food, the kite perished. This hawk seems totally unable to shift its appetite to another species of prey, even as the black-footed ferret seems unable to shift to another food source after the prairie dog decreased in numbers due to 1080 poison campaigns.

By the mid-1950's the damage had been done in Florida, and the Everglades kite population reached its low point. Some slow and steady comebacks progressed through the period of 1960-1971, but an extreme drought situation in 1971 reversed the trend. The population declined sharply, indicating again, as if a reminder was ever needed, how vulnerable this specialized species of raptor is. Since that 1971 drought year, slow but heartening increases have been noted.

Florida has given protection to the endangered kite since 1943, and the federal government has given legal protection under terms of the Endangered Species Act and under amendments to the Migratory Bird Conservation Act, which concluded a treaty with Mexico and Canada.

National Audubon Society employee Alexander Sprunt has protected the birds in the Lake Okeechobee area for many years. He is a member of the Recovery Team. Fish and Wildlife Service employees patrol the Loxahatchee National Wildlife Refuge to protect birds, and large areas have been closed to human entry during the critical nesting season. The National Park Service provides good protection for the kites in the Everglades National Park. A private security patrol protects the birds in the St. Johns Reservoir, Indian River

County, and entry is not permitted for other than official business. This effectively reduces human disturbance of the birds.

The Recovery Team plans on continuing protection measures by stepping up publicity as to the needs of the kites. This group also is entering upon a long-range program of inventorying suitable habitat and making plans for the acquisition and future management of critical areas of habitat. Unfortunately, they recognize that the bird may become extinct while we make plans for its increase. A natural catastrophe could eliminate the species, for we have all of our Everglades kites in one basket. With this in mind, the team is planning captive breeding programs.

The Patuxent Wildlife Research Center has been rearing the similar, but different, South American snail kite in captivity since 1966. This group is developing rearing techniques and gaining invaluable knowledge of life histories, needs and problems of the birds. The staff at Loxahatchee National Wildlife Refuge has been experimenting with the propagation of apple snails, and with other techniques for increasing the total production of *escargot* dinners for Everglades kites.

Management of water levels in the existing habitat for the Everglades kite is the most important factor in the fight for survival of this species. Acquisition of other lands and changes in management of other lands may come too late for the Everglades kite. Only time will tell.

While we must assume the blame for altering its habitat and causing its demise, the Everglades kite has contributed to its own precarious situation by being such a picky eater. This again demonstrates that extreme specialization is dangerous for any species.

20

The Kit or Swift Fox

One of the fastest runners of all North American predators, this diminutive fox was once fairly well distributed over the western half of the continent. Farm boys know him as the "too small" fox which didn't bring a good price on the fur market (or at the "skunk house," as it was often called where I grew up).

South Dakota research suggests that the northern prairie swift fox may have had a limiting effect upon prairie dog numbers. It seems more logical to me that the fox might NOW limit prairie dog numbers when the total 'dog' population is so low. The fox didn't have any effect upon populations when the dog towns stretched for miles along the fertile grasslands bordering the Missouri River.

The jackrabbit is one species which surely would not mourn the passing of the swift fox. The actual chase and capture of a healthy adult jackrabbit by a swift fox has been recorded on movie film. I have never failed to marvel at the blinding speed of this racer, no matter how many times I have seen the film. The coyote has also been known to run down jackrabbits by coursing the long-eared hoppers in relays and tiring them out. The kit fox simply spots the rabbit and, cheetah-like, runs it down.

Perhaps the kit or swift fox lacks the wariness which we normally associate with the red fox. In fact, the kit is less careful than the gray fox in keeping out of sight. Perhaps the knowledge that no one can catch him in a race is the reason for this lack of prudence.

The species has declined in numbers drastically over the past eighty years, probably due in great part to the poisoning campaigns launched against the coyote and lobo wolf which also killed some of the smaller meat eaters. As organized campaigns, these poisoning operations are now over. The swift fox seems to be holding his own in suitable habitats. Colorado claims a stable, hale and hearty population. Remnant populations survive in both Dakotas, Oklahoma, Montana, Nebraska, Kansas and Wyoming. Both Kansas and Wyoming feel that their populations are increasing. There is little downward pressure exerted against the swift fox. Low numbers don't warrant its exploitation by the fur trade, and this small fox doesn't arouse the animosity of the farmer and sheepman as the coyote does.

The "meat and potatoes" of the swift fox was probably the prairie dog at one time, but this source of food has disappeared. Where enough prey species exist, the swift fox still exists. Many laymen think that predators control the numbers of prey species, but close observation has taught me that the opposite is true. The scarcity or abundance of prey species actually determines the number of predators on the scene. Where there are goodly populations of ground squirrels, rabbits, mice and hares, the swift fox will do just fine. Where that food supply is threatened, so the fox will be also.

One particular population of swift foxes, the so-called San Joaquin kit fox, which is named for its type locality in California, was especially hard hit by the poisoning campaigns and other man-caused environmental changes of several decades ago. Its rebound has been very slow. This animal is now the target of a Recovery Team effort similar to those we have learned about for other species.

Although not very wary, the swift fox is well adapted to earn his own way in the world. His blinding speed allows him to run down any small prey which cannot burrow into the ground to escape. If the plow leaves him some of his native prairie, he'll make out.

The males may weigh as much as six pounds, although most will average less than five. Brownish grey over most of their bodies, the colors shade to reddish sides and a white underbelly, with a black-tipped nose and tail. This is a very long-legged creature for its small size, and its long legs are remarkably efficient.

The animals evidently form a stronger pair bond than we usually observe in the fox and coyote families. I remember strong evidence of this in northwestern South Dakota. A poison-killed swift fox's body was stretched out upon the clean white snow in Harding County. It was a female. Forty-five dead mice, by actual count, mysteriously appeared next to the dead body! When the fox was lifted away, the mice formed an outline sketch of the fox's body. The male fox, unable to comprehend what had happened to his mate, must have continued to try to feed her, even after her death.

The swift fox is an interesting animal and one that has had very little impact upon mankind. Surely there is room for him in this land we hold dominion over.

21

The Blind Salamander

In the limestone escarpment of Texas which is the dividing line between the long flat prairies sloping very gradually to the sea and the rolling rocky hills, there is a series of caves with a water supply provided by an underground river. In the endless blackness of this cave, a species of salamander took up residence millennia ago. Did this salamander deliberately choose to live in eternal darkness away from the light and warmth of our sun, or was it trapped within the underground chamber by some freak accident of geology? No one will ever know.

After thousands of years of never using eyes, the necessity for having eyes no longer existed. Where there are no light rays to fall upon a retina, there is no retina. Evolution eliminates superflous characteristics. Sometimes it takes many thousands of years to remove an unnecessary appendage, as in the case of our own tail bone which still occurs in rudimentary form despite the fact that we no longer have a tail. But we are a species with a long life span and a slow cycle of about twenty years from one generation to the next. The salamander has a much shorter reproductive cycle, regenerating itself every year. The salamander got rid of its unnecessary sight capability much sooner than we would have, faced with life in the absence of light.

Because there is no light, the Texas blind cave salamander now lives without eyes. Because there is no light, there is no need for color; so the salamander is a colorless creature.

Is this an endangered species, which must be preserved? Or is this one of the failures of evolution, already doomed before man knew of its existence? Should we try to preserve the blind cave salamander? What do you think?

22

Masked Bobwhite Quail

The masked bobwhite, a smaller bird than the northern species of bobwhite quail, is distinguished by a brick red breast and a black head and throat, with some white almost always present on the head. Females closely resemble the "regular" bobwhite and are almost indistinguishable from the female of several other quail species or subspecies.

These quail were found in goodly numbers over the wide grasslands of Arizona and Sonora, Mexico when the white man moved into those areas. The settler's cattle and sheep overgrazed those same pastures and did irreparable damage to the habitat of the masked bob. Overgrazing was continuous over most of the best range in south central Arizona from 1870 to the end of the century. Cattle numbers rose from 5,000 in 1870 to 1,500,000 in 1891. Added to that, there were severe drought conditions over most of this area in the 1890's. By 1900, you couldn't find a single masked bobwhite in the United States of America.

Small populations hung on in similarly overgrazed ranch lands in Sonora, south of the border in Old Mexico. Pioneer ornithologist Ligon said that even the Mexico populations were gone in 1950. But a small population was discovered near Benjamin Hill in Sonora in 1964. That remnant population is still hanging on by the narrowest of margins.

The brothers Jim and Seymour Levy, sportsmen-ornithologists from Tucson, found feathers of the masked bobwhite in cactus wren nests in Sonora. They looked into the situation and found that there were indeed masked bobwhites in the wild in Mexico. The Levys attempted to raise the birds in captivity in Tucson and to reintroduce them into coverts in Arizona where they had once flourished. Vandalism and destruction of their birds and pens discouraged that attempt, but the Levys kept a steady pressure on the government to take a hand in saving a species that was very near the brink of extinction.

Roy Tomlinson, a Spanish-speaking biologist, was assigned to study the masked bobwhite. From his headquarters in Tucson, Roy began a long search through Sonora and down into Sinaloa, looking for populations of the masked quail. He carried with him a pair of mounted birds, male and female, and visited countless hundreds of *ranchos* to ask the same question, "Have you seen a bird that looks like this?"

He succeeded in locating two separate populations and began a scientific, systematic study of the birds in order to assess their needs and to estimate their numbers. I had the privilege of making the rounds with Roy over some of the worst roads in Mexico, while he continued his study of the masked bobwhite in the deteriorating habitat of that country. Simultaneously, Roy was studying habitats within the historic range of the masked bobwhite in Arizona to seek new transplant ranges. Tall grass was needed for the denuded, badly eroded soils of southern Arizona if the bird was to have a chance at successfully reestablishing itself in the United States. The Bureau of Land Management, the Arizona Game and Fish Department, the University of Arizona, and the U.S. Forest Service all cooperated in programs to make southern Arizona suitable for the masked bobwhite quail once more.

After successfully negotiating the proper protocol hurdles, Tomlinson got permission from the Mexican government to live trap some masked bobwhite quail stock from the dwindling populations in Sonora. These birds went by air express to Patuxent, Maryland, with a side trip to Mexico City.

Artificial propagation experts in Patuxent found the masked bird easy to raise. Quickly a breeding stock was working hard to perpetuate that particular group of genes. Some of the earliest production went directly to Old Mexico, to be released into favorable coverts down there in repayment for the birds we had trapped. However, the pen-raised birds stood little chance of surviving in the wild in Old Mexico with its big wintering populations of raptors as well as ground predators. Pen-raised quail simply didn't have enough smarts to hide when the hawks flew overhead. The high-priced hawk food disappeared quickly.

Various other release methods were tried to give the birds a better chance of surviving in the wild. I remember nights when volunteer students from the University of Arizona slept on cots alongside the temporary pens of the quail, guarding them through the night.

With a plentiful supply of birds available from the Patuxent Center, the Fish and Wildlife Service tried holding the birds over a full year and releasing them as adults. Although there were hopeful signs that the birds might learn to live in the improved pastures, there was little optimism for returning a viable population to southern Arizona until some budding genius thought of the foster parent program.

"Why not use adult males, livetrapped in Texas, to teach the youngsters how to get along in the wild?" he asked.

"Because those livetrapped Texas bobs would hybridize with the masked bobwhites and defeat our purpose," he was told.

"Not if those Texas males were caponized before release," he retorted.

The experiment succeeded. The young masked bobwhites were introduced to the broody Texas males during normal nesting seasons. They were given a day or two to get accustomed to each other, then gently released as a family. The adult male taught the youngsters to freeze at his danger call, to follow him to good food, to stay out of sight when possible, to protect themselves. It worked, and the young masked bobwhites grew up wild and wary.

Populations had been introduced into suitable habitat in 1971 and 1972, but failed to adjust. Using the foster parent system, populations were again put into those same habitats in 1976 and took hold. They have persisted and have nested successfully.

But remember that these birds must survive in a land which is nowhere near as hospitable to them as it was in 1850. The lesson has been learned. You cannot raise wildlife on abused pastures any more than you can raise livestock on abused pastures. Many decades are necessary to restore the natural grasses—given favorable rainfall conditions. Without favorable rainfall, the job may become impossible.

We now have tiny populations living in the wild in Arizona, which is reason for hope. We also have a goodly population of breeding birds in Patuxent. But what about Old Mexico?

Since Roy Tomlinson first began running call count transects in Sonora, the trend had been steadily—and steeply—downward. Continued destruction of critical habitat was steadily shrinking the known range of the masked bobwhite in Mexico. A quick trip to extermination appeared certain—although we knew that the tough little masked bobs had hung on in Mexico for thirty years after they were given up for gone in 1950.

A caponized male Texas bobwhite teaches young pen-reared masked bob-whites to adopt to the wild.

Then in September of 1979 two things happened. First of all, rains came at the right time for the late summer-nesting masked bobwhite. There was new green grass and a new crop of insects when the hatch came off in 1979, which gave reason for slight optimism. At the same time, there was a resurgence of interest in the masked bobwhite on the part of Mexican authorities. This was evidenced by two events: (a) the Mexican authorities got several captive pairs from Patuxent and took them to Mexico City to start some kind of an artificial propagation program of their own, and (b) it was decided that Patuxent-reared birds, "fathered" by caponized Texas bobwhites would again be reintroduced into suitable coverts in Sonora during the summer of 1980.

The prognosis for the masked bobwhite must be regarded as hopeful, but a long way from secure. Easily propagated in captivity, the bird profits from its excellent reproduction potential. Yet arrayed against it are poor ranching practices in both nations. The good cooperation of Mexican authorities is a definite plus for the species in its fight for survival. If it makes the grade, this will be a splendid example of international cooperation. Let's review the sitaution for a minute. The bird was assumed extinct in both nations for thirteen years—1950 through 1963. Then survivors were found in Mexico. Mexican birds were live-trapped and propagated in the United States. Now with viable wild populations existing in both nations, the United States is furnishing birds for restocking Mexican coverts.

The masked bobwhite had to make several trips back and forth over the border to avoid extinction. Poor ranching practices forced the moves. Without improvement of the overgrazing situation, there is no hope that the bird will ever become numerous again.

23

Of Flying Mice and Men

If there is any mammal in the world which ought to have the full support and friendship of the human race, it is the bat. These completely harmless little flying rodents—the famous *Fledermaus* of opera—provide the most perfect insect control ever devised. Most bats are never seen by humans. They come out only at night when they fly an erratic zig-zag path across the sky, their tiny mouths engulfing thousands of flying insect pests.

Bats were the first creatures to develop airborne sonar. They emit high-pitched squeaks which echo from solid objects, allowing them to navigate with eyes closed, guided by echoes. This has been proved by scientific experiments in which bats' eyes were hooded, removing all chances of seeing. Certainly, bats must be able to navigate without sight, for some colonies of bats fly into the Stygian darkness of deep caves to find their daytime roosting place. Research shows that they can even avoid wires hung in the darkness.

On the roost, bats cling to the ceiling in thick concentrations, hanging upside down. In this position they give birth and nurse their young.

The bat doesn't bother man in any way. Conversely, it destroys man's insect pests in unbelievable numbers and roosts far from the usual haunts of man. How on earth could man and bat collide? Man's exploration of roosting caves has caused troubles for many species of bats. Only by protecting the bat's roosting habitat from disturbance can we help the bat. He asks nothing more than to be left alone. Is that too much?

Let's see how the present situation looks for several species of bats:

On October 16, 1976, Dr. John S. Hall, a professor of Biology at Albright College in Pennsylvania, and Dr. Michael J. Harvey, a professor of Biology at Memphis State University, petitioned the United States Fish and Wildlife Service to place the Virginia big-eared and the Ozark big-eared bats on the list of Endangered Species.

After preliminary investigation showed that the petition seemed valid, these two bats were proposed for listing on December 2, 1977. At the same time, the Service proposed five caves in West Virginia and one in Kentucky as critical habitat for the Virginia big-eared, but no critical habitat was identified for the Ozark big-eared bat.

Before these proposals could be acted upon, Congress passed the Endangered Species Act Amendments of 1978, which greatly changed the critical habitat designation procedure. To bring everything into order legally, the Service reissued the proposal for the Virginia big-eared bat on August 30, 1979. According to the law, this proposal called for a ninety day comment period. This would have extended it to November 30, 1979, more than three full years after the original proposal was received. There was considerable discussion by students of these bats, and the Service considered designating Stillhouse Cave in Lee County, Kentucky, as critical habitat for the Virginia big-eared bat. However, the Kentucky Fish and Wildlife Resources Commissioner pointed out that critical habitat designation would only call attention to the cave and increase public use of that cave. He pointed out that the present owners of the cave were affording protection to the cave. The decision was not to name Stillhouse cave as critical habitat.

This is a perfect example of a species which only needs to be left alone to prosper. Designating that particular cave as critical habitat would be a case of "killing with kindness." This is similar to the fate suffered by some of our most beautiful rivers in the state of Missouri. By designating them "Wild and Scenic" rivers, we have increased boat traffic tenfold. The result is the destruction of the very values the designation was intended to protect.

If we hurt the bats when we try to help them, what can be done? It is not always true that our efforts call attention to the existence of the bats and thus hurt their chances for continued existence. Sometimes we can help.

Consider the gray bat, the largest member of this genus in the eastern U.S. Although it is the biggest of its kind, this bat weighs less than sixteen grams. Bats are very small creatures. The "wing of the bat" is a membrane which, in the case of the gray bat, connects to the ankle bone, rather than to the base of the first toe as is the case with other members of the *Myotis* family. The gray bat is a monotypic species which occupies scattered parts of a limestone karst range in the southeastern United States.

At one time there were individual hibernating populations of gray bats estimated to contain more than a million and a half bats. About 95% of this huge population often hibernated in one cave! From these huge wintering concentrations, the gray bats spread out to summer roosting colonies (maternity caves) sometimes several hundred miles from winter quarters. Breeding takes place immediately upon arrival in the hibernation colony. Gray bats go into hibernation as early as the first of September, and all have entered their winter quarters by the first of October, as befits a species which finds insect food scarcer in the winter time.

Migration to summer homes occurs in April and May. The single young is born in late May or early June. At "birthing" time, the females congregate in the warmest cave, while males and non-reproductive females live in smaller groups in peripheral caves which are still within the home range of the colony. The bats are extremely loyal to the home range and do not simply "move to another cave" when they are disturbed. By crowding together in the caves, the need for body heat is reduced and the newborn can be tended by their mothers with less total food being consumed than would be the case if the mother-young pairs lived singly, or in small groups.

112

This raising of the young is the dangerous part of the bats' life cycle. If the colony is disrupted and becomes smaller, the young take as much as thirty-five days to become adept fliers, instead of the twenty to twenty-five days that it takes the bats to fly in normal (high concentration-high temperature) situations. If the colony is reduced in size by disturbance or vandalism, the colony finds itself unable to maintain the necessary high temperatures. The young simply die.

Bats prefer to forage over water, although they do find insect food over land areas also. When water pollution removed a mayfly population from one of their favorite feeding areas, the bats simply disappeared from that feeding area. Whether or not they were able to adjust and find another feeding area is not known. There is some evidence that bats do establish territorial rights over feeding areas. These territories are controlled by lactating females. There is no evidence that the mother bat teaches her young to fly and to feed; evidently that comes naturally.

Gray bats have exceptionally rigid habitat requirements. They usually winter in deep vertical caves where the temperatures fluctuate between 6°C and 11°C, and where the shape of the cave tends to trap cold air and hold it. In the summer, maternity colonies prefer caves that have high-domed ceilings capable of trapping and holding the body heat of the thousands of mother-young pairs that hang from these high ceilings. Summer caves are almost always within one kilometer distance from a water area which provides the preferred foraging area. A heavily forested land area between the cave and water feeding areas is ideal, for the bats prefer to fly in the protection of the forest canopy as they go to and from their feeding areas. In fact, gray bats will often abandon a feeding (overwater) area if the vegetation is cleared from the edges of the water area.

The gray bats face the greatest danger from human disturbance and from vandalism in their hibernating caves. Consequently, most experts predict that the gray bat will continue to decline in numbers and probably will face extinction.

Disturbances need not come from a club-swinging goon who smashes the bats against the wall—although this has happened. Any disturbance in maternity caves or in hibernating caves can be very serious. When the bats are disturbed in maternity colonies, there is a drop in the all-important temperature. Several arousals and the young die! If you walk into a cave and the bats flutter around for a minute or two and then settle back to their roosting places, you may feel that no harm has been done. Unfortunately, thousands of young bats may die because of this single disturbance.

The disturbance of a hibernating colony is even more deadly. The bat must store enough fat in the late summer and fall to carry him through the winter. If he is disturbed during hibernation, he uses up expensive energy. As a result, his stored fat is burned at a rate greater than normal. This may cause the bat to come out of hibernation in a weakened condition, or—if he is disturbed enough—not to survive the hibernation at all.

Tuttle's unpublished observations on gray bats show that they normally lose only .01 gram of body weight per day while hibernating. When aroused from hibernation they may lose as much as .48 grams of body weight in the first hour of disturbance. If human disturbance on the hibernating roost uses up too much of the bat's limited supply of stored energy, the bat will have to leave the cave too early—to search for food. Insect life is scarce in the early spring, and the bat's early departure may mean a death sentence.

Routine uses of insecticides in bat foraging areas has resulted in loss of numbers in the bat colonies. Residues of PCB, DDT, DDE, heptachlor epoxide or lead at dangerous levels has been found in the guano (bat manure) deposits in bat caves.

Forest clearing has had a detrimental effect; so has the siltation of water areas over which the bats forage, for it limits the insect life available to them. Any detrimental factor is important, for the gray bat has a very poor reproductive potential. Females do not produce until their second year, and only produce one offspring per year. Given the very critical temperature requirements for reproduction plus these other requirements, the gray bat cannot easily stage a comeback from low populations.

How bad is the situation? Gray bats are notoriously difficult to census, but the best informed guesses made by the Recovery Team indicate that perhaps something over 1,600,000 gray bats still exist. How can we call a species endangered if it still boasts of more than a million and a half members? Surely this cannot put the gray bat in the same class with the slightly more than one hundred whooping cranes? Yes, it certainly can.

Consider the bat's short life span, its poor reproductive potential, and above all, its strict requirement for huge numbers in its maternity colonies needed to produce body heat necessary to keep young bats alive.

In one cave in Missouri, the gray bat colony has decreased from more than one hundred thousand to less than three thousand in the last fifteen years. The decline in gray bat numbers over the last two decades has been estimated to be in the neighborhood of 50%.

To quote from the Recovery Team Report, "the decline in gray bat numbers began in the nineteenth century when the exploitation of caves was first begun on a large scale (mining of saltpetre, onyx, and other cave materials). The rate of decline has accelerated drastically during the past two decades, reflecting the soaring popularity of spelunking as a sport. If populations continue to decrease at the rate of 54% every six years, there would be as few as 100,000 gray bats left in the year 2000. Since gray bats require large colonies for successful rearing of young, a population of 100,000 scattered among many caves in six states might not be able to sustain itself. Thus the species might be doomed to extinction if the population is ever allowed to drop anywhere near that level."

Is the situation hopeless? Not by a long shot.

The Fish and Wildlife Service has purchased the major gray bat wintering cave in Kentucky as well as the most important known summer cave and is considering other acquisitions. A summer cave on the Wheeler National Wildlife Refuge has also been fenced and posted. As a result of that fencing and posting, the colony has improved from less than 10,000 males and non-productive females to the status of a maternity cave with more than 19,000 bats. It can be done!

The Recovery Team is actively pursuing a policy of protecting known gray bat caves. They have enlisted the cooperation of owners in preventing intrusion by humans. They have earmarked for acquisition many other caves which contain—or did contain—colonies of the Indiana gray bat. They have engaged in an active program of calling the attention of the spelunking fraternity to the great dangers of even a short, minor intrusion. The bats need to be left alone in their caves.

If they are not left alone in their caves, we may soon require other methods of controlling insects. Frankly, the bats do a better job than DDT, without the lethal side effects associated with it.

24

The Dusky Seaside Sparrow

As a great river moves along toward the sea, eddies and small whirlpools are formed where the water swirls against the bank. Parts of the bank are constantly pulled down forming tiny niches in which separate mini-ecosystems are created. The river throws up chunks of floating refuse, upon which the silt lodges, forming other tiny ecosystems. These tiny ecosystems are interesting, but they are not really an integral part of the mainstream of the river—a mainstream which flows inexorably toward the sea. Or are they?

As the river of evolution moves along its path, guided by experiments which are both successful and unsuccessful, small ecosystems develop along the edges of the mighty river. In each niche of these mini-systems, species begin to evolve differently. Often the mini-system is destroyed by the same process which built it, before the new species can evolve to fit it perfectly. Other times the evolutionary river forms a quiet whirlpool along its moving edge, different from the countless other habitats along the path of the river. Sometimes the quiet eddy, or backwater, persists long enough for a species to evolve which is admirably suited to life in that backwater. When the backwater forms, it is impossible to predict whether the backwater will slowly silt in, clog up and die, or whether the species inhabiting it will perish. Perhaps the eddy will slowly become larger, more important, and even become the main channel of the river.

We cannot decide when an evolutionary process is a dead end. Mankind does not possess that intelligence. How can we decide in advance that a species is doomed to failure? The extreme specialization of a black-footed ferret makes its survival doubtful, but we cannot be sure. The Texas blind salamander may develop to fit an evolutionary backwater and may be doomed to extinction because its habitat is so limited that it is unable to survive in other habitats. We can say that—but we are never sure.

The dusky seaside sparrow *(Spartina bakerii)* appears to occupy a shrinking nook in the environment. It has adapted beautifully to a specialized ecosystem not in the main stream of evolutionary development. Now that habitat is disappearing. Does this mean that the dusky seaside sparrow is also disappearing?

The dusky seaside sparrow was discovered in 1872, near Salt Lake, west of Titusville, Florida. Less than a hundred years later the bird was classified as

117

being endangered. Now the sparrow only exists in a small area of east-central Florida. It has been eliminated—for all intents and purposes—from its traditional breeding areas on Merritt Island. Although early ornithologists reported that they could see as many as twenty seaside sparrows from one spot at the turn of the century, the bird is now sought in vain in its tiny ecosystem, a strip about a quarter of a mile wide and ten miles long, on Merritt Island.

The bird is a ground feeder, nests in only one forb, and is difficult to observe. For most of this century, many sparrows were plentiful in the specialized habitat on Merritt Island. Because it was locally abundant there, nobody noticed that the bird was scarce or absent over the rest of the world. We had many dusky seaside sparrows on Merritt Island and along the St. Johns, so we failed to note that this tiny ecosystem was the only one that the duskies favored. This was specialization to a greater degree than any other case we have previously discussed, including the Kirtland's warbler.

Then that specialized habitat began to change. Man started to control the water levels to control mosquito larva. Mosquitoes require fluctuating water levels for successful reproduction. Man kept a constant water level, thus foiling the mosquito, and built dikes to maintain the constant level. By flooding the prairies of Florida, vegetation which the duskies needed for nesting disappeared. The permanent flooding changed the species composition of the insect life available to the dusky. The small bird is almost exclusively an insect and spider eater.

Man needed more pastures for his livestock, as Florida ranks only behind tremendous Texas in numbers of cattle. Man set fires to burn off the dead vegetation and allow grass to take over. This further constricted the habitat available to the dusky, leaving man with even less *Spartina* than were available before the burning.

Early students of the dusky seaside sparrow described the preferred habitat as being "damp, but not flooded, salt marsh." When mankind flooded it, he destroyed the habitat upon which the existence of the species depended. On the St. Johns Refuge, the effects of fire are demonstrated by the census figures. Sharp counted 143 singing males in 1970, and James Baker found 110 in the same area in 1972. Two wildfires in the winter of 1972-1973 burned about 700 hectares. The 1973 count produced only 54 singing males. In 1974, two more wildfires reduced the habitat even more. The spring of 1974 found only 37 singing males serenading the coming of the nesting season. A couple of years without fires brought the number of singing males up to 47 before fires fanned by strong northerly winds covered 75 percent of the refuge in 1975 and 1976. After that disaster, the count was 11 in 1976; 12 in 1977; and 9 in 1978.

Insecticides had reduced the population of sparrows even before the disastrous series of wildfires finished the job. But fires—set by lightning or other natural causes—have always been a part of the environmental picture on Florida's savannahs. Why did the dusky seaside sparrow coexist with wildfire for millennia, and then succumb to it in a few years? Because its habitat was so severely restricted that the loss of one more acre was crucial. Furthermore, its population was so low that the loss of a single individual was calamitous.

The unit value of habitat and the unit value of an individual bird have both inflated with the collapse in population numbers.

Destruction of habitat can be a final blow to a dusky seaside sparrow population because the species is reluctant to colonize a new savannah, unless a corridor of unbroken habitat exists. Small areas of suitable habitat are rendered unsuitable in the eyes of the sparrow, because they are not large enough.

The species was dealt another hammerblow in 1972, with the construction of the Beeline Highway through its limited habitat. Not only did the construction remove great areas of its prized nesting area, but we learned something else about dusky psychology. For endless generations, this bird had grown accustomed to the pancake flat savannah which was his home. When spoil piles created hills on his horizon, the dusky moved away from those hills which were foreign to him. Before construction, there had been 94 singing males—afterwards, only 12 remained.

Insecticides, flooding, wildfire and highway construction are the four causes of the decline in numbers of the dusky seaside sparrow.

In the spring of 1979, surveys revealed only thirteen singing males in existence! Using helicopters to find suitable habitat, the Fish and Wildlife Service and cooperating members of the recovery team have sought in vain for signs of female duskies, or of nesting activity. We know of no production of young since the spring of 1975. Considering the short life span of the sparrow family, this situation is extremely precarious. By the time you read this, the species may be extinct. If an active nest is found, the Recovery Team proposes to guard that nest against predation until the young birds are four days old. Then the young birds will be taken into captivity. The scientists may never have the opportunity!

The Recovery Team admits that its job is very nearly hopeless—and surely a realistic appraisal could hardly come to any other conclusion. They do not feel that the cause is lost, yet. If only they can locate one or more females and take them into captivity, they will have a chance.

The Game and Fish Commission in Florida has built an aviary. Three male duskies and a larger number of Scotts seaside sparrows are in captivity. They are experimenting with artificial propagation of the similar Scotts sparrow; so that they will know how to proceed with the dusky seaside sparrow if a female is ever located.

In a personal communication to me, Recovery Team leader Dr. Baker said that the three requisites right now for the fight against extinction are captive propagation, management of habitat, and a public awareness of the plight of the sparrow. He adds, "We have had a difficult time getting publicity for the dusky. Possibly if the bird were much larger, or had a name other than 'sparrow' it would help."

Dr. Baker's eye is on the sparrow, but the passing of the dusky seaside sparrow will not be noticed, nor mourned, by many. Was this species just an evolutionary experiment in a backwater ecosystem? Or was it an important part of the evolutionary process which man ruined by the four plagues of insecticides, wildfire, flooding and spoil piles?

25

The Light-footed Clapper Rail

Southern California is one example of mankind's unhappy proclivity for destroying what he loves by crowding in on it. Man's love for the seacoast, and his propensity for making his home on the seacoast, may have placed the final nail in the coffin prepared for the light-footed clapper rail, a geographical subspecies of the clapper rail, one of twenty-six separately recognized subspecies. Human alteration of the salt marshes which are home to the rail is only the latest calamity to befall these birds. Their numbers had been shrinking long before man's actions became a serious factor.

Ornithologists began to write of the scarcity of these rails as early as 1915. Their original range was thought to extend all the way along the salt marsh coast from Santa Barbara County in the state of California down to San Quintin Bay, Baja California in Old Mexico. However, no sightings have been verified from Santa Barbara since 1875. Was the light-footed clapper rail losing the battle as long ago as that?

There is some evidence that these rails do move from one marsh to another; marshes devoid of rails have been known to repopulate. The birds are non-migratory, however, and remain year-long residents of the marshes they choose.

The secretive and wary clappers are strange-looking birds. Long legs and splayed toes give them support when walking on their usual habitat, the soft marsh. They bob their heads when they walk, and twitch their comical, too-small tails from side to side. Among the rails, they are unfortunate in being big enough to attract the meat hunter.

Yet the hunter has probably not been the main cause of their decline. The clapper rails lead a precarious existence at the mercy of tides and winds. They build their nests, usually in cordgrass, at the spot where earth and water meet. Unexpectedly high tides or storm-driven tides can flood them out. Both the adults and the chicks can swim, but if forced to stay afloat very long, a heavy loss of clapper rail life usually results.

Food has never been a problem for the clapper rails. Their diet includes almost all of the mollusk and crustacean life of the marsh. Food in quantity always seems to be present as long as the marsh habitat is not disturbed by mankind's canals, levees, dikes and buildings. Food quality is another story. During the nightmarish years during which DDT was used indiscriminately for control of insects, the clapper rails found themselves at the top of a food chain which concentrated DDT and DDE to dangerous levels. What losses they suffered during those years immediately after World War II have not been well documented.

Overshooting by hunters had some effect and DDT probably added eggshell thinning to the list of mortality factors. But the greatest danger has been the destruction of salt marshes. According to the Recovery Team report, "Dredging and filling for various reasons has continued at an accelerated rate until only about 8,500 acres of salt marsh now remain between Santa Barbara and the Mexican Border, an area that at one time had an estimated 26,000 acres of salt marsh. Particularly hard hit were several areas known to have supported large populations of light-footed clapper rails: San Diego Bay reduced from 2,450 acres to 350 acres; Mission Bay, reduced from 2,400 to 21 acres; and the Los Angeles-Long Beach area, from 6,800 to 70 acres. Because this species is dependent on the coastal salt marsh environment, entire local populations have been exterminated."

The light-footed clapper rail is also found in Old Mexico, in the marshes at Bahia San Quintin and Bahia de Todos Santos. Very little is known of the bird's status in Mexico.

The last little bit of salt marsh environment important to the light-foots is the San Diego Bay-Tijuana Estuary area. About one half of all the known light-foots live here. The fate of this remnant of endangered birds is dependent entirely on our efforts to save some of this habitat. This means that the fate of the United States portion of the light-footed clapper rail population hangs by a very slender thread indeed.

The Recovery Team has set a goal of stabilizing the light-footed clapper rail population at about 400 nesting pairs. To let even this tiny number have a good chance of survival, four thousand acres of prime habitat must be provided for their use.

There can be no question that habitat is the key to survival. Yet preservation of habitat in land-hungry southern California is not easy. The California Department of Fish and Game is currently trying to restore the Bolsa Chica marshes—which will benefit many species including the clapper rails. The forward looking California Department and the U.S. Fish and Wildlife Service have agreed upon a report which says that the five areas now occupied by light-footed clapper rails are the highest acquisition priority of all California coastal wetlands.

In some areas, human alteration of the habitat has blocked out the tidal flow, which seems to be a requisite for clapper rail populations. Restoring tidal flows is very expensive in most areas and impossible in others. This remains the key to rail restoration. In some cases, good coastal salt marshes seem to be supporting fewer rails than they formerly did, because of the interruption or cessation of tidal flow. Restoration of the tidal flow seems to automatically upgrade the food supply, with beneficial results to the clapper rails.

Basically, the Recovery Plan envisages saving the existing rail habitat, buying up some of the areas lost to human development and returning them to tidal marsh conditions. This will provide complete protection for existing populations so that they might increase in numbers. Finally, birds from existing populations must be trapped and transplanted to the optimum habitat that becomes available. Because its recovery will be expensive and time consuming, and because the rails' needs conflict with man's plans for "progress" in the tidal marshes, there are many questions asked as to whether or not the bird is worth the effort.

Most of these questions are rooted in the undeniable fact that the light-foot is only a family of the clapper rail species—a species which is abundant in other parts of the country. However, there are three "families" of clapper rails which are now threatened or endangered in California alone: the Yuma rail, a family which developed along the Colorado River and the Salton Sea; the California clapper rail of San Francisco Bay; and the light-foot. All three of these families are endangered.

If three of the twenty-six known families of clapper rails are exterminated, there will only be twenty-three families left. In other words, we may be witnessing a "nibbling away" at the clapper rail family by those factors under man's control which have reduced habitat so disastrously in California. Because California's climate and scenic attractions have caused it to suffer most from a burgeoning human population, the clapper rails suffer there **first.**

Exactly the same factors, to varying degrees, are affecting the destiny of other "families" of clapper rails. If we cannot save the light-footed clapper rail, can we save the other families of clappers?

26

The Aleutian Goose

A tenet of good wildlife management is to not introduce exotic species into an environment without having first studied all possible results of that introduction. It is probably not a good idea to introduce the exotic animal even if your studies show no possible damage to the ecological niche being invaded.

A classical example of the damage that can be done by the introduction of an exotic is the German carp. A praised and desired food fish in Europe, the carp proved to be the bane of North American waters where its bottom feeding habits ruined spawning beds, muddied waters, destroyed aquatic vegetation and caused the extirpation of desirable fish from some waters.

The desire to make money also caused the introduction of exotic Arctic foxes onto the uninhabited islands of the Aleutians where the Aleutian goose nested. After all, there was a chance to turn the few pairs of foxes loose, avoid the costs of pen raising them, the cost of fences and caretakers, and still be able to harvest the crop of valuable furs when the time came to do so. The Russian-American Company began this practice in 1836 and it was continued by American citizens until about 1930.

The fogbound, rocky, cold, wet and isolated islands of the Aleutian chain were the nesting grounds for the Aleutian goose. The goose is a ground nester, and its nests and young were easy prey for the introduced foxes; for the Aleutian race of Canada goose had evolved into a successful life form during millennia free of foxes. No defense or escape mechanism had evolved to help the geese cope with the foxes. They simply served as meals for these foxes. The decline of Aleutian geese was immediate and catastrophic.

Agattu Island is a case in point. There were no native foxes on Agattu Island, and the Aleutian goose bred by the thousands. In 1923 four Arctic foxes were released on Agattu, five more in 1925 and another twenty-three in 1930. Between 1929 and 1936 at least one thousand foxes were killed for their pelts on Agattu Island. This tremendous explosion in fox numbers was due largely to abundant food on the island. Part of that food was Aleutian geese. Instead of the thousands which had formerly nested there, an observer in 1937 reported less than six pairs of geese in four days of traveling on the small island! Extermination was nearly complete. Similar tragedies occurred on most of the other islands of the Aleutians.

By 1962, the only known nesting population of Aleutian geese was on Buldir Island—which had escaped the introduction of Arctic foxes. In 1963, goslings were trapped on Buldir and removed to far-off Monte Vista National Wildlife Refuge in Colorado. That's where I saw my first Aleutian geese.

There is very little to identify the Aleutian from other small races of Canada geese. As I explained in my book, *GOOSE HUNTING*, plumage coloration is a poor means of differentiation between races of Canadas. To the goosehunter who must make a decision on the spur of the moment while looking at a bird which is flying past, there are only two kinds of Canada geese, big ones and little ones.

Sometimes the distinction between big and little is very difficult, for the gradation is gradual. Experienced observers say that there is a distinctive narrowing of the beak of the Aleutian, when seen from above. The problem is that we so seldom get to see our geese from above. Others point to a lighter coloration of breast feathers to distinguish between Aleutian and Cackling. These differences are so slight, however, that they fail me entirely as field identification aids.

In size, Aleutian geese usually rate between the Cackling geese and the Lesser Canada—but not always. Some Aleutians are larger than the smallest Lessers, and some Aleutians are smaller than the largest Cacklers. However, the long process of evolution which so perfectly fitted the Aleutian goose for life on the Aleutians—in pre-Arctic fox days—developed a goose which was definitely different in habits, in food preferences, in wintering grounds, and in many other qualities from other small races of Canada geese.

Starting with the first captured goslings from Buldir, the Fish and Wildlife Service built up a captive flock which was later transferred to Patuxent to take advantage of the expertise possessed by that remarkable facility in the field of avian physiology and in captive rearing of wild birds.

With a slow buildup of the captive flock, the gene pool seemed to be safer, but there was still the fact that the Aleutian Island home of these geese was no longer suitable for their continued existence. In 1949, the refuge branch of Fish and Wildlife had begun a program to eliminate the foxes on the more important goose nesting islands. They dropped strychnine baits and the incomparably more effective and species-selective Compound 1080 baits on Amchitka Island. Follow-up work continued through 1967, when the determination was made that no more foxes were alive on Amchitka.

A similar control program was begun on Agattu in 1964, using lethal baits dropped from airplanes. Follow-up ground work eliminated the remaining foxes by 1967, or so it seemed. However, in 1974, about 100 foxes were reported to be alive on Agattu. Scientists had to start the work of elimination all over again. Control measures are continuing, but in 1979 only one fox was taken on Agattu. Control measures are now underway on Alaid/Nizki Islands, and are planned for Kanaga Island which has a population of more than 700 foxes.

As the foxes were being eliminated from the Aleutians, the geese were breeding in captivity at Patuxent, and goslings were available to start reintroduction work. The first release was made on Amchitka in 1971, but the birds disappeared. No one knows why.

In 1974, the Fish and Wildlife Service decided to try again. They used forty-one wing-clipped adult geese from Patuxent's production line. They were released on Agattu. Four pairs nested and produced a total of five goslings. 139 more were released on Agattu in 1978, and another 244 geese were brought to Agattu in 1979. Nine molting geese were captured from the wild in Buldir and brought to Agattu for release with the captive-raised birds. The birds which had already migrated at least once would hopefully lead the captive-reared birds south on the long trip to California and return.

Aleutian geese from Buldir and perhaps from other islands in the Aleutian Islands have continued to migrate south to California each winter. Observers have searched carefully for signs that some of the Patuxent-reared birds were with them. Sadly, we do not have proof that Patuxent-reared birds have yet made the southward migration, even with wild-reared birds to lead the way. This may prove to be an insuperable difficulty born of the strong family structure of the Canada goose. Perhaps the young goslings follow only their own parent; perhaps they are driven off by other birds when they attempt to follow. These hardly seem likely, but to date we have not had artificially reared Aleutian geese on their traditional migration path.

Perhaps the new "Patuxent strain" of Aleutian goose has found a new southern wintering ground? We do not know.

An interesting ethical question came to light when the Fish and Wildlife Service stocked twenty-two pen-reared birds onto Amchitka Island in 1976. Bald eagles ate them. Obviously no released birds migrated from Amchitka, either. The ethical question is this: Is it justified to use predator control measures to manage the meat eaters in order to ensure that the rare and endangered species is not eaten before it has a chance to reproduce? Can we poison the endangered red wolf in Texas to save the endangered Attwater's prairie chicken?

The bald eagle, our national emblem, is definitely endangered in the lower forty-eight, but he is plentiful in Alaskan (including Aleutian) habitats. Should we have killed the bald eagles to protect the Aleutian geese? How about transporting some of the eagles to other states?

The judgment of Solomon is needed to answer those questions, but fools rush in where wise men fear to tread. I feel that it would be unwise to kill red wolves to save Attwater's prairie chicken, because the red wolf was always a part of the environment in which the Attwater's evolved.

The same thing is true of the bald eagles. They have always been part of the environment in which the Aleutian goose evolved; so I would not favor poisoning the bald eagles, even though they are numerous and the Aleutian goose is scarce.

However, I definitely favor poisoning the Arctic foxes, because they were introduced to the Aleutian goose habitat by meddling man. They are not native to the islands of Buldir, Amchitka, and Agattu; hence they do not belong there. The Aleutian goose never had a chance to develop a means of competing with the Arctic fox—he would never have had to if it had not been for man's meddling. What man caused by his meddling, man has an obligation to correct by more meddling.

Because the Aleutian goose breeds readily in captivity, for the moment we have saved the gene pool of this subspecies. But we still have not established this subspecies in sufficient numbers on its traditional migration paths. The gene pool of the goose may be safe now, but the bird may have been changed. Perhaps the geese will never be satisfied with the cold and fog of Agattu after they've seen Patuxent. "How you gonna keep them down on Agattu, after they've been to Maryland?"

Good News!

Late in the winter of 1980-1981, biologists of the California department and of the federal Fish and Wildlife Service positively identified Aleutian geese from Buldir Island wintering in their ancestral grounds in California. The progeny from artificial propagation have successfully adapted to their usual migration paths. The future for the Aleutian goose is now much brighter!

27

The Houston Toad

Biologists have described this relict population of toads sometimes as a sub-species of the much more common *Bufo americanus*, and sometimes as a species called *Bufo terrestris*, in acknowledgement of its soil-dwelling charac-teristics. More correctly we refer to it as *Bufo houstonensis*, in deference to its type locality.

The peculiarities which mark this toad were first described by John Wootring and then more formally described by Sanders in 1953. Even a taxonomist has trouble with identification of this species. The classical description includes a dorsal pattern consisting of dark spots on a tan background, coupled with obviously thickened postorbital and interorbital cranial crests. Then the sci-entist goes on to say, "...the absence of the obviously thickened postorbital and interorbital crests in many specimens leads to confusion." I will agree with that statement.

Actually the best identification of the male Houston toad is its very distinctive mating call, consisting of a 7 to 22 second high-pitched call in the 1646-2300 cps range with trills at pulsing rates varying between 14 and 36 pulses per second. That is very technical. Yet once heard and identified, the call of the Houston toad can be easily separated from related toad serenades.

Very few hard facts document the assumption that the Houston toad was formerly found over Burleson, Bastrop, Austin, Colorado, Fort Bend, Harris and Liberty Counties in Texas. Today it is found only in Bastrop and Burleson Counties.

The Houston toad prefers the type of loose, sandy soil commonly associated with loblolly pine in the parts of Texas named above. This secretive toad spends most of the year buried, or partly buried, in that loose soil. Active only at night, and almost unknown except in its mating season, the Houston toad is one of the hardest species to locate, let alone to census.

Reproduction of the Houston toad is associated with breeding ponds, where temporary water—present at just the right time—causes the males to get in a singing mood and the females to become receptive to that same singing. When spring rains do not come at just the right time, the Houston toad males are not much apt to go serenading their lady loves. The males in which the mating urge is strongest will go looking for non-existent temporary water supplies.

Failing to find them, they go to larger semi-permanent water holes favored by other related species of toads. Singing (and mating) from these areas results in hybridization with the more common subspecies of toad—a case of a particular gene pool being literally drowned in a larger gene pool of a more numerous species.

The species is fortunate in that its present day range, although greatly reduced from its historical distribution, includes two large state parks in Bastrop County where it is relatively safe. Changing land use patterns, including the changeover from undisturbed sandy soil to housing developments, are the greatest danger to this small toad. Yet if sufficient undisturbed habitat is left and the rains come at the right times each spring, the Houston toad is in no danger of extermination.

Researchers have discovered that this toad is easily propagated in captivity, and they are currently gaining proficiency in artificial propagation in the hopes that they can bring off some reproduction every spring, even in years when the wild toads are not romantically inclined. If the production from the toad nursery results in recruitment of a numerous age class each spring, the adult population should have no worries.

28

The Bald Eagle

Although Benjamin Franklin spoke eloquently in favor of the wild turkey, the United States of America chose the bald eagle as its national emblem. With a seven-foot wingspan, this bird is a majestic flier, and is capable of catching live fish near the surface of the water by swooping down and simply grabbing them with its sharp talons. The eagle is dark brown (almost black) over most of its body. The strikingly beautiful white head which gives it its name appears after three years. However, the younger birds, colored a lighter brown and splotched with white, give a very different appearance. These young eagles are often mistaken for hawks.

Besides catching fish from the water, the eagle is also a carrion eater and feasts on dead animals wherever they can be found. By harassing the far more skilled osprey into dropping the fish it has caught, the bald eagle is also a thief. The abandoned fish is usually caught in mid-air by the eagle.

Once plentiful over all of the North American continent, excluding Mexico, the bald eagle has fallen upon hard times during the last half century. It was placed on the endangered species list in 1978. Forty-three of the lower forty-eight states listed the bald eagle as "endangered"; in Michigan, Minnesota, Oregon, Washington and Wisconsin, however, it was listed as "threatened". There are lots of bald eagles in Alaska—probably more than in all of the other states combined. They are most numerous in the southeastern panhandle of Alaska. Admiralty Island has been found to have as many as 1200 active nests in one year! In the lower forty-eight, however, you would have to know something of the ancestral nesting grounds and be well acquainted with the country to find even one bald eagle nest a summer. Eagles are opportunists who follow the source of easily obtained food whenever possible. During the salmon runs, they will be found on the salmon rivers, sharing the profligacy of nature with the brown bears and with every other fish-eating species of bird or animal.

During cold winters, many bald eagles follow concentrations of wintering waterfowl. I have never seen an eagle take a healthy duck out of a flock, for a duck is too strong a flier to be easily caught. But the natural mortality rate among waterfowl will provide a steady supply of duck carcasses. Therefore the eagle often takes up residence near a large wintering concentration and dines well throughout the winter.

In 1958, when I was employed by the U.S. Fish and Wildlife Service in Mitchell, South Dakota, a typical "little old lady in tennis shoes" walked into the office and asked if I might help her locate a bald eagle. I told her that she would find about 200 on the tall cottonwoods near the Lake Andes National Wildlife Refuge, a half day's drive to the south. She looked at me very reproachfully as she said, "Please don't make fun of me, sir. I **know** that the bald eagle is rare."

Bless her heart, she came back the next afternoon to tell me that she had seen so many eagles at Lake Andes that she was afraid they "would eliminate ducks" that wintered there. She based this fear upon the fact that she saw no less than seventeen eagles feeding on duck carcasses at one time. She didn't know, of course, that the ducks on the eagles' menu were only part of one night's normal mortality out of a flock of nearly 250,000 mallards that were wintering in the area. That area is still an important wintering place for eagles, especially the part within the boundaries of the Karl E. Mundt National Wildlife Refuge.

With such an unlimited food supply, what has caused the decline of the bald eagle? Four reasons usually given are (1) habitat loss, (2) loss of nesting trees, (3) illegal shooting and (4) DDT and its metabolite DDE.

The eagle is quite intolerant of human intrusion in the area near the nest site. If observers come to the nest site several times, even within binocular distance from the nest, the eagles may desert the nest. The same nest is used by eagles over several decades. Each year they add to its mass until it may measure ten feet wide by fifteen deep.

Both parents bring food to the young and watch over them until they have learned to fly. The adults become increasingly stingy, however, with the free lunches as the youngsters learn to forage on their own.

Today's monoculture in forests has caused a gradual loss of big nest trees through attrition. As the big hardwoods die and fall, they are replaced with conifers for lumber, not with more hardwoods. This means that the eagle cannot find a suitable nest site and moves on, or—as is too often the case—does not nest at all.

Illegal shooting was once a serious cause of mortality among eagles. The passage of the Bald Eagle Protection Act slowed the illegal shooting to the point of almost being negligible (statistically, at least) in the dynamics of bald eagle population. The killer of a bald eagle could be hit with a fine of $5,000 or a year's imprisonment, or both. The law was rigorously enforced by state and federal officers. An educational program was developed to tell the story of our endangered national emblem. This has also been helpful in reducing illegal eagle shooting.

The fourth reason for the bald eagle decline is DDT. Its peril almost caused the total extermination of the bald eagle in the lower forty-eight states. During the bad old days when DDT was thought to be an unmitigated blessing, the number of active nests in Florida dropped from five hundred in 1940 to eighty in 1958. Add that bit of data to the known fact that DDT use was highest in the period following World War II and ending in 1960, and you get the picture.

The bald eagle was the unprotected top of a food chain made up of efficient bio-accumulators. Algae, at the bottom of the chain, were good at storing the poison. Algae were consumed by fish, which concentrated the DDT in their own fatty tissues where it was very soluble. The fish-eating bald eagle got the full impact of the stored DDT. There was no visible effect upon the eagle itself, but the drug reduced its ability to reproduce in many ways. Most dramatically, it reduced the bird's ability to manufacture eggshell. The too-thin eggshells broke when the bird tried to incubate its eggs.

Since the outlawing of DDT and the passage of the eagle protection laws, we have seen signs that the trend is being reversed. The bald eagle is no longer sliding precipitously toward extermination. The National Wildlife Federation annually conducts a bald eagle survey during January. In 1980 this count turned up a total of 13,127 bald eagles in 45 of the lower 48 states. No eagles were seen in Rhode Island, West Virginia and Vermont. The total was about 35% higher than the total recorded one year earlier. The good news has to be interpreted correctly to be of value, though, according to NWF's top eagle man, William S. Clark. He points out that improved methods, better area coverage and better trained observers account for a lot of the increase noted. He also points out that many of these birds have flown from Alaska and from Canada to spend the winter near open water and wintering concentrations of water-fowl.

After a few more years of these annual counts being fed into the computer, we will have good data upon which to decide whether the bald eagle is decreasing or increasing in numbers. The early indications are very optimistic, but it would be wrong to get our hopes up without hard data to allow for base line comparisons.

The total of more than 13,000 bald eagles in 1980 includes those which have flown down from Alaska to spend the winter. This is shown by the total of 1,623 bald eagles reported in the state of Washington. Mr. Clark estimated that as many as 80% of the total winter count was made up of "immigrants" from farther north.

The lingering effects of DDT are probably coming to an end at last. As the dregs of the chemical finally pass through the food chain, they become diluted past the point where they can cause eggshell thinning. The legal protection given to the bald eagle, combined with new public awareness of the plight of our national emblem may have almost eliminated the illegal shooting. The fact still remains that nesting habitat is being steadily destroyed throughout the range of the eagles in the lower forty-eight.

The realistic student of such affairs doesn't really believe that the destruction of habitat will be reversed in the foreseeable future. Bright spots are the national wildlife refuges which are being managed to provide nesting sites, near water, for the big white-headed birds. This is especially true of the Upper Mississippi River Refuge between Minnesota and Wisconsin, and Iowa and Illinois. Historically, this was prime eagle habitat and can be again. The Karl E. Mundt Refuge, mentioned earlier, is of importance farther west, as is the De Soto Bend and several other refuges near the Big Muddy.

Timber companies owning most of the prime eagle habitat in the Pacific

Northwest have shown an awareness of public opinion regarding wildlife on their lands. They can be expected to show more concern for nesting sites of the eagles along their waterways.

It's too early to tell, but there is hope for the bald eagle. We really must save this bird. What a national tragedy if we failed to save our own national emblem! But if the unthinkable happens and our national emblem becomes extinct, I second the motion made by Benjamin Franklin so long ago, to nominate the wild turkey as our national emblem.

29

California's Least Tern

The smallest North American member of the large family of gulls and terns, the least tern is one of the most beautiful shore birds. The adult in breeding plumage is a striking combination of white and black, making it a picture of diminutive elegance. Its very elegance, though, was once its greatest peril, for its skins were used to furbish the bonnets worn by ladies of fashion.

The leading "bird book" of the 1950's was mistaken when it stated that the market price of twelve or fifteen cents was responsible for the near-complete extermination of the least tern in the gay nineties. This guide credited the Audubon movement with stopping the traffic in least tern feathers and chronicled the complete recovery of the bird from the low ebb of the turn of the century. Freed from the millinery menace, one might expect the least tern to prosper in new found immunity from man's threats to its existence.

Not so.

What has happened to the least tern? Why have its numbers declined in California where it was once so common? Let me answer that question by quoting from a series of status reports compiled by employees of the California Department of Game and Fish. According to Paul Kelly, "Once widespread and common in California coastal habitats from the Mexican border to San Francisco Bay, this tern is currently threatened by numerous human-related environmental disturbances."

The California census showed only an estimated eight hundred breeding pairs in the entire state in 1978. What caused this? Paul Kelly continues, "As a result of destruction and increasing disturbance of historic nesting areas, the California least tern is evidently being forced to nest on smaller, often times substandard nesting areas where unnaturally dense colonies may form. Such high concentrations of birds may serve as strong predator attractants, which enable predators to locate colonies quickly and to repeatedly prey upon them." A little farther along he notes: "The presently used techniques of enclosing colonies with posts, signs, flagging tape and twine, has proved relatively ineffective in excluding ORV's (off road vehicles) which have done serious damage to several colonies."

Do you mean to tell us, Paul, that we have brought the least tern to its low estate by simply being careless and running over its nest with our play toys? Maybe it's worse than that.

From a report by Elsie Roemer: "I saw so many least terns that I tried to find their nesting colony. I thought I'd found it, but bulldozers were at work covering the area as I watched. Workmen told me later that they had covered many nests."

From a report by Jonathan Atwood: "Least terns did not attempt to nest at nearby Ormond Beach in 1978. The increasing use of this area by ORV's is very likely the primary factor in the abandonment of this nesting area in 1978."

From the same report: "Least terns did not breed at the nearby Beethoven Street Fill in 1978. Large mounds of sandy dredge material from the Ballena Creek channel were placed on the site prior to this year's breeding season, rendering the area unsuitable for least tern nesting."

Again from Atwood: "...and subsequent use of a portion of the nesting site for auto storage apparently resulted in abandonment of this area in 1978.

"Since this portion of the beach receives extremely heavy human use during the summer months, the only possible nest sites west of Pacific Coast Highway are the two meter wide planters between the road and the parking lot and the flat roofs of the restroom facilities in the area. Either possibility would be amazing."

From a report by Philip Unitt: "Marine Corps personnel erected a conspicuously posted barrier of elastic cord and metal posts extending the length of the beach on the seaward side of both the south and north dunes. Although tanks (underlining supplied by CLC) were seen rolling along the beach on almost every visit, they stayed outside of the barrier and did not flush the birds off their nests."

Later from Unitt's report: "...helicopters from nearby Palomar Airport had been conducting test flights over the lagoon, at times hovering low over the colony site.

"The Navy plans to build an athletic field at the north end of the land where the colony is situated, covering most of the present nesting area. At least thirty-six pairs of least terns attempted to nest on the asphalt helicopter landing area north of the control tower."

By now you have gotten the picture. Man has simply waged a war on the California least tern's nesting areas. Attacking with tanks, helicopters and off-road vehicles, humans have caused the vast decline of these attractive little birds which do no harm to anyone. Our activities still threaten the very existence of the least tern as a species.

Can anything be done?

Yes, and Californians are beginning to take affirmative actions which may save the bird. There's a lot of imagination in California and a lot of civic pride; once it has been awakened.

By again looking at California reports, we can see that sand fences are being erected to stop off-road vehicle traffic, and, indeed, all human intrusion in some of the bigger nesting colonies. Paul Kelly says: "Sand fencing, erected seasonally, was employed successfully at Venice Beach for the second year; although not a substantial barrier, this fence excluded dogs and most beach goers. Through local public support and awareness, the Venice Beach colony has become one of the largest and most successful in the state."

See what great things can be accomplished by simply giving the bird un-hindered use of an area for the two months of its breeding season? I mentioned imagination, and Californians have a good supply. Witness the fact that they used *papier-mâché* least terns to decoy the wild birds to the nesting areas where they would be safe from such slight annoyances as tanks, helicopters, motorcycles, dune buggies and parking lots. It worked! The least terns came to the dummy birds and took up residence.

The terns prefer bare stretches of beach upon which to form their loosely knit nesting colonies. When terrestrial vegetation grows up on newly prepared nesting sites, the terns move on. So Californians tried pumping salt water from the inexhaustible supply in the Pacific Ocean over the emergent vegetation in an effort to kill it off. All the tools of our imagination are needed to help the birds.

I hope that I haven't given the impression that the armed forces are intolerant and uncaring about the birds which share their lands with them. This is not the case. To quote from a Richard Erickson report: "Naval Air Station personnel placed a log barrier around the site this year. Logs about one foot in diameter completely surrounded the nesting area and effectively isolated the colony from the rest of the airfield. Vehicular traffic, apparently the problem in the past, was eliminated. Many chicks managed to exit through cracks in the barrier but generally did not wander far. Aside from the log barrier there was no site preparation. Concrete blocks provided for shelter in 1977 were well used this year and the log barrier provided additional shelter for the chicks."

Civic pride in a nesting colony of least terns can be the greatest protection the birds can have. If left to reproduce without fear of human intrusion, the California least tern can probably be depended upon to maintain its numbers at the mark of about eight hundred breeding pairs, the highest observed in the last ten years. If nesting sites are protected from predation by man's dogs, cats and rats, the birds will probably double that number very quickly. But they have a long way to go to replace even a fraction of their former abundance.

The California least tern is a striking example of man's carelessness toward the other life forms which share this limited planet with us.

The present trend toward environmental awareness may conceivably lead to the development of an ecological conscience. Unfortunately the signs of such a development are very few, even today. If the California least tern is saved from extinction, mankind will be taking another small step toward its own evolution as a thinking animal, and a small step away from callous neglect for others. In the case of the California least tern, the jury is still out. Its deliberations may take several decades.

Robert C. Belden working with a Florida panther.

30

Florida's Panther

When the white man came to this continent, the mountain lion was found from northern British Columbia to the Everglades, from Maine down through all of Mexico and on into the South American continent. He was known by many names: painter, catamount, puma, cougar and American lion. The mascot for Pennsylvania State University is the Nittany lion. His natural food was the whitetailed or mule deer and all of its subspecies found across his tremendous range.

Deer populations were much smaller at that time than they are now. The mountain lion was a population-controlling factor in some areas, but not in many. After all, panthers had been eating deer for millennia, without decreasing the overall population.

When mankind began to change the face of this loveliest of all continents, he tipped the scales heavily in favor of the deer and weighted them against the cougar. Man's agricultural practices removed the primeval forest and replaced it with a variety of crops which the deer found tasty. Mankind also introduced a great increase in "edge" habitat of the kind that deer like most—the edge of trees left along a field of sweet corn at the side of a managed pine forest, which offered quick escape routes yet was never too far from food. Deer prospered in this habitat.

At the same time, man hunted the cougar with dogs which tracked him by scent and treed him for the hunter to shoot. Man trapped the mountain lion with steel leg traps, for the lion had already shown a liking for such succulent meals as pigs, calves and colts. The monoculture type of forestry practice which converted hardwood forests into even-aged stands of one marketable pine tree species did little for the lion—except destroy the mature forest where he had found safety in the past.

Today the range of the panther is greatly shrunk. For all practical purposes, he is found in the Rocky Mountain states and west to the Pacific, but only in reduced numbers and in the most inaccessible habitat.

He is almost gone from east of the Mississippi. The one exception is the Florida panther.

Few in numbers, this secretive nocturnal cat is still living in the Everglades National Park area of Florida. Biologists call it a separate subspecies *Felis* _olor coryi_, but its own mother couldn't tell a _Felis concolor coryi_ from a _.iis concolor_ at twenty paces. This claim of belonging to a different race is justified only by a few differences which distinguish it from the more numerous western race of cougar. The Recovery Team leader describes the Florida panther as being a medium-sized, dark subspecies with short and rather stiff pelage. Long limbs distinguish the Florida panther from the other subspecies along with small feet and a rich ferruginous color, particularly in the mid-dorsal region. The skull has a relatively broad, flat frontal region with remarkably broad and high arched or upward expanded nasals. Practically all specimens have white-flecked head, neck and shoulders.

This slightly different Florida panther once was found over most of the southeast: Arkansas, Louisiana, Mississippi, Alabama, Georgia and Florida, as well as parts of Tennessee and South Carolina. Now it is found only in the Florida Everglades, with relict populations probably hanging on in Arkansas and Louisiana. The reasons are simple. Mankind took away much suitable habitat from the big cat's range, so it is now found only in the small areas where habitat is suitable.

Documented evidence of its existence today can only be found in the Fakahatchee Strand, Big Cypress National Preserve, and Everglades National Park, in Florida.

Although the Florida panther receives protection against hunting of any kind, the inexorable growth of mankind's homes and towns has squeezed the big cat farther and farther into the last bit of suitable habitat.

Although very little is known about the needs of the few remaining panthers, the Florida Panther Recovery Team has formulated a Recovery Plan which calls for (1) maintaining any existing populations of Florida panthers, (2) improving public opinion and behavior toward the panther by means of an educational program, and (3) the re-establishment of populations where feasible.

Robert C. Belden, Florida biologist, is the leader of the team. He points out that the biggest problem with preserving the existing populations is that you first have to find those populations. The Florida panther is definitely not cooperating with those who wish to study him. This cat is one of the most secretive of all wild animals. In a lifetime spent in the out-of-doors, I have only once seen a free, wild mountain lion—except for those I saw chased by hounds, or taken in traps.

A process of systematic searching is now underway coupled with establishment of clearing houses for the evaluation of sighting reports, to get a better idea of how many Florida panthers exist and where they exist.

The Recovery Team urges acquisition of the Fakahatchee Strand area as critical habitat for the panthers. It wants to go into radio-telemetry as the quickest and surest way of finding out how big an area the animals range over, what their foods are, and what population density can be sustained by the various habitats.

After the critical habitat is safeguarded, and after basic knowledge of the cat's needs is gained, a captive breeding program may be used to provide stock for reintroduction into the wild in suitable habitats which will be chosen after careful analysis. Although zoo experiences show that almost all of the big felines can be bred in captivity with relative ease, this has not yet been the case with the Florida panther. Four males and four females are kept in captivity by Everglades Wonder Garden, and one male belonging to the Florida Game and Fresh Water Fish Commission is kept at a youth camp in High Springs, Florida. With one exception, all of these animals are captive-born. They show abnormal conformations resulting from deficiencies in their diet during the developmental stage. These captive animals have all failed in breeding attempts. Biologists feel that these animals might be "human imprinted," or that the males are all impotent due to old age.

One suggestion that has been made is that a wild male be trapped and used to breed the captive females before being returned to the wild.

How would that needed male be captured? One suggestion is that the Florida panther be treed by a professional lion hunter and his experienced hounds; then captured. It would make an exciting movie. The daring captor climbs within reach and then slips a noose over the head of the lion. If possible, a second line is fastened around a foot as the lion fights against the noose. Then the animal is pulled out of the tree—the dogs having been tied safely where neither they nor the lion would get hurt. Roy McBride, professional lion hunter from West Texas has taken his hounds to Florida and actually proved that they can track and tree a Florida panther. I worked with Roy in Texas back in the 1960-1962 era, and know him to be a thoroughly competent outdoorsman, with great experience in tracking lions with dogs. If anyone can do it, Roy can.

Today the future of the Florida panther is very much in doubt. Its habitat is restricted, and is becoming more so. Captive propagation might be the answer, but that is very doubtful right now due to the problem of teaching the cage-reared lion cub how to go about the business of feeding himself.

The big job of educating the public to the fact that the Florida panther needs help is now underway. Team leader Chris Belden has proved to be able and prolific in writing about Florida's last big cats. He has authored a pamphlet on recognizing panther tracks and has described the few known panther facts very well.

But—and it is a very big but—is it possible to maintain a viable population of a specific race of mountain lion in the small habitat still available to him in Florida?

The fight is going on now.

Attwater's Prairie Chicken performing his prenuptial dance on the booming grounds.

31

Attwater's Prairie Chicken

A subspecies of the more common prairie chicken of the north, the Attwater's prairie chicken is one of our rarest endangered game birds. The steady destruction of its best habitat, caused by the spreading megalopolis which now straddles much of the Texas Gulf Coast, has left the Attwater's with very little room. This grouse has many friends, though, and they have come to his rescue in a big way.

By the time mankind noted that the Attwater's was in trouble, his numbers had declined to the point where only 1,070 birds were recorded on the 1967 census. This was the low point. Census figures for past years give a good idea of the population trends:

1937........8,711	1970 1,440	1975 2,240
1950........4,200	1971 2,212	1976 2,088
1956........3,450	1972 1,650	1977 1,500
1963........1,336	1973 1,772	1978 1,500
1967........1,070	1974 2,004	1979 1,802

Even though we have only a remnant population now, the bird seems to be in no immediate danger at the present time.

Just as destruction of its habitat for real estate development has been the biggest cause for the numerical slide of the Attwater's, the setting aside of critical habitat will certainly be the stabilizing factor. We can only hope that this stabilizing factor will continue to operate and that the bird will adapt to today's conditions and change some of its stubborn ways.

Stubborn ways? Yes sir, the Attwater's prairie chicken yields to few species when it comes to stubborn refusal to change its habits. Each spring when sex rears its lovely head and the male birds get excited, they gather on "dancing grounds" or "booming grounds" to put on their spring display which is supposed to lure females to them. With wings stiffly distended so that the primary feathers scrape along the ground, and heads stuck straight out in front, the birds "dance" in a strange pirouetting motion, circling again and again in this strange position. While this performance is going on, the male bird inflates yellow gular pouches along the sides of his neck. At the conclusion of each phase of his dance, he releases the pent up air in a noise which is usually called booming, but sounds more like a sodden "plop" to me. The dance is usually performed at or near sunrise. As the hens stroll nonchalantly through the dancing grounds, they seem to pay no attention to the performances of the males. But they must be watching out of the corner of their eye, for they do pair off for a brief romantic interlude. This system has perpetuated the species for thousands of years; so we can't knock it.

There has to be one constant in this weird performance—the location of the dancing ground. If there were no designated place for the ritual to take place, male and female would not meet. The species would perish. There is a very strong and instinctive desire on the part of the birds to return to an ancestral dancing ground, one that has always been theirs to perform their nuptial dances upon.

So what happens when an unthinking nation builds an air force base upon the dancing ground? What happens when the Attwater's prairie chicken comes out to dance and finds that spot is now a concrete runway? Experience has given us the answer to that question—the indomitable and stubborn chicken dances on the runway. What happens when jet plane and prairie chicken collide? The chicken dies and sometimes the plane crashes (a chicken sucked into the air intake causes a flame out and crash).

There have been occasions when there was no prairie chicken in sight at pre-sunrise time, but the roaring departure of a jet plane would bring out the males, each one ready to dance his challenge to the big plane. Obviously in such a confrontation the prairie chicken has two chances. As Dizzy Dean said about the baseball player caught in a rundown—"two chances, slim and none."

There have been many attempts to trap and relocate the chickens where an air base was being built. Most have failed; a couple have shown good results. At best, the trapping and relocating is apt to lose a complete year out of the reproductive cycle, with resulting damage to population totals.

In 1979, thirty-nine Attwater's were trapped on the Houston Gulf Airport, using the latest technique of a "helinet" dropped over the birds from a helicopter. They were moved to a ranch in Victoria County, in prime habitat. Observers reported that the birds scattered badly upon release, probably each one seeking the lost airport home. But six months later about sixteen of the birds remained on or near the release site. Perhaps they will succeed in establishing a colony. But can you imagine the consternation in their little heads when it came time to do the courtship dance in the spring of 1980? How could the birds reach a consensus that "this is the place"?

The future of the Attwater's has been considerably brightened by the establishment of the Attwater's Prairie Chicken National Wildlife Refuge, 5,600 acres of good habitat along the San Bernard River in Colorado County, Texas. There are about one hundred and fifty Attwater's chickens on the refuge today, and the principal management objective of the refuge is the protection of the Attwater's. Intensive study there may guide the way to other measures which will ensure their future.

The Tatton family gave 7,500 acres of prime Texas Gulf Coast land to the Aransas National Wildlife Refuge, to try to help the Attwater's. This 7,500 acres was appraised at more than $1,750,000 when the gift was made. Today it would be at least double that. This addition to the home of the whooping crane is also home to about sixty Attwater's prairie chickens. On both the Aransas and the Attwater's National Wildlife Refuges, there has been an attempt to improve habitat for the prairie chicken by means of brush clearing and selected burning. This changes the environment from the scrub oak thicket to the ancestral tall grass prairie which was home to these birds long before the white man arrived.

An interesting sidelight on the Attwater's fight for survival is the fact that one of the predators of the chicken in days gone by was the red wolf, itself an endangered species. Attempts to "clean out" populations of coyotes which hybridized with the red wolf may have resulted in lowering the total predator population in the chicken's favor. We have discovered that experiments in eliminating the larger predators have resulted in an increase in numbers of smaller predators. Raccoons and skunks are probably greater dangers to the chicken than the red wolf used to be.

With only about 200 Attwater's prairie chickens on the federal refuges and another 1600 to 1700 depending upon privately owned land, the future of the species depends upon the attitude of the Texas ranchers.

32

Sonoran Pronghorn Antelopes

Some taxonomists claim that the Sonoran pronghorn is merely a color phase of *Antilocapra americana*, a pronghorn which is numerous across the wide grasslands of Wyoming, Montana, and a dozen other western states. Others claim that this antelope differs in several ways from the other, more numerous race.

The question of which set of taxonomists is correct may become moot, for the Sonoran pronghorn appears to be on the way out, moving very slowly through the door to extinction.

At the present time, the Sonoran pronghorn is one of the most forgotten of all wildlife species. This is easy to understand if you live where this speedster lives. I've never known a more cruel, difficult, and forbidding place to eke out a living than the furnace-hot expanses of the Sonoran Desert. No man really wants to be stationed in a climate of waterless, charred lava fields and burnt red rocks, where daytime temperatures regularly reach 120° F.

In 1975 the Director of the U.S. Fish and Wildlife Service named a Recovery Team for the Sonoran pronghorn. Five years later that recovery team had not even come up with a preliminary recovery plan. In fact, to the best of my knowledge, in more than five years they have not produced even a single report; not one bit of evidence acknowledges that someone cares about the future of this beast.

How big a population are we talking about? There are roughly—no one knows for sure—eighty Sonoran pronghorns on the Cabeza Prieta National Wildlife Range in southern Arizona. For fifteen years, biologists have added the words "and another hundred or so in Mexico directly south of Cabeza Prieta." I do not know where the original estimate came from, nor do I see any evidence to believe that there are 100 pronghorns in Mexico. No one has counted them in two decades, to the best of my knowledge. The U.S. Fish and Wildlife Service did some aerial survey work in Old Mexico a year or so ago, and they tell me that they did count about fifty antelope in Mexico. They have no idea whether or not they found them all, nor even if they looked in the right places.

My guess is that there are about 140 Sonoran pronghorn in the world today— 80 head in the United States and 60 in Mexico. No one knows if that population is decreasing, holding its own, or increasing. My guess is that the population is slowly decreasing due to the inroads of motorized travel on that expanse of Mexico where the antelope is now hunted occasionally, and where previously a motor-equipped hunter was not seen from one decade to the next.

The pronghorn, like the desert bighorn sheep which also inhabits this seared and sere desert, benefits from the benign neglect and splendid isolation that come with living in a roadless desert. The only serious predator of the antelope is man—for the Mexican grizzly is gone, and the panther was never numerous in this treeless expanse. How many Sonoran pronghorn once roamed this area? We cannot know. Perhaps they were never numerous, considering this hostile environment.

We know so little about the desert and about the place of the pronghorn in that environment. Does this antelope eat the fruit of the prickly pear, or of the barrel cactus? The names of the plants he may feed on are foreign to most of us. We are unaccustomed to words like tasajillo, ocotillo, cholla, palo verde, boojum, lecheguilla and saguaro.

Water is a scarce commodity on the Cabeza Prieta and is even harder to find outside the boundaries of the refuge. Papago Well, Charlie Bell Well, Antelope Wells—the names of the waterholes are easy to remember, for they hold life and death in their balance. Was Antelope Wells, New Mexico, once named for Sonoran pronghorns? We don't know. The usable range of the pronghorn here in the desert is limited to that area which is within an hour's walk—in 120° F—of the water supply.

I have lain in wait for wildlife, armed with a movie camera, in the furnace heat of the Cabeza Prieta. I have had desert bighorn rams pick out my photo blind from miles away, and stay away for hours. Finally, though, they all had to come to water and within range of the camera. Their wariness as they approached was evident. They knew that a man hid in waiting for them, and they feared that man. Yet they had to come to the water. If they did not, they would have died. Life is often reduced to simple equations in the desert Southwest.

As mentioned above, we do not know much about the food habits of the Sonoran pronghorn. Does he range so widely, and move so often because his preferred foods are scarce—few and far between? There is so much we don't know.

What we do know is that a remnant group of slightly different pronghorn antelopes, less than two hundred animals, ranges across an awesome piece of cruel desert aggregating perhaps 900,000 acres in two nations. Almost no attention has been paid to it by anyone in a position of responsibility since the inception of the Endangered Species program. We can hope that they are holding their own. All we can do is hope, because we do not know their numbers. And we can also hope that their gene pool has not been so severely constricted that the race may have already lost its ability to survive. We may never know if there is something of value in the building blocks of this gene pool, some key to successful survival in a land of heat and bare rock, of desiccated cacti and blast furnace winds. Mankind may one day find himself in a similar environment.

We may never find many answers about the Sonoran pronghorn, for a species is easily ignored by mankind when its home is an ecological niche so hostile to man himself. The Sonoran pronghorn has been forgotten during the decades that the Johnny-come-lately white man has attempted to manage this continent's wildlife resources.

Nene Geese of Hawaii

33

The Hawaiian Picture

The bird life which has evolved on the islands of Hawaii in the centuries since those lava mountains thrust up out of the sea is one of the most varied and beautiful to be found anywhere.

Because they evolved in the total absence of large animal predators, and because they were limited in territory to the comparatively small island or islands which they occupied, these bird species are infinitely more specialized in their choice of habitat, choice of food, and acquired protective reactions than are birds of a larger mainland territory.

A glance at the situation which affects one of these specialized birds, will serve to indicate the scope of the "endangered species" problem in the Hawaiian Islands.

A finch-like member of the Hawaiian honeycreeper family, the palila is limited to the Kona district of Hawaii. Its historic range around the top of the mountain has now shrunk to about one fourth of its former size. Today it ranges only in the mamane-naio ecosystem of Mauna Kea at an elevation above 6,000 feet. "Mamane" and "naio" are names of trees native to the area, and the mamane is of paramount importance to the palila. The mamane tree furnishes food, nesting habitat and protection from the elements for the palila. The bird builds its nests in the mamane. When the young hatch out, they are fed the seeds of the mamane during most of the fledging period. Without the mamane, the palila is in trouble.

European colonization of the Sandwich Islands began with Captain Cook. Successive waves of humans from almost every corner of the earth have since been attracted to the beautiful islands. These waves of colonists brought their domestic animals with them. And these INTRODUCED animals sounded a death knell for the wonderfully varied bird life of Hawaii.

Feral goats, sheep and pigs all eat the mamane tree, which can be destroyed by overgrazing. Because they have eaten the seedling mamane trees, they have almost stopped regeneration of this tree in the Mauna Kea area. In 1937 about 30,000 sheep roamed Mauna Kea's slopes, which is about one sheep for each two acres. The damage they did brought about the need for a control program. More than 3,000 sheep were killed in two days in 1937, but the damage had already been done.

Now feral sheep, goats and pigs have been reduced or eliminated at the lower elevations—at least to the point where the forest deterioration has been arrested. Above 8,000 feet the degradation of the ecosystem continues.

Census studies in 1975 and 1976 gave us a palila population estimate of about 1,400 birds. To protect these 1,400 birds, the Recovery Team wants to eliminate entirely the feral flocks of sheep and goats, to manage the numbers of feral pigs and introduced mouflon sheep (a sport-hunting animal of some value), and to acquire extensive habitat to ensure protection for the palila. This seems to make the price of protection abnormally high, but there are five other species of endangered birds present in the same habitat. The work done to help the palila will also help the dark-rumped petrel, the Hawaiian hawk, the Hawaii creeper, the Hawaiian akepa, and the akipolaau.

The Recovery Team must manage an entire ecosystem—the mamane-naio forest areas—for the benefit of these native species. Without the INTRO-DUCTION of exotic species, there would be no need for a protection program. The Hawaiian species evolved to fit particular niches in the ecosystem. They didn't need any help from mankind until mankind changed their essential habitat with the introduction of exotic mammals against which the birds have no defense.

Perhaps the most celebrated of the Hawaiian species is the state bird, the nene goose. This beautiful cousin of the plentiful Canada goose was once numerous throughout most of the islands in the Hawaiian chain. Then sugar cane planters, attempting to reduce the population of introduced commensal rats, introduced the mongoose in the hopes that the mongoose would eat the rats. Since there had been no preliminary research to guide the introduction, they forgot a simple fact. Mongooses are diurnal; rats are nocturnal. The mongoose had no affect upon the rat population, but feasted on ground nesting birds and their eggs. The once plentiful nene goose is a dryland nester, hence the population plummeted dramatically—to the point where no more than forty nene's existed in the wild during the mid-1940's.

Strangely enough, the nene goose seldom goes near the water but inhabits the lava slopes of the islands where it feeds mainly on berries. Introduced feral goats and pigs have destroyed its favorite nesting cover; introduced mongooses have eaten the exposed eggs and, all too often, the nesting female.

Wild house cats have also added to the woes of all ground nesting birds on these "islands of Paradise." Researchers on Mauna Loa found that every single wild nene nest in the 1978-1979 season failed. They failed to produce young nenes because of predation upon the nests by mongoose, cats and feral pigs.

How many nenes have withstood the assault of the INTRODUCED enemies against which they had never known the need to develop a defense? Researchers right now feel that there are about 245 on Hawaii and another 100 on Maui. The state game department has released about 1500 nenes since 1962, in hopes of bolstering the numbers of the wild flock.

Happily, there is a good nucleus of breeding stock held in captivity all around the world. If our fiftieth state can solve the problems which have rendered its paradise unsuitable for the nene, then it should be relatively easy to reintroduce a native flock. Can the new birds be considered wild? The wild nene is remarkably tame, allowing humans to approach within ten or fifteen feet at times before taking flight. This lack of wariness may be a trait of the species, not just of pen-raised nenes.

The nene is a waterfowl which no longer goes near the water, but three other real waterbirds are also endangered. They are the Hawaiian stilt, the Hawaiian coot and the Hawaiian gallinule. All three are non-migratory subspecies of their more common namesakes found in the continental United States. Their habitat has been destroyed and their numbers have diminished with the destruction of their habitat.

Originally the Hawaiian Islands boasted a surprisingly large marsh area which was attractive to these specialized birds. The marsh area was planted into taro by the original Hawaiians, and fortunately the change did little harm to the birds because taro grows in a marshy habitat. There must have been huge acreages planted to taro at one time, as the food helped to support a human population estimated at 300,000.

Introduced diseases decimated the endemic human population, however, and intermarriage of human races from all over the world changed the nature of the human population remaining. The biggest racial change was from taro-eating Polynesians to rice-eating Orientals. Yet even rice was good habitat for the stilt, the coot and the gallinule; so they were not in trouble yet.

Real estate on the islands has always been very valuable. Rice could be grown in Asia and shipped to Hawaii cheaper than it could be grown on the islands; also, California rice growers were able to undercut rice production in Hawaii. Hence, no more rice was grown on the islands and the habitat for these birds disappeared.

Hunting played an important part in reducing the high numbers of the coot and gallinule, and even of the stilt which was hunted regularly. Note that when their habitat was abundant, these birds could support considerable sport hunting. When they were crowded into sparse habitat they became easy prey for the hunter and even easier prey for the introduced mongoose.

The facts of the Hawaiian picture are:

1. Introduced humans have had a bad effect upon native wildlife in the Hawaiian Islands.

2. Introduced mammalian predators have had a disastrous effect upon native wildlife species. There were no mammalian predators when Captain Cook came to the islands.

3. A good case can be made for the elimination of all mammals on the islands. This would be a sensible Recovery plan, but almost impossible to implement.

Elimination of feral goats, sheep and pigs is possible—although terribly costly and very difficult. Elimination of feral mongooses is quite another story. I doubt that they can be eliminated, but the wealth of native bird life that they threaten is so valuable that their elimination should be attempted. The resultant reduction will doubtless have a positive effect on the special bird population.

Elimination of feral cats is an impossibility in my estimation. However, continuation of the good publicity campaign being mounted in Hawaii to appraise residents of the fight against the extinction of these birds to the abandoned cat, the feral goat and the introduced mongoose can do much to help the feral cat situation.

The beauty and variety of Hawaiian bird life was one of the greatest wonders of the world. The elimination of many of these species and the great reduction in numbers of many others is a great tragedy. A tragedy in Paradise, where the unsophisticated species which never knew predators for thousands of years now are easy prey for enemies that should never have been introduced to Hawaii.

Puerto Rican Parrot

34

The Puerto Rican Picture

The Commonwealth of Puerto Rico politically occupies a unique place in the United States of America, as well as a geographic and ecological position of great interest. This large island in the Caribbean is the overlapping meeting place for life forms which are not found elsewhere in the United States. This is the southernmost part of the range for many U.S. species and the northernmost part of the range of some South or Central American species. As a land of mountains and forests, it provides a markedly different environment than is found on the other low lying tropical islands.

Puerto Rico has been densely populated for many more years than the oldest settlement in the continental United States. Problems of coexistence with its animal neighbors date from exploration by the Spanish conquistadores in the early 1500's. Consequently, the destruction of entire species started much earlier than on the continental mainland. Most of the great hardwood forests of this rich land were falling to the axe back in 1900-1920 to make room for expanding villages, towns and cities.

Faced with widespread poverty, illiteracy and burgeoning human populations, the Commonwealth had great obstacles to overcome to provide meaningful help to endangered species. In some cases, these obstacles have been overcome; in others the obstacles have won and the wildlife species have lost. To serve as examples of the situation in this beautiful part of the States, we will briefly discuss the plight of two species, the Puerto Rican parrot—because there are so many interesting sidelights to its struggle; and the Puerto Rican plain pigeon—because the danger it faces is typical of so many species which have failed to adjust to the overwhelming flood of increasing human populations.

In 1975, there were probably no more than thirteen Puerto Rican parrots in the wild. These were located in the Luquillo Mountains within the Caribbean National Forest. Like the California condor's precarious situation, the plight of the parrot is better measured in numbers of breeding pairs than in number of individuals. The breeding pair is the only hope for survival. Although the parrots have increased in numbers since that bird census in 1975, the number of known breeding pairs only increased to three in 1976 and 1977.

Unlike the California condor, the parrot has a good reproductive potential and can increase its numbers in a few years under complete protection and with protected habitat.

Almost all of the Puerto Rican parrot work takes place in the National Forest. Almost all of the facilities, including an aviary which breeds captive parrots, are on U.S. Forest Service lands. A major part of the funding comes through the Forest Service. Leadership for the endangered species work is provided by a trained aviculturist from the Fish and Wildlife Service's Patuxent Center. Manpower and cooperation also comes from the Commonwealth. The great lengths to which this group of agencies and people have already gone in defense of the parrot is remarkable.

Several years ago wildlife biologists watched closely as three breeding pairs laid a total of fourteen eggs. Eleven of them hatched. These young birds were beset by many dangers before they learned to fly. In one case, biologists watched nervously along with parrot mothers as three fledglings attempted to learn to fly. All of the young birds crash-landed, unable to fly. Examination showed that their feathers were besmirched with a gooey black substance which had formed in the bottom of their nest. Cavities in trees form the preferred nesting sites for these birds, and this one had leaked rain water into the nest, forming the "goop" which grounded the birds.

The gooey young birds were rushed to the aviary where they got their feathers scrubbed clean with a toothbrush. Then they were subjected to a thorough "blow drying" with a commercial hair dryer. This treatment enabled two of the three fledglings to get airborne. The third again tumbled ignominiously to the ground. Its feathers had been weakened by the cleaning effort and were unable to carry the youngster's weight. Back at the aviary scientists transplanted a complete set of tail and flight feathers molted by captive parrots onto the little bird. Amazingly, the youngster promptly flew—a triumph of tender loving care, scientific observation and prompt action dictated by the needs of the species.

In another nest, observers found that several eggs had been damaged by the parent bird. Although an egg was badly cracked, it was taken to the laboratory where the shell was actually patched. The patched egg was successfully hatched in the incubator and the fledgling is now part of the captive flock!

One of the greatest dangers for the wild Puerto Rican parrots is the danger of egg destruction caused by the "pearly-eyed thrasher," a native bird species which likes to dine on parrot eggs. The U.S. Forest Service solved part of this problem by providing artificial nesting boxes of polyvinyl chloride materials which made it much more difficult for the thrashers to see the eggs, and much harder to get to them. Biologists were unsatisfied with this improvement and found a method of using the pearly-eyed thrasher to *protect* the parrots!

The thrasher is a territorial bird, and one that will drive away other members of its species if they invade its territory. So the biologists placed nesting boxes, designed for the pearly-eyed thrasher, within a short distance of the parrot nests. The thrashers promptly took to the nests and set up their defense perimeter. Because thrashers drove off other thrashers when they invaded this territory, they were defending the parrot's nest as well as their own. This evidently worked, because none of the eggs were lost from wild nests in 1977 or 1978, although the pearly-eyed thrasher had been thought to be the most important single cause of parrot egg mortality before that time.

In 1978 fertile eggs were produced by captive pairs of Puerto Rican parrots for the very first time. This raised the level of scientific optimism considerably. As of January 1979, there were fifteen Puerto Rican parrots thriving in the Forest Service aviary, including the one pair which had formerly resided at Patuxent, Maryland.

Scientists are certain that artificial insemination can be used successfully on this species. They are aware that a parrot can be induced to lay a second clutch of eggs if the first clutch is removed or destroyed. They feel that they are making progress in protecting the very small wild population. There is hope for the Puerto Rican parrot—hope engendered by a group of men who use every means (including toothbrushes and blow driers)—to help an endangered species.

Further hope comes from the fact that the Commonwealth of Puerto Rico has stepped up its efforts to protect all wildlife species. There are now more than 160 rangers on patrol duty in the Commonwealth. Their duties are definitely oriented toward the endangered species. They patrol the beaches to prevent human intrusion into the nocturnal egg laying rites of the hawksbill and leatherback turtles, both endangered species. Rangers are stationed on Mona and Culebra Islands where they can protect the turtles and also watch over the endangered Mona ground iguana. These rangers enforce the hunting regulations which have placed such endangered species as the Bahama pintail duck, the ruddy duck and the purple gallinule on the "closed to all hunting" list of game species on the island.

The manatee exists in very small populations in the Commonwealth, and Puerto Ricans are optimistic about preserving it. The white-crowned pigeon also supports a remnant population, and rangers enforce the no hunting laws which protect that formerly abundant species. Like the plain pigeon, the white-crowned is very good to eat, which explains its decrease in a land where meat is scarce and expensive.

The plain pigeon is a subspecies of the much more abundant (in Central and South America) red-billed pigeon. Other subspecies exist in Cuba and across Hispaniola. We are here concerned only with our own species, the Puerto Rican plain pigeon. It has been in dire straits for many years. Wetmore studied the situation in 1911-1916, and did not report seeing any of the birds. In 1956, one of the most knowledgeable of all "birders" in Puerto Rico reported that the species was almost certainly extinct.

We should not be too quick to write off any species, even when it has not been reported for several years. In 1963 the Puerto Rican plain pigeon was rediscovered in a small population near Cidra in the interior of the island territory. They have been counted yearly ever since. Their numbers have gone as high as 120 individuals and as low as 75.

Why did they decrease in numbers? Natives call this bird the "paloma boba" or fool pigeon, because it is unwary and unafraid of man. It is also delicious eating. Formerly appearing in huge flocks, this colony nester was extremely vulnerable to the hunger of the unarmed human who could remove the squabs from the nest before they learned to fly. The pigeon, described as "exquisite eating," was sold for food as late as 1961. After that date they became too scarce to support a market hunting industry.

In addition to this lack of native caution, the pigeon was a bird of the hardwood forests, where it was relatively safe in large colonies from human intrusion by nesting high in the big trees. But before 1920 most of the best hardwood forest had been put to the axe and the saw. Agriculture had taken over the best lands, leaving no room for the pigeons. Their doom appeared to be sealed by the inexorable advance of mankind into their world.

Don't count this bird out, however. Although it lays only one egg per year in a flimsy nest—as bad as the mourning dove's—the Puerto Rican plain pigeon has the mourning dove's ability to produce more than one nestling per year. Multi-brooded birds are capable of amazing reproduction. More than one natural catastrophe, such as a hurricane or heavy rain storm, is needed to knock out one year's age group entirely.

The Commonwealth has closed the areas used by the plain pigeon to hunting, but illegal hunting still takes a toll of these rare birds. This should not be considered heinous for the bird is difficult to distinguish from the legally-hunted red-necked pigeon. Because of the danger of illegal hunting, the Recovery Team has asked for one or more Commonwealth agents to be assigned full time to the Cidra area to protect the birds. The Recovery Team is also trying to establish other nesting colonies, to avoid the ever present danger of having all of its eggs (and Puerto Rican plain pigeon eggs) in one basket.

The Recovery Team has also recommended the use of the Forest Service aviary in the Caribbean National Forest to produce a flock of captive pigeons (they are known to do well in captivity) as a source of future transplant stock.

There is hope for the endangered species of Puerto Rico. This is doubly important. Not only is the prevention of the loss of endangered species important, but this good work may serve as an example and as a source of inspiration for wildlife workers in Caribbean nations which are the custodians of a remarkably variegated and fascinating wildlife legacy.

35

List of U.S. Endangered Species

Mammals

COMMON NAME	SCIENTIFIC NAME	WHERE FOUND
Bat, gray	*Myotis grisescens*	Central and Southeast U.S.A.
Bat, Hawaiian hoary	*Lasiurus cinereus semotus*	Hawaii
Bat, Indiana	*Myotis sodalis*	East and Midwestern U.S.A.
Bat, Ozark big-eared	*Plecotus townsendii ingens*	Missouri Oklahoma Arkansas
Bat, Virginia big-eared	*Plecotus townsendii virginianus*	Kentucky, West Virginia, Virginia, Indiana, Illinois, Ohio
Bear, brown or grizzly	*Ursus arctos horribilis*	Western U.S.A.
Bison, wood	*Bison bison athabascae*	Northwest U.S.A.
Deer, Columbian white-tailed	*Odocoileus virginianus leucurus*	Washington Oregon
Deer, key	*Odocoileus virginianus clavium*	Southern Florida
Ferret, black-footed	*Mustela nigripes*	Western U.S.A.
Fox, northern swift	*Vulpes velox hebes*	Northern plains
Fox, San Joaquin kit	*Vulpes macrotis mutica*	California
Jaguar	*Panthera onca*	Texas, Arizona, New Mexico
Jaguarundi	*Felis yagouaroundi cacomitli*	Texas

Jaguarundi	*Felis yagouaroundi tolteca*	Arizona
Manatee, West Indian (Florida)	*Trichechus manatus*	Southeastern U.S.A.
Margay	*Felis wiedii*	New Mexico Arizona
Mouse, salt marsh harvest	*Reithrodontomys raviventris*	California
Ocelot	*Felis pardalis*	Southwest U.S.A.
Otter, southern sea	*Enhydra lutris nereis*	West coast U.S.A.
Panther, Florida	*Felis concolor coryi*	Southeastern U.S.A.
Prairie dog, Utah	*Cynomys parvidens*	Utah
Pronghorn, Sonoran	*Antilocapra americana sonoriensis*	Arizona
Rat, Morro Bay kangaroo	*Dipodomys heermanni*	California
Squirrel, Delmarva Peninsula fox	*Sciurus niger cinereus*	Delmarva Peninsula to Southeastern Pennsylvania
Wolf, gray	*Canis lupus*	Minnesota
Wolf, red	*Canis rufus*	Southeastern U.S.A., to Central Texas

Birds

Akepa, Hawaii (honeycreeper)	*Loxops coccinea coccinea*	Hawaii
Akepa, Maui (honeycreeper)	*Loxops coccinea ochracea*	Hawaii
Akialoa, Kuai (honeycreeper)	*Hemignathus procerus*	Hawaii
Akipolaau (honeycreeper)	*Hemignathus wilsoni*	Hawaii
Albatross, short-tailed	*Diomedea albatrus*	Alaska, California, Hawaii, Washington, Oregon
Blackbird, yellow-shouldered	*Agelaius xanthomus*	Puerto Rico
Bobwhite, masked (quail)	*Colinus virginianus ridgwayi*	Arizona

Condor, Calfornia	*Gymnogyps californianus*	California Oregon
Coot, Hawaiian	*Fulica americana alai*	Hawaii
Crane, Mississippi sandhill	*Grus canadensis pulla*	Mississippi
Crane, whooping	*Grus americana*	U.S.A., Rocky Mountains east to Carolinas
Creeper, Hawaiian	*Loxops maculata mana*	Hawaii
Creeper, Molokai (Kakawahie)	*Loxops maculata flammea*	Hawaii
Creeper, Oahu (alauwahio)	*Loxops maculata maculata*	Hawaii
Crow, Hawaiian (alala)	*Corvus tropicus*	Hawaii
Duck, Hawaiian (koloa)	*Anas wyvilliana*	Hawaii
Duck, Laysan	*Anas laysanensis*	Hawaii
Eagle, bald	*Haliaeetus leucocephalus*	U.S.A.
Falcon, American peregrine	*Falco peregrinus anatum*	U.S.A.
Finch, Laysan (honeycreeper)	*Telespyza (Psittirostra) cantans*	Hawaii
Finch, Nihoa (honeycreeper)	*Telespyza (Psittirostra) ultima*	Hawaii

Ivory-billed Woodpecker

Gallinule, Hawaiian	*Gallinula chloropus sandvicensis*	Hawaii
Goose, Aleutian Canada	*Branta canadensis leucopareia*	Alaska, California, Oregon, Washington
Goose, Hawaiian (Nene)	*Branta sandvicensis*	Hawaii
Hawk, Hawaiian (Io)	*Buteo solitarius*	Hawaii
Honeycreeper, crested (akohekohe)	*Palmeria dolei*	Hawaii
Kite, Everglades (snail kite)	*Rostrhamus sociabilis plumbeus*	Florida
Millerbird, Nihoa (willow warbler)	*Acrocephalus familiaris kingi*	Hawaii
Nukupuu (honeycreeper)	*Hemignathus lucidus*	Hawaii
Oo, Kauai (Oo Aa) (honeyeater)	*Moho braccatus*	Hawaii
Ou (honeycreeper)	*Psittirostra psittacea*	Hawaii
Palila (honeycreeper)	*Psittirostra bailleui*	Hawaii
Parrot, Puerto Rican	*Amazona vittata*	Puerto Rico
Parrot, thick-billed	*Rhynchopsitta pachyrhyncha*	New Mexico Arizona
Parrotbill, Maui (honeycreeper)	*Pseudonestor xanthophrys*	Hawaii
Pelican, brown	*Pelecanus occidentalis*	Southeastern U.S.A. Carolinas to Texas and California
Petrel, Hawaiian dark-rumped	*Pterodroma phaeopygia sandwichensis*	Hawaii
Pigeon, Puerto Rican plain	*Columba inornata wetmorei*	Puerto Rico
Poo-uli	*Melamprosops phaeosoma*	Hawaii
Prairie chicken, Attwater's greater	*Tympanuchus cupido attwateri*	Texas
Rail, California clapper	*Rallus longirostris obsoletus*	California
Rail, light-footed clapper	*Rallus longirostris levipes*	California
Rail, Yuma clapper	*Rallus longirostris yumanensis*	Arizona California
Shearwater, Newell's Manx	*Puffinus puffinus newelli*	Hawaii

Shrike, San Clemente loggerhead	*Lanius ludovicianus mearnsi*	California
Sparrow, Cape Sable seaside	*Ammospiza maritima mirabilis*	Florida
Sparrow, dusky seaside	*Ammospiza maritima nigrescens*	Florida
Sparrow, San Clemente sage	*Amphispiza belli clementeae*	California
Sparrow, Santa Barbara song	*Melospiza melodia graminea*	California
Stilt, Hawaiian	*Himantopus himantopus knudseni*	Hawaii
Tern, California least	*Sterna albifrons browni*	California
Thrush, large Kauai	*Phaeornis obscurus myadestina*	Hawaii
Thrush, Molokai (*olomau*)	*Phaeornis obscurus rutha*	Hawaii
Thrush, small Kauai (*puaiohi*)	*Phaeornis palmeri*	Hawaii
Warbler (wood), Bachman's	*Vermivora bachmanii*	Southeastern U.S.A.
Warbler (wood), Kirtland's	*Dendrocia kirtlandii*	U.S.A., principally Michigan
Whip-poor-will, Puerto Rican	*Caprimulgus noctitherus*	Puerto Rico
Woodpecker, ivory-billed	*Campephilus principalis*	Southcentral and southeastern U.S.A.
Woodpecker, red-cockaded	*Picoides (Dendrocopos) borealis*	Southcentral and southeastern U.S.A.

Amphibians & Reptiles

Alligator, American	*Alligator mississippiensis*	Southeastern U.S.A.
Anole, Culebra giant	*Anolis roosevelti*	Puerto Rico: Culebra Island
Boa, Mona	*Epicrates monensis monensis*	Puerto Rico
Boa, Puerto Rico	*Epicrates inornatus*	Puerto Rico
Boa, Virgin Islands	*Epicrates monensis granti*	U.S. and British Virgin Islands

Crocodile, American	*Crocodylus acutus*	Florida
Iguana, Mona ground	*Cyclura stejnegeri*	Puerto Rico; Mona Island
Lizzard, blunt-nosed leopard	*Crotaphytus silus*	California
Lizzard, Island night	*Klauberina riversiana*	California
Lizard, St. Croix ground	*Ameiva polops*	Virgin Islands: Green Cay Protestant Cay
Rattlesnake, New Mexican ridge-nosed	*Crotalus willardi obscurus*	New Mexico
Snake, Atlantic salt marsh	*Nerodia fasciata taeniata*	Florida
Snake, eastern indigo	*Drymarchon corais couperi*	Alabama, Florida, Georgia, Mississippi, South Carolina
Snake, San Francisco garter	*Thamnophis sirtalis tetrataenia*	California
Turtle, Plymouth red-bellied	*Chrysomys (Pseudemys) rubriventris bangsi*	Massachusetts
Coqui, golden	*Eleutherodactylus jasperi*	Puerto Rico
Salamander, desert slender	*Batrachoseps aridus*	California
Salamander, Red Hills	*Phaeognathus hubrichti*	Alabama
Salamander, Santa Cruz long-toed	*Ambystoma macrodactylum croceum*	California
Salamander, Texas blind	*Typhylomolge rathbuni*	Texas
Toad, Houston	*Bufo Houstonensis*	Texas
Treefrog, pine barrens	*Hyla andersonii*	Florida, Alabama, North and South Carolina, New Jersey

Fish

Bonytail, Pahranagat	*Gila robusta jordani*	Nevada
Cavefish, Alabama	*Speoplatyrhinus poulsoni*	Alabama
Chub, bonytail	*Gila elegans*	Arizona, California, Colorado, Nevada, Utah, Wyoming
Chub, humpback	*Gila cypha*	Arizona, Utah, Colorado, Wyoming

Chub, Mohave	*Gila mohavensis*	California
Chub, slender	*Hybopsis cahni*	Tennessee Virginia
Chub, spotfin	*Hybopsis monacha*	Alabama, Georgia, North Carolina, Tennessee, Virginia
Cisco, longjaw	*Coregonus alpenae*	Lakes Huron, Erie, and Michigan
Cui-ui	*Chasmistes cujus*	Nevada
Dace, Kendall Warm Springs	*Rhinichthys osculus* *thermalis*	Wyoming
Dace, Moapa	*Moapa coriacea*	Nevada
Darter, bayou	*Etheostoma rubrum*	Mississippi
Darter, fountain	*Etheostoma fonticola*	Texas
Darter, leopard	*Percina pantherina*	Arkansas Oklahoma
Darter, Maryland	*Etheostoma sellare*	Maryland
Darter, Okaloosa	*Etheostoma okaloosae*	Florida
Darter, slackwater	*Etheostoma boschungi*	Alabama Tennessee
Darter, snail	*Percina tanasi*	Tennessee
Darter, watercress	*Etheostoma nuchale*	*Alabama*
Gambusia, Big Bend	*Gambusia gaigei*	Texas
Gambusia, Clear Creek	*Gambusia heterochir*	Texas
Gambusia, Goodenough	*Gambusia amistadensis*	Texas
Gambusia, Pecos	*Gambusia nobilis*	New Mexico Texas
Killifish, Pahrump	*Empetrichythus latos*	Nevada
Madtom, Scioto	*Noturus trautmani*	Ohio
Madtom, yellowfin	*Noturus flavipinnis*	Georgia, Tennessee, Virginia
Pike, blue	*Stizostedion vitreum* *glaucum*	Lakes Erie and Ontario
Pupfish, Comanche Springs	*Cyprinodon elegans*	Texas
Pupfish, Devil's Hole	*Cyprinodon diabolis*	Nevada
Pupfish, Owens River	*Cyprinodon radiosus*	California
Pupfish, Tecopa	*Cyprinodon nevadensis* *calidae*	California

Pupfish, Warm Springs	*Cyprinodon nevadensis pectoralis*	Nevada
Squawfish, Colorado River	*Ptyshocheilus lucius*	Arizona, California, Colorado, New Mexico, Nevada, Utah, Wyoming
Stickleback, unarmored threespine	*Gasterosterus aculeatus williamsoni*	California
Sturgeon, shortnose	*Acipenser brevirostrum*	Atlantic Coast
Topminnow, Gila	*Peociliopsis occidentalis*	Arizona New Mexico
Trout, Apache	*Salmo apache*	Arizona
Trout, Gila	*Salmo gilae*	New Mexico
Trout, greenback cutthroat	*Salmo clarki stomias*	Colorado
Trout, Lahontan cutthroat	*Salmo clarki henshawi*	California Nevada
Trout, Little Kern golden	*Salmo aguabonita whitei*	California
Trout, Paiute cutthroat	*Salmo clarki seleniris*	California
Woundfin	*Plagopterus argentissimus*	Arizona, Utah,

36

The Endangered Species Act

December 28, 1973 is a very important date to those concerned with endangered species, for it marks the effective date of legislation under which the federal government operates in the field of endangered species. There have been many changes and added regulations since 1973, but the fundamental purpose of the Act, as originally stated, remains the same.

The Act applies to all threatened or endangered species that warrant federal protection—whether or not the species concerned has any commercial or sport value. The Act governs the taking of any species of animal so listed, regulates interstate commerce in the animals and provides the legal authority for the acquisition of habitat needed by the species. Of great importance is the section of the Act which provides federal assistance (federal money) to several states and to foreign countries.

The Act assigns primary responsibility to the Secretary of the Interior, who delegates the responsibility to the Director of the United States Fish and Wildlife Service. The Director's position is almost always filled by a career civil servant who has worked his way up through the ranks of the Service. To assist him in this work, the Office of Endangered Species (OES) was established. The OES is the focal point for all federal activities on behalf of endangered species.

For much of its early life, the OES was under the direction of Keith Schreiner. Schreiner deserves credit for maintaining the integrity of the program against pressures from many sources—often times congressional—which could have distorted the original purpose of the Act by allowing for individual exemptions to its provisions. I've known Keith Schreiner since 1950, having worked with him in the North Dakota State Game and Fish Department before we both entered federal service. I know him to be a dedicated wildlifer and a competent administrator who will stick to his guns under fire. Some detractors have called him "stubborn as a mule." I reply, "Thank God for that stubbornness!"

The responsibility for marine species was assigned to the Secretary of Commerce, who works through the Director of the National Marine Fisheries Service. Although this dichotomy has interposed another layer of bureaucracy which must be penetrated before cooperation can be achieved, the division into land and marine areas of responsibility has worked fairly well to date. Similarly, responsibility for endangered plant species has been delegated to the Department of Agriculture. Cooperation between Interior and Agriculture along these lines seems to be functioning normally.

How does it all work? The Act tries to help species that are threatened by destruction of habitat, overharvest for any purpose, disease and predation, inadequate regulatory mechanisms, and almost any other threat you can imagine.

The machinery of listing is simple. When a species is proposed for listing, either by a concerned individual or by Interior's OES, the OES makes a thorough study of the situation and solicits opinions from qualified sources. If the available evidence suggests that the species is threatened, OES publishes a "proposed rulemaking" in the Federal Register. The public is given at least sixty days in which to comment. In the case of "resident" species, the governor of the affected state is given at least ninety days in which to respond to the proposed rulemaking. There may also be a public hearing, if one is requested within forty-five days of the publication of the proposed rulemaking.

Sifting through all the evidence and all the recommendations from outside its own office, the OES makes the final "determination" and publishes a final rulemaking, which usually becomes effective thirty days after publication.

Once listed, the species is covered by a large body of law and regulation. The rules prohibit import, export, taking, possessing, transporting in interstate commerce, and selling or offering the protected animals for sale in foreign or interstate commerce. The states regulate interstate commerce.

There are exceptions to the rules: (1) A grandfather clause exempts listed animals held prior to the enactment of the law. (2) Alaskan natives are allowed to use listed species for subsistence and handicraft purposes. (3) Listed animals may be taken in defense of human life. (4) Taking of sick or injured animals by qualified federal or state employees is permitted.

A detailed Fact Sheet about the Endangered Species Act is available free upon request to the U.S. Fish and Wildlife Service, Department of the Interior, Washington, D.C. 20240.

37

Critical Habitat Laws

In an effort to help endangered species survive, the Congress of the United States passed the Critical Habitat Provisions of the Endangered Species Act.

Although these provisions have the potential for being a tool of great significance in maximizing the effect of Federal actions upon the fight for survival of many species, they have been one of the most misunderstood parts of the entire endangered species program.

The first Administrator of the Endangered Species program, Keith M. Schreiner, wrote about Critical Habitat laws in the second issue of the Endangered Species Bulletin, back in August of 1976. His words are worth quoting here, inasmuch as they do a lot to dispel the misconceptions about the bill.

CRITICAL HABITAT: WHAT IT IS-AND IS NOT

Keith M. Schreiner
Endangered Species Program Manager

In recent months, my staff and I have been barraged with innumerable queries and comments concerning critical habitat. It is clear that Federal and State administrators, Congressmen, biologists, reporters and private citizens are wondering about the meaning of critical habitat and its potential effects on their own activities and interests.

The most important point I can make about critical habitat is that in no way does it place an iron curtain around a particular area; that is, it does not create a wilderness area, inviolable sanctuary, or sealed-off refuge. Furthermore, I would stress that it does not give the Fish and Wildlife Service or any other government agency an easement on private property nor will it affect the ultimate jurisdiction regarding any public lands.

*Critical habitat is provided for by section 7 of the Endangered Species Act of 1973, which charges Federal agencies—and **only** Federal agencies—with the responsibility for ensuring that actions authorized, funded, or carried out by*

167

them do not either 1) jeopardize the continued existence of Endangered or Threatened Species or 2) result in destruction or adverse modification of the habitats of these species. (State and private actions that do not involve Federal money or approval do not come under the terms of the Act.)

Simply stated, critical habitat is the area of land, water, and airspace required for the normal needs and survival of a species. As published in the Federal Register on April 22, 1975, the Service has defined these needs as space for growth, movements, and behavior; food and water; sites for breeding and rearing of offspring; cover or shelter; and other biological or physical requirements. Determination of a critical habitat may include consideration of certain biological, physical, or human elements of a species' environment, if—but only if—the element is required for the continued survival or reasonable recovery of the species.

We are taking special pains to make sure that every shred of biological data is obtained and analyzed before any critical habitat is determined. Federal and State agencies are being contacted in writing prior to publication of a proposal. Once the proposal has been published, written comments on its biological adequacy are actively sought from all interested parties. In some cases, if the situation warrants, public hearings are being held in the affected states to seek the views of local residents. It is only after all of this biological information has been collected and carefully analyzed that a final determination is made.

Once the final determination has been published, its only effect is to cause Federal agencies managing lands or administering programs within the area to examine their actions in light of section 7.

The actions of private individuals (farmers, ranchers, trappers, etc.), firms, and State agencies are not affected unless funding or approval from a Federal agency is involved.

If an action does require Federal funds or approval, then the particular Federal agency having jurisdiction must decide whether or not the action would jeopardize the continued existence of the species or result in destruction or modification of its critical habitat.

There is no way to predict how Federal agencies will decide about particular actions in particular areas. The agencies simply consider them on a case-by-case basis as they arise. Nevertheless, I should emphasize that there are many types of existing land uses that are compatible with the continued survival of species and maintenance of the quality of their habitats. In addition the Service is prepared to provide assistance and consultation on the biological impacts of proposed activities whenever such consultation is needed. However, the final decisions will be made by the appropriate Federal agencies.

In short, the determination of critical habitat is a means of helping all Federal agencies meet their responsibilities under the Endangered Species Act of 1973. It is a tool to help save and restore species, not a weapon to hinder economic or social progress.

38

CITES: The International Treaty

The Convention of International Trade in Endangered Species, which we will call CITES from now on, is an international treaty which seeks to protect endangered species in all countries by making it illegal to sell these species across international boundaries. It was designed to remove the source of profit from poachers. Or so it was thought.

For example, in South American countries, there is only a small domestic market for specimens of rare monkeys. Outside of the inconsequential demand for use in native decorations and clothing, no real market exists. However, there is a huge market for monkeys as zoo specimens and pets in the United States and in Europe. It was reasoned that there would be no profitable market if we made it illegal to sell these commodities across international boundaries. If no middle man would be willing to pay a native poacher a goodly sum of money for the animals he took illegally, he would stop taking these animals illegally. Right? Let's see if it has worked out that way.

First, let's make sure we understand what CITES is all about. In May of 1977, the United States government published regulations designed to enforce the Convention of International Trade in Endangered Species of Wild Fauna and Flora. At last count, more than sixty nations had signed this convention along with the United States. The convention established procedures to control and monitor the export of imperiled species from a country and the import of an imperiled species into a country that is a signatory to CITES.

CITES regularly publishes a list of wildlife species which are considered to be in danger. Our own (United States) Office of Endangered Species also publishes a list of endangered species. Although they overlap considerably, these lists are not the same, and this only adds to the inherent confusion surrounding the CITES provisions in our country.

Because Uncle Sam is such a big customer for everything the world sells, and because the United States public is perhaps more ecologically aware than in other countries, Uncle Sam carries a big stick in CITES business. If America will not buy the species (or parts of animals, such as pelts or horns) from an exporting country, that exporting country might just as well stop trying to sell them. This is true in the majority of cases, though certainly not in all.

Some strange things have happened in the world arena of endangered species. First, let's consider the American alligator, which is not endangered as a species, and which never was endangered as a species. However, many crocodilians of several species definitely were endangered in southern Asia. A couple of species were so low in numbers that they rated among the most endangered of all wildlife!

Once the skin is removed from this animal and salted and rolled to go into international trade, it is difficult for the layman to tell the endangered crocodile from the abundant American alligator.

Spurred by the hyperactive American ecological conscience, Uncle Sam put the alligator on the endangered species list, which effectively stopped its export to France. France was not a member of CITES. France bought most of the alligator and crocodile hides offered in international trade because France was skilled at transforming these raw 'gator hides into ultra chic and ultra expensive alligator handbags, belts and shoes.

The result was that Americans lost a lucrative market for gator hides which could have been exported in international trade. The people of Louisiana went up in arms because they were told to protect—as endangered—a species which they could see in great abundance. As one Louisiana man told me, "We're up to our butts in 'gators, and the damned fools in Washington tell us they're endangered." As a result, other states stopped expending state funds on projects that would have benefited the American alligator. Why manage and develop a resource that you are forbidden to crop?

A side effect of this action was to make a lot of enemies in France. Because of the completely unnecessary action of the United States (in over-protecting the 'gator), the French lost most of their world supply of reptile hides. They protested mightily.

As a result of French protests, a few years later Uncle Sam took the American alligator off the list of endangered species (where it should never have been put in the first place). Only a fool refuses to change his mind; and along these lines, perhaps not coincidentally, France has signed CITES!

Many of the world's spotted cats are considered to be greatly reduced in numbers. This surely holds true of the Central and South American jaguar, ocelot and margay cats. The cheetah, fastest of all cats, certainly is in danger of extinction. For some reason I've never yet understood, the CITES people placed the spotted leopard on the endangered list in 1972, and this stopped its importation into any country which is a signatory to CITES. First and foremost, this meant that trophy big game hunters could not legally bring a leopard skin, or a mounted leopard back into the United States after a big game safari into Africa. As a result, many American big game hunters stopped going to Africa to hunt leopards.

Estimates of how much a big game hunter spends on an African safari vary greatly. The price has escalated sharply in the seventies and into the eighties because of rampant inflation in many of the emerging countries of Africa. But it is certain that the average big game hunter leaves more than five thousand American dollars in each African country in which he hunts. This supply of foreign exchange was very important to many of the developing nations. As a result, these nations were beginning to manage their leopard hunting with wisdom, seeking to preserve the goose which laid such a golden egg.

But when they could not sell their product, the leopard trophy, they immediately lost all interest in protecting the leopard or in managing it for future generations. Several of the small African nations stopped expending money to stop poaching, because they had lost the income which formerly financed their anti-poaching efforts.

All very interesting, but what's the point? The point is that the African leopard is **not** endangered. It's numbers are **not** dwindling. It does **not** need any protection from the trophy hunters who used to seek it, at great expense, in these countries. I have not been able to find even one competent wildlife manager who will say that the leopard needs CITES protection. By placing the leopard on the endangered list, mankind has done the leopard no favor. In fact, by thus reducing the monetary value of the leopard, we have caused it to be ignored by African wildlife managers.

Oscar Wilde told us that "each man kills the thing he loves," and we may have killed with kindness many CITES species by overprotecting them internationally. That overprotection has resulted in a feeling of apathy toward the species at home—where it counts the most.

CITES has also given the enemies of hunting a weapon to use against the wildlife managers who consider hunting a normal form of wildlife management. For an example, look at the situation regarding the bobcat, one of America's most common predators. While the United States wasn't looking, the United Kingdom succeeded in having the protection of CITES extended to all members of the order *Felidae*. We awoke to find out that this meant the country of origin of any cat would have to issue export permits before any parts of any member of the order *Felidae* could be exported to another country in international trade!

Thousands of bobcat skins are taken each year in the United States, and most of these skins are sold to European markets. There is no shortage of bobcats. They are numerous and thriving over all parts of their former range, excluding those covered up by cities or highways. One would assume that the United States, through its Fish and Wildlife Service, would simply issue permits for the exportation of bobcat skins to Europe. The Fish and Wildlife Service thought so too but they failed to take into account the Defenders of Wildlife, who ignored the commonly accepted belief of all knowledgeable wildlife managers and told the courts that the United States did not have scientific evidence to back up the claim that the bobcat was numerous. Therefore, the Defenders of Wildlife maintained that "they must bring forth their scientific evidence to prove that there are enough bobcats to allow for their export (in pelt form) to Europe."

The Endangered Species Scientific Authority (ESSA) agreed, and required research proof to elucidate the obvious fact that there was no shortage of bobcats.

State and federal wildlife managers were caught without any scientific proof. It was like a hypothetical situation where a court says "Prove that there are 100,000 illegal aliens crossing the Mexican border into our nation every year." We can easily prove that the number of aliens IN the country had increased by 600,000 in the last six months, but we can't prove that they had actually crossed the border.

The very fact that hundreds of thousands of bobcats are trapped each year, without any visible reduction in numbers, should have been accepted by ESSA as proof that there were enough bobcats to justify export permits. But we are not dealing with common sense; we are dealing with the exact wording of the law, and with a judicial mentality which says, "Do species population numbers research for three years, and then present the proof to us." We have a pressing need for good wildlife research in this nation; we can ill afford research to establish known facts.

One of the worst aspects of the CITES treaty and its application in the United States is the obvious fact that foreign affairs take precedence over domestic affairs when wildlife is concerned. During a career spent in wildlife work, I often noticed that when the Department of the Interior and the State Department butted heads in Washington, decisions were automatically awarded to the State Department without hearings. This happened more often than coincidence would allow. The automatic stand taken at the White House and in the Executive Office Building, where America's decisions are made, was "If State is against it, Interior has no chance to get it through."

As of the end of 1980, the operation of the Endangered Species Act in the United States is overshadowed by the exaggerated need to cooperate with CITES in every way possible. Congressional action to free the Endangered Species Office from the control of the Endangered Species Scientific Authority (ESSA) has been swiftly negated by executive orders which have undercut the legislation passed by the Congress. This "over-cooperation" with CITES, to the detriment of beneficial programs of wildlife management in this country, is a weakness of CITES.

However, I certainly would not advocate withdrawal from CITES, for that would wreak incalculable harm to wildlife species all over the world. Such a withdrawal would surely destroy our credibility as an international friend of wildlife.

39

Getting On (or off) the List

At the formal beginning of the Endangered Species Program, there were lite-rally thousands of endangered species—or at least there were thousands of species proposed for inclusion in the list of threatened or endangered species. Dedicated scientists, worried about the future of their particular species, pro-posed many species for listing. So did a very few taxonomists who wished to "discover" a new subspecies and so publicize their own name and fame. These people with various motivations asked for listings of species and subspecies which were not usually recognized as being different from the more populous species or subspecies which they closely resembled. They were not entirely wrong.

New species are constantly being discovered, as a matter of routine, by hard-working scientists. They are also constantly evolving through the process of biological selection. If it were not possible to recognize new species as they develop, or as they are discovered and classified, biology would be a prosaic, exact science with limited boundaries, rather than an exciting inexact science without limits for the trained observer.

Let us describe a hypothetical case. A dedicated herpetologist, Mr. Basil Meredith Nurd, III, finds that a particular skink in the southwest corner of Stuffiness County, Arkansas, has an elliptically-shaped nicitating membrane over its eyes, while the run-of-the-mill skinks of this genus have a more rounded nicitating membrane. The dedicated herpetologist feels that this is reason enough to describe a new species of skink. With parental pride he names it *Eumeces skiltonianus nurdii*. He feels that it is sufficiently different from the regular *Eumeces skiltonianus* to merit the new subspecific designation which, of course, honors the finder, Mr. Basil Meredith Nurd, III.

It is true that many of the proposed subspecies were in grave danger of extinction, yet other subspecies did not really even exist as a separate group of animals. Many of the requests for sub-speciation listing were rejected by the original work force at OES. Some of them found their way onto the list, for a time at least. I should not be poking fun at the taxonomic "splitters" as opposed to the taxonomic "lumpers-together", for I am not scientifically qualified to know which claim to subspecies designation is worthy and which is not.

The great majority of the names proposed for listing came from concerned scientists who had already spent a good part of their working career studying a particular species. Because this great body of evidence and backlog of research study existed, the work of the early listers was eased considerably.

No one is happy about putting a name on the list. To list a species as being endangered is obviously to express another example of human failure. To remove a name from the list may be cause for celebration, as in the case of the Trumpeter swan, or it may be the cause of a small sadness, as in the case of the pupfish. The pupfish were removed from the list because they were found to be extinct. An extinct species is surely no longer endangered!

From time to time I have read accounts purporting to prove that more species have become extinct in the last decade than in the preceding century. Although I would agree that we **know about** more species becoming extinct in the last decade than we knew about in the last century, I have to take these accounts with a large helping of salt. No one can know how many species became extinct in the past century. A human may never have known that a species even existed, much less have noted the exact date of its final passing from the scene.

As we stated in the first chapter, extinction of entire species is nothing new. The extinction of species is just as much a part of the evolutionary process as is the development of new species. Passage of the Endangered Species Act could not have been made retroactive to save the dinosaurs. That is a fact worth noting.

A species can get off the list in three ways: (1) it can become extinct, as in the case of the pupfish which went into the shades almost unnoticed and unmourned, (2) it can be taken off the list because research proved that it didn't belong there in the first place, like the Trumpeter swan or the American alligator, or (3) it can increase its numbers to the point where it is no longer in danger.

If we are speaking of red tape and paper work, a species is delisted in much the same manner it becomes listed in the first place: with a preliminary notice of intent to remove from the list, followed by a time period for public comment and the presentation of evidence pro or con, followed by final action published in the Federal Register.

Because I have watched the fight of the whooping crane for more than thirty years, I have a fond hope that I may live to see that ungainly symbol of the endangered species battle removed from the list. What would be a safe number of whoopers? How many separate flocks going to how many scattered wintering grounds would be considered safe? How many different, discrete flocks would be enough to guarantee genetic variability and survival as a species? The recovery teams set their goals. Their aims seem modest enough, but surely the day might come when we could be willing to share the bounty of the earth with more than a "survival" population of our fellow creatures?

The transition from "listed" to "non-listed" can occur in a few generations in a species with a short life cycle and good reproductive potential, such as a snail darter. The transition in the case of a slow reproducer like the California condor might be the result of a century of hard work.

No two species are exactly alike in needs, reproduction potential or habitat requirements. The addition of each new name on the list is cause for sorrow and reason for concern. The removal of a name from the list by reason of improved status is cause for justifiable celebration.

Attwater's Prairie Chicken

40

Must We Decide?

Does mankind have the right to sit in judgement upon the question of survival or extinction for an entire species?

Usually the question does not occur in such a clear-cut, recognizable form; it is mixed with other concerns. In most cases, the measures which ought to be taken into account to improve the living conditions for one species will improve living conditions for all species in that environment. Deterioration of habitat is usually the reason for a particular species being at risk. If we improve living conditions for red-cockaded woodpeckers by maintaining a supply of trees suitable to their particular needs, we have not caused a deterioration of the environment, but rather have replaced monoculture with variety which usually benefits all species.

If we improve the habitat for the Delmarva fox squirrels by leaving some deciduous hardwoods to provide the hollow trunks and high-up hiding places which these squirrels seem to like, we are also improving the environment for all mast-eating species such as turkeys and deer. The squirrels will harvest many of the acorns from a white oak, but many more will fall to the ground and be eaten.

True, there are times when improving the chances for one species will cause deterioration of living conditions for another species. If this is so, are we justified in causing the death of members of one species to protect another species? I say, "yes", because the unit value of the rarer species is greater than the unit value of the more common species. Should we kill foxes which threaten the nesting success of the endangered Aleutian goose? That is an easy question to answer, because the unit value of the common Arctic fox and of the introduced silver fox is less than the unit value of the Aleutian goose. By unit value, I refer to the value of the rare species as a building block in the environmental laboratory, not the intrinsic value of the pelt of the furbearer. In addition, the fox is not indigenous to the nesting islands of the Aleutian goose, so we have no duty to preserve the status quo in a situation which should never have existed in the first place. We should never have introduced these foxes into a foreign environment.

Should we kill raccoons which threaten the nesting success of the whooping crane or the Trumpeter swan? My answer is "of course," because we have no shortage of raccoons and because that adaptable animal is capable of quickly replenishing its numbers after it is reduced.

These have been easy questions. Let's move to a more difficult one. The Attwater's prairie chicken is an endangered species; its numbers have been reduced to the point where the unit value of each Attwater's prairie chicken is very high. Should we resort to predator control programs in the few East Texas counties where they are still found? Should we use traps, poisons and den-hunting (with subsequent destruction of the young) to reduce the numbers of coyotes which prey upon the rare prairie chicken? Sounds logical to me. The unit value of the ubiquitous and resourceful coyote is very low and its reproductive potential greater than that of the prairie chicken. So we agree to reduce the number of coyotes in order to increase the numbers of chickens.

The larger predator in this same area is the endangered Texas red wolf. Red wolves love to eat prairie chickens; they have been a part of their natural diet since time immemorial. Should we reduce the numbers of the red wolves in hopes of increasing the numbers of chickens?

Now we are on the sharp horns of a dilemma. Do we have the right to decide which species is to be allowed to continue, and which species is to be sacrificed so that another species can live?

My reply is that we do not have to decide and should not decide. The decision can be avoided by proper management. In the case of red wolves and chickens, let's see what actually did happen. The endangered red wolf was in peril because of hybridization with the coyote, as we have seen in an earlier chapter. The accepted solution was to trap and relocate those red wolf individuals which exhibited most clearly the characteristics of the true strain. These red wolves were then propagated in captivity, or were released in other parts of their historic range where they could prosper without unduly endangering another species, rare or common. The red wolves were propagated in the Pacific Northwest, far from the Attwater's prairie chicken, and were released in the far-off coastal marshes of Carolina. This was truly a Solomon-like decision, one which allowed us to keep both of our endangered species, at least for the time being.

The opposite situation prevails much more often. Frequently we fail to make any decision or take any action, and thus allow the species to perish by default. An example of this is the decision to allow pumping of underground waters in the desert southwest, without even knowing that pumping would lower the water table enough to cause the demise of entire species of pupfish. In this case, we did not make a conscious decision; we did not play the part of God. Rather, we failed to consider the needs of the pupfish. By this failure we doomed the species.

No, we shouldn't play God. Neither should we play the part of the fool by failing to anticipate the consequences of our actions, and by not understanding the interdependence of species which cause the interweaving of entire environments. To avoid this in the future, we must learn about every living species, and we must realize that a tug upon any part of the web of life will result in a tremor in every part of the ecosystem.

Knowledge is the key to the lock that protects endangered species.

41

Captive Propagation?

In the chapter on the California condor we discussed the question of whether or not pen-reared birds would be markedly different from wild-reared birds.

There are many questions as to whether birds raised in captivity can adjust to life in the wild and whether or not we can ever reintroduce a captive-reared strain into the wild successfully. We admit that a captive-reared animal will lack certain characteristics of the wild-reared animal. He will be less wary, less apt to evade attack instinctively. The first attempt to reintroduce pen-reared masked bobwhite quail to the Arizona grasslands failed because of this lack of wariness. Wintering Harris hawks joined the resident predators in enjoying an easy meal. The young quail had not learned "from their mother's knee" that the warning call meant either a motionless alertness to avert detection or a dash into cover.

Raptors swooped down on the unsuspecting youngsters and converted them into expensive meals. The pen-reared birds were unwary. Did that mean that we could not introduce them to the wild? Absolutely not. It meant that human ingenuity had to develop a procedure which would give the young quail the necessary education for survival. Biologists used caponized Texas bobwhite quail males as foster fathers for the young. It worked, and the adult males taught the brood in ways which we do not yet fully understand to stay alive in the dangerous world outside of the pen.

Most mammals are easily propagated in cages. Zoos use surplus young to trade for other species. But life in a cage does not provide the exercise and physical conditioning which is a part of the life in the wild. A puma which has spent its entire life in a concrete floored jail cannot possibly have the muscle tone, heart and lung capacity of its brother who grew up in the mountains.

If large numbers of pen-reared mammals are reintroduced to the wild directly from their cages, survival will be very low. However, this certainly does not mean that we cannot help endangered species by pen-rearing.

Animals can be pre-conditioned to release into the wild. Elsa, the African lioness, is perhaps the most publicized example of teaching wild carnivores to forage for themselves and of fitting them for life in the wild.

The New Mexico Game and Fish Department has much experience with this problem, for they have long years of captive propagation of exotic ungulates. Kept in zoos for more than a generation to guard against introduction of a

179

foreign disease or parasite in domestic livestock herds, the oryx, ibex and Barbary sheep were allowed to take their time in adapting to wild life; they slowly learned to rely more and more upon themselves, and less and less upon their human attendants until they were truly wild.

Pre-conditioning can be accomplished, but not easily.

Cornell University has led the way in pen-rearing the fast-flying peregrine falcons. Usually, if these birds are reared in captivity, it is very difficult for them to acquire the powerful muscles required to fly like a wild-reared bird. Without those flight muscles, the peregrines starve, for their preferred diet is birds caught in flight. But Cornell developed an answer to the problem: produce the eggs in captivity, and hatch them under wild birds. This program has been very successful. The descendents of pen-reared peregrines have now nested successfully in coverts from which the peregrine had disappeared during the DDT years.

When we produce wildlife in captivity, many problems arise. The whooping crane, which has its own neuroses and hang-ups to overcome, demonstrated this when hatched in captivity at the Patuxent Research Center. The young whoopers "imprinted" upon the first long-legged thing they saw after they hatched out of their eggs. The first thing they saw was the attendant who cleaned the incubator area. Each young whooper started life with the complex that the man in overalls was his mother. Think of the problems that youngster could take to his psychiatrist! Trying to work around this, the biologists stayed out of sight as much as possible and wore white smocks when they had to come within eyesight of the young whoopers, hoping that the young birds would thus be predisposed toward big white birds when they finally did see them.

This imprinting problem can be avoided now by hatching the whooper eggs under foster parents of greater sandhill cranes. Obviously, the young whooper will be better off thinking that another crane is its parent rather than a human. The sandhill crane makes a better model than a human anyway, for humans cannot migrate long distances by flapping their wings; nor can they catch mice with their beaks—all important skills to a whooping crane.

Whether or not the whoopers resulting from foster-rearing will mate and reproduce normally remains to be seen. What will happen if a whooper thus reared falls in love with a greater sandhill (thinking that they are the same species), and the sandhill crane won't have anything to do with him? Unrequited love can be very painful. We won't know the answer to that question for two or three more years. Whoopers mature slowly.

Sometimes it is possible for the aviculturists to prepare for a "last-ditch" pen-rearing project by practicing on a closely related species. The Andean condor has furnished the practice to teach us how to propagate the California condor in captivity.

When a species becomes rare, many factors which are needed for normal reproduction may be missing. Some species require colony nest-building to stimulate egg production. Courtship displays, such as the prairie chickens on their dancing grounds, are needed to bring male and female together at the right time of the year. Rivalry is an important part of this courtship ritual. If too few individuals show up on the booming grounds, that year's production may be lost. If this happens in consecutive years, a short-lived species would be doomed.

In some species, the males attach more importance to establishing territorial dominance than they attach to the sexual act of reproducing. A male bird will leave a receptive female to drive off another male who encroaches on his territory. Rutting season combat of male against male is necessary in some horned-animal species to start the reproductive process. When there are too few males in a given area this combat is forsaken. Reproduction may not take place.

In captivity, scientists have the added tool of artificial insemination. In the losing battle to save the black-footed ferret, artificial insemination was resorted to, albeit too late, and a young female was inseminated with semen from an aged and cancerous male. Artificial insemination procedures for rare cranes are now known. Artificial insemination of condors, Puerto Rican parrots and many other species is now an accepted part of a concerted effort to save these species from extinction.

Pen-rearing is part of a struggle to prevent extinction, but no one of us would feel that a captive-reared individual is the equal of its wild-reared brother. Yet almost all of us are ready to admit that pen-rearing is the only way in which some species can be perpetuated.

Captive propagation is a means to an end; not an end itself. If we knew that there would never be any chance that a pen-reared species would ever return to the wild, I would not invest a dime nor an hour in captive propagation of that species. But it **cannot** be said that there is **no** hope for release into the wild. We do not know what techniques will be developed in the future. Perhaps it will be something simple like using caponized male bobwhites to "father" the artificially propagated masked bobwhites. Perhaps we will discover a complicated technique using three-dimensional motion pictures and automated models, à la Disneyland, to teach the young.

If you will grant me that there is one chance in a million that we can some day release into the wild those descendents of pen-reared species, then I am in favor of using captive propagation for that species. But if there is no chance ever, then why bother?

A mounted specimen in a museum, or a good photograph, is just the same as an animal in a pen. Both the specimen and the caged animal can give us an idea of what the animal once looked like. Either can tell us what the animal once was but can never be again.

42

Are They Really Gone?

In 1851, biologists classified a new species of fish, the Leon Springs pupfish. Its only known habitat was Leon Springs, near Fort Stockton, Pecos County, Texas. Between 1851 and 1900 there were many changes and modifications in its habitat, and before 1900 the fish was though to be extinct. In 1938 it was listed as extinct by those few who had known that the pupfish existed in the first place. Here was another case of a species which had been discovered after is was (a) already extinct, or (b) after its population and its habitat were both so reduced that its doom was sealed.

In 1965, icthyologists rediscovered the living pupfish species just nine miles north of Fort Stockton, in Diamond Y Spring. The species which had been written off was found to be alive. The lost was found, almost as if the dead had risen. The particular population in the Diamond Y Spring seems to be in no danger at the moment; it is stable. But Pecos County is dangerous territory for any fish because of the heavy demand for underground water to grow cantaloupes and other produce on the irrigated lands.

No passenger pigeons have been seen for years; so they must be extinct. Right? Well no, because no Leon Springs pupfish were seen for decades either. But the passenger pigeon with its migratory habits would certainly be more visible than the tiny pupfish.

Perhaps a small-sized species can survive long after we have given it up for extinct, while large animals cannot easily escape detection. Yet the Sinai leopard was presumed extinct since the end of the 19th century until it was rediscovered by Giora Ilani in 1975. This was after more than a century of presumed extinction.

For quite a while most of us presumed that the Florida panther was either extinct or so reduced in numbers that it might just as well be extinct. Not so. The large cat, nocturnal and secretive, has survived almost within sight of Miami. No one knows how many prowl the palmetto scrub land, unseen by man.

The dusky seaside sparrow seems surely headed for extinction, despite efforts to save it. There might be other colonies of the bird, however, which have never been located, much less censused or studied. True, the odds are against it, but this bird is hard to find. A colony might exist for years without our knowledge.

When the world's population of wild whooping cranes was down to twenty-one individuals in 1941, we were almost willing to concede that the bird was, for all practical purposes, extinct. With a population above the hundred mark now, and with two separate populations rather than one, the whooper is still not out of danger. But it has proved those doomsayers wrong who predicted that it was already "genetically extinct". To many students of such matters, the total population of only twenty-one was a guarantee that line inbreeding would occur, resulting in genetic defects and a decreased chance for survival of a species. This is still a danger. All whooping cranes are more closely related than the inhabitants of a small town in Ireland. Has this already doomed the whooper species? Today, there are hopes that this is not the case.

No one knows the exact date of the passing of the last pigeon, that member of mighty flocks which once darkened the skies in their flight and broke down big trees with the weight of their nests. We can study the reference books and find that the last heath hen perished on such and such a date, but no one can guarantee that other individuals didn't linger on past that date.

If the population of great whales is reduced to the point that a lonely male cannot find a lonely female during breeding season—if they become so few that the lonely querulous song of the whale echoes unheard through the ocean canyons—then that species can be considered to be extinct. If an isolated male meets with an isolated female in breeding season, another calf will probably be provided to delay the obvious extermination by another forty years. But the birth of that lonely whale calf will not change the end result. When the numbers of an endangered species are reduced to the point where they cannot be relied upon to replace their own numbers every breeding cycle, then that species is in grave danger of extermination. Unaided, they will surely pass from the earth.

The coelecanth, a particularly unlovely type of fish, must have been one of the most successful life forms, existing almost unchanged through countless millennia. First known as a fossil, this fish was considered extinct long before it was discovered to live in our modern age. A surprised fisherman brought one to the surface of the ocean off of South Africa. Since then, the species has been found and even studied to a limited degree. It did not come back to life, for it was never gone.

Reincarnation of a species is not something we can hope for, nor expect to happen. Extermination is forever. Genes once lost can never be formed again.

Today we are slow to remove a name from the endangered list by reason of extermination of that species. This is not just red tape and time-consuming legalities. This is a well-learned caution taught by the coelecanth and the Sinai leopard. Let's not be in a hurry to declare that we have lost the battle.

A Florida Key Deer in natural habitat at the National Key Deer Refuge

43

The Role of Wildlife Refuges

Without the Aransas National Wildlife Refuge, there is little chance that the whooping crane would exist outside of zoos today. But the Aransas is not our only refuge. More than three hundred refuges are important to wildlife species throughout the country. For tiny finches in Hawaii and bison in Oklahoma, national wildlife refuges are found from the swamps of Louisiana to the foggy cold of the Aleutians.

In Florida, the key deer find safety from poachers on the national wildlife refuge established for their benefit. The Sonoran pronghorned antelope ranges across the more than 800,000 acres of burned rock and lava mountains that make up the Cabeza Prieta National Wildlife Range, a part of the refuge system. Like the desert bighorn sheep which shares this awe-inspiring wasteland, the pronghorn is often dependent upon the water provided by windmills on the refuge. It's a long hard trip without roads for the four-wheel drive vehicles which service the windmills and "gallinaceous guzzlers" on the refuge, but it's a trip which must be made regularly. If the windmills stop, so does life itself.

This is nothing unusual. Endangered species routinely depend upon wildlife refuges for their survival.

In New Mexico, the Bosque del Apache National Wildlife Refuge provides wintering grounds for most of the continent's greater sandhill cranes and—not coincidentally—for the newly established second flock of whoopers. Therefore, the refuge system no longer has all of its whoopers on one refuge. Cranes winter on the Bosque and on the Aransas; in the summer they live in the Grays Lake National Wildlife Refuge in Idaho and on Wood Buffalo Park in Canada. Thus refuges and parks provide protection for the cranes on both ends of their long migration. Normal stopping places during the spring and fall flights are almost all on or near other federal refuges, such as Salt Plains in Oklahoma and Sand Lake in South Dakota.

Since Theodore Roosevelt created the first federal refuge—an insignificant spit of land off the Florida coast, but important to the pelicans for whom it was created—the system has grown to include the most intensely managed waterfowl production areas as well as the loneliest, harshest environments in our nation. Many of these areas are almost completely untouched by man.

185

The Red Rock Lakes refuge in Montana provided sanctuary for the (then) endangered Trumpeter swan. Refuges like this stretch all across the nation. Far out in the Pacific a spit of rock extends the chain of the Hawaiian Islands a bit father. This is Nihoa, home of the endangered Nihoa finch, a bird found nowhere else in the world. The Hawaiian Islands National Wildlife Refuge protects many species found only in Hawaii—species such as the Laysan duck which lives on one of these lonely, uninhabited islands.

At the other end of the spectrum are the important waterfowl refuges which attract and hold as many as half a million geese at one time, even though the refuges are located in thickly populated areas. Horicon, Crab Orchard, Necedah, Blackwater, and a dozen other are all wintering homes for a very great portion of this nation's migratory waterfowl.

The National Wildlife Refuge system and the National Park system are approximately equal in size, although the proposed addition of huge parcels of Alaskan land to each system will change this balance greatly. Just as some national park areas are of strictly historic value, offering nothing to wildlife, so some of the wildlife refuges serve special wildlife interests which do not have a bearing on endangered species.

Bear River, Utah, is the home of a refuge which is a production factory for migratory waterfowl. Very few waterfowl, on the other hand, are produced on the Wichita Mountains refuge near Lawton, Oklahoma, which is famed for its big herds of bison and elk; two species which would have disappeared from that state long ago had it not been for the refuge.

The management philosophy of parks and refuges is very different. National parks **prohibit** sport hunting whenever they possibly can; wildlife refuges **provide** hunting whenever they possibly can.

There are exceptions, of course. Elk hunting is allowed in Grand Teton National Park in an effort to avoid the ghastly spectacle that occured in Yellowstone Park when park rangers slaughtered elk to reduce the herd and keep it within the carrying capacity of the park. The hunting fraternity, through the purchase of the federal duck stamp, and through their sponsorship of the Pittman-Robertson law which earmarked an 11% excise tax on hunting arms and ammunition, pays most of the cost of refuge land acquisition. Hunting on refuges mirrors the feeling that hunting is an efficient management tool.

Philosophically, the National Park Service feels that its mission in a "natural park area" is to keep the area natural, and all of its wildlife in a "natural" state with as little interference from man is as possible. The refuge system, in my opinion, holds an opposite view. They feel that they should intensively manage every square foot of the refuge area to protect wildlife values to the utmost.

Manipulation of the environment is considered good practice in the refuge system. This includes controlled burning and construction of dikes and levees to change water areas. Such manipulation is considered heresy by the National Park Service. NPS feels that parks are for people to enjoy; NWR feels that refuges are for wildlife. People are only tolerated as temporary intruders in that environment.

Both systems are vitally needed; both systems are of great importance to some endangered species of wildlife. Because the refuge system has figured so strongly in the preceding chapters, we will not go into detail of its work with endangered species. More needs to be said about the work done by the National Park Service, and by our nation's biggest land manager, the Bureau of Land Management.

44

The Role of National Parks

The National Park System in the United States plays a very important role in the protection of rare and endangered species of wildlife. Because of the great importance I attach to the efforts being made by the NPS, I asked Park Service veteran John Vosburgh to describe the activities of his agency.

John's reply is as follows:

NATIONAL PARKS AND THE CRUCIAL PROTECTION OF NORTH AMERICAN WILDLIFE

Many endangered and threatened species of wildlife are making their last stands in the national parks. The parks provide wildlife protection and a natural habitat.

Everglades National Park alone is crucial to the survival of the Southern bald eagle, the Florida panther, the American alligator, the Cape Sable sparrow and the American crocodile.

Everglades' 1.4 million sub-tropical acres at the south tip of Florida also have been instrumental in protecting the brown pelican, Florida manatee, roseate spoonbill, Everglades kite and loggerhead turtle.

Yellowstone National Park's 2.2 million acres in Wyoming, Montana and Idaho have played a similar role in the survival of the Trumpeter swan, the bison and the grizzly bear.

Isle Royale National Park, Michigan has proved to be an unexpected haven for the wolf. At least eight parks contain American peregrine falcons and are sharing in the effort to prevent the bird's extinction. One park has seen a remarkable recovery of the arctic peregrine.

At least four parks are trying to save rare fishes from extinction: Big Bend National Park in Texas; Death Valley National Monument in California-Nevada;

Rocky Mountain National Park in Colorado; and Dinosaur National Monument in Colorado-Utah.

Here is a park-by-park look at National Park System areas containing endangered and threatened species of wildlife whose populations have fallen to a critical level at one time or another.

EVERGLADES NATIONAL PARK, Florida

Southern bald eagle—*The park has the highest population of bald eagles in the lower forty-eight states, with fifty-five nests of breeding birds. Outside of the park, the Southern bald eagle, an endangered species, is being steadily pushed out of its habitat by land development.*

American alligator—*The Everglades contained possibly a million alligators before Columbus; by 1969 the population was down to 29,000. Hunting for hides was a principal cause of the decline, but poor water management also was a factor, accentuating the effects of fire, flood, and drought. In 1969, the Secretary of the Interior flew to the park and announced: 'The danger of extinction of the alligator is so critical that I am assigning ten additional park rangers to the Everglades.' Poaching was virtually stopped. Today the alligator population is substantial both inside and outside the park, but the species is still on the endangered list.*

American crocodile—*The 100 to 300 remaining American crocodiles range from Biscayne Bay to the Florida Keys and Florida Bay. The bay is in the park, thus offering protection from shooting and vandalism. Raccoons, salinity changes in the water, and Australian pine growth on nesting sites are adverse factors, however. Four of sixteen crocodile nests on the bay were destroyed by raccoons in one year. The Fish and Wildlife Service says only ten to twenty-five females try to nest each year. The National Park Service is trying to control the Australian pine and considers Florida Bay the most suitable habitat for the crocodile's survival.*

Florida panther—*Yes, there **is** a Florida panther. Biologists have difficulty seeing one, but motorists killed two in six months in 1979-80. The largest weighed 110 pounds. The panther inhabits the darker recesses of Everglades National Park, Big Cypress National Preserve just north of the park and the state's nearby Fathahatchee Nature Preserve. The scheduled and protected habitat may save this endangered species from extinction.*

Cape Sable sparrow—*The park and Big Cypress National Preserve are the principal habitat of this endangered species. The population is estimated at 3,000.*

Brown pelican—*Since DDT (dichloro-diphenyl-trichloroethane) was outlawed, the brown pelican has recovered from a population decline caused largely by DDT-caused thin eggshells. The park provides an ample food source and nesting sites.*

Florida manatee—*A tough state law protects the Florida manatee or sea cow. The park and Biscayne Bay National Park help to preserve this en-*

dangered sea mammal by providing winter feeding grounds. About 100 of the estimated 1,000 manatees winter in the park. Cold waves take a toll of manatees staying too far north. Steller's sea cow, a close relative in the Bering Sea, was exterminated in the 18th century.

Roseate spoonbill—For a bird whose population in this country was down to fifty nesting pairs in 1919, the roseate spoonbill has staged one of the comebacks of the century. By 1941 it numbered 5,698; by 1976, close to 6,000. New laws, new sanctuaries, new wardens and new spoonbills from Latin America helped. So did the proposed Everglades National Park, authorized in 1934. By 1941 the park had 303 of the colorful flamebirds; today it has 600 to 700. Five-sixths of the spoonbills are in Alabama, Mississippi, Louisiana, and Texas.

Everglades kite—The survival of this rare and endangered species was considered only "problematical" thirty years ago. The bird feeds exclusively on a certain type of snail called the Pomacea, but Florida's expanding human population has steadily reduced the snail supply. Now the kite visits Everglades National Park from its habitat to the north to feed. The park has plenty of Pomacea snails.

Loggerhead turtle—The success of this species in nesting Cape Sable in recent years may prevent its going the way of its relative, the green turtle; now a scarce and endangered species. The loggerhead, a threatened species, is holding its own with a population of about 1,000 in the park.

YELLOWSTONE NATIONAL PARK, Wyoming-Montana-Idaho

Trumpeter swan—This huge bird was considered near extinction in 1913, but eighteen years later five pairs were nesting in the park. Thirteen young survived; by 1941 there were 211 trumpeters in the park and nearby Red Rock Lake Migratory Waterfowl Refuge. The world's largest swan—thirty pounds and an eightfoot wingspread—had escaped the endangered species list. In 1954 a significant breeding colony was found in Alaska. That state has some 4,000 trumpeters; the lower 48 about 750.

Bison—The park's bison numbered no more than fifty in 1902; the American buffalo was being killed off. Some plains bison were brought into the park to breed with the remnant mountain bison herd. By 1968 the herd numbered 471 animals; today the count is 1600. Though not an endangered species, the national park bison are closely watched to prevent the species' return to the brink of extinction. Wind Cave, Theodore Roosevelt and Badlands National Parks also have substantial buffalo herds.

Grizzly bear—Without the protection of Yellowstone and Glacier National Parks, the grizzly possibly would have been eliminated in the lower forty-eight states by now. An Interior Department committee put the grizzly population at 1,200 in 1940, all in Montana and Wyoming. Nearly thirty years later the population was down to an estimated 1,000—a fourth of them in Yellowstone National Park. Though not an endangered species, the grizzly bear appears heavily dependent on Yellowstone and Glacier National Parks just to survive in the lower forty-eight states.

KATMAI NATIONAL MONUMENT, Alaska
GLACIER BAY NATIONAL MONUMENT, Alaska
ANIAKCHAK NATIONAL MONUMENT, Alaska
LAKE CLARK NATIONAL MONUMENT, Alaska
KENAI FJORDS NATIONAL MONUMENT, Alaska

Brown bear—*This endangered species is a popular target of sports hunters. Until President Carter set aside Aniakchak, Lake Clark and Kenai Fjords National Monuments by proclamation on Dec. 1, 1978, the Alaska brown bear was fair game for sports hunters except in Katmai and Glacier Bay National Monuments, a state sanctuary and one closed area tip of the Alaska Peninsula. Hunting of the big bear, largest land carnivore, is permitted in Kodiak National Wildlife Refuge. The President also added 1.87 million acres to Katmai and 550,000 acres to Glacier Bay. The Katmai addition is expected to assure a self-sustaining habitat for 200 to 300 brown bears. The species is found throughout much of Lake Clark National Monument, less frequently in Kenai, and numbers about 2,000 south of Katmai. Sport hunters took forty-eight bears on the Alaskan Peninsula in 1972.*

WIND CAVE NATIONAL PARK, South Dakota

Black-footed ferret—*This member of the weasel family is the rarest native wild mammal in North America. The ferret feeds on prairie dogs. These have been heavily poisoned to clear lands for farming or grazing. The prairie dog population fell sharply; the ferret has practically vanished. One ferret was seen outside the park in 1979. The species hasn't been seen inside the park for five years. The outlook for survival of the black-footed ferret is poor.*

ISLE ROYALE NATIONAL PARK, Michigan

Wolf—*Wolves crossed the ice to this island in Lake Superior in the 1940's, finding an abundance of moose. By 1957, Isle Royale had fifteen to twenty-five wolves. The island population of this endangered species is now close to ninety. Despite a high death rate among pups, the wolf benefits from the plentiful supply of moose. Except for some wolves in northern Minnesota, the Isle Royale population is the principal remnant of this species in the lower forty-eight.*

DEATH VALLEY NATIONAL MONUMENT, California-Nevada

Devil's Hole pupfish—*The warm pool in which this endangered species had been isolated for 20,000 years was proclaimed a sanctuary by President Truman in 1952. The pool area became a detached portion of the national monument. Pumping outside the sanctuary had threatened to lower the pool to a critical level. Protests halted the pumping; the pupfish population remained* stable. In June 1980 the count was 333. Then work started on nearby real estate subdivisions. The park recommended that applications of the builders for water permits be disapproved. Heavy withdrawal of water could lower the pupfish pool to a level fatal to the species.

BIG BEND NATIONAL PARK, Texas

Big Bend gambusia—*The world population of this tiny species was down to three fish in 1959 but now numbers more than 1,000. The fish was separated from the more aggressive common gambusia and was provided a pool of its own. A warm aquifer furnishes a high volume of fresh water.*

ROCKY MOUNTAIN NATIONAL PARK, Colorado

Greenback cutthroat trout—*Believed extinct in 1937 as the result of human tampering with its environment, the greenback was later found in two Colorado streams. In 1976, sixty-five greenback cutthroats were transplanted to the park's Bear Lake. The park population is one of nine which may save this endangered species.*

BISCAYNE NATIONAL MONUMENT, Florida

Green turtle, Hawksbill turtle—*Both of these endangered species are frequently observed in Biscayne National Monument. The park has few nesting grounds but 1980 brought the first nesting of sea turtles since the park was authorized in 1968. The manatee, Southern bald eagle and American crocodile are other endangered species in the park.*

PADRE ISLAND NATIONAL SEASHORE, Texas

Kemp's Ridley turtle—*The seashore is trying to prevent extinction of this endangered species. The turtle is native to Mexico where its survival is threatened by egg hunters and oil spills. The park contains a few natural nests of this species and is working with the National Marine Fisheries Laboratory in Galveston to hatch incubated eggs at the seashore.*

Arctic peregrine falcon—*The park is a stopover for the migrating arctic peregrine falcon. The park is considering designation of a critical habitat where this endangered species would be protected.*

YUKON-CHARLEY NATIONAL MONUMENT, Alaska

Arctic peregrine falcon—*The best nesting area for this bird in the United States extends along the Yukon River westward from the Canadian border. Most of the nests are in the new national monument. In 1973 only ten pairs were nesting. Pesticides, ingested by waterfowl which were consumed by the falcon, had an adverse effect on the falcon's reproduction. Pesticides controls proved effective, however. The count of nesting falcons increased to 11 pairs in 1975,*

12 in 1977, 16 in 1978 and 19 pairs in 1979. These 19 pairs reproduced 39 young. Fifteen of the 19 pairs and 33 of the young are in the national monument. In addition to these 63 falcons in the park along the Yukon, several more are believed active in the Charley River part of the park.

DINOSAUR NATIONAL MONUMENT, Colorado-Utah

American peregrine falcon—*The park has two aeries and is working on a recovery program for this endangered species. One pair fledged young in 1980.*

Colorado squawfish—*The upper Colorado River basin is the habitat of this endangered species. The fish may hold its own without further impoundments.*

Humpback chub—*This endangered species frequents the Yampa and Green Rivers. It needs free flowing conditions to assure survival.*

Bonytail chub—*The outlook for this endangered species in the Yampa and Green Rivers is poor. Any water impoundments would probably doom this fish.*

GRAND TETON NATIONAL PARK, Wyoming

American peregrine falcon—*The park is conducting a recovery program for this endangered species. Biologists set out "hack sites" which are falcon nests containing young falcons. The birds are expected to become imprinted with the nest location and form the nucleus of a permanent nesting population in the park.*

MOUNT RUSHMORE NATIONAL MEMORIAL, South Dakota

American peregrine falcon—*This park also has a recovery program in progress.*

ZION NATIONAL PARK, Utah

American peregrine falcon—*The endangered species is frequently seen here; the park keeps a monitoring record.*

CAPITOL REEF NATIONAL PARK, Utah

American peregrine falcon—*The park monitors the falcon flights.*

GLEN CANYON NATIONAL RECREATION AREA, Utah-Arizona

American peregrine falcon—*This park also has this rare species and monitors its flights.*

BIGHORN CANYON NATIONAL RECREATION AREA, Colorado-Wyoming

American peregrine falcon—*The falcon flies here and its visits are monitored.*

BLACK CANYON OF THE GUNNISON NATIONAL MONUMENT, Colorado

American peregrine falcon—*The park had a falcon nesting two years ago and is considered good falcon habitat.*

CHANNEL ISLANDS NATIONAL PARK, California

Brown pelican—*In 1970, West Anacapa Island was the only nesting site of the brown pelican in the western United States. Only one egg was hatched successfully. In 1974 NPS made the nesting site a research natural area off limits to all except nesting pelicans and the scientists studying them. In response to a park request, the state closed off the area to boating. DDT, which had caused thin eggshells, was outlawed, and by 1980 the brown pelicans were fledging 1,000 young. Nesting had spread to Santa Barbara Island where fifty young were hatched. The brown pelican is still an endangered species.*

Guadalupe fur seal—*The park is frequented by this rare species, once possibly near extinction in this country. Young males visit Anacapa Island for brief periods. The seal is an endangered species.*

GLACIER BAY NATIONAL MONUMENT, Alaska

Humpback whale—*Glacier Bay attracted twenty to twenty-four humpback whales every summer during the 1967-77 period. The number fell off in 1978, and in 1979 only three of this endangered species moved into the bay. A heavy increase in vessel traffic is believed to be a major factor in the decline. The park is increasing its research of the species. On June 1, 1980 a permit system was begun for small boats, limiting them to five per day, or a cumulative total of no more than fifteen a day. Permits are not required of commercial fishermen, charter boats and cruise ships. The bay has been a choice summer feeding location for this whale.*

CANAVERAL NATIONAL SEASHORE, Florida

Atlantic green turtle—*This national seashore, established in 1975, has one of the country's best nesting records for the endangered green turtle—eighteen nests in 1979 and eight by July 1 in 1980, including beaches of the adjoining Kennedy Space Center. Canaveral National Seashore also contains six other endangered species:*
West Indian (or Florida) manatee

Southern bald eagle
Brown pelican
Kemp's Ridley turtle
Arctic peregrine falcon
Atlantic hawksbill turtle *(one observed by Merritt Island National Wildlife Refuge)*

Canaveral also is a prime nesting site of the loggerhead turtle, a threatened species. Supervised small groups of visitors are allowed to witness the nocturnal nesting. The nest count is estimated at 2,700.

45

The Bureau of Land Management

Because he is an old friend and fellow worker in the wildlife vineyard, I asked Bureau of Land Management Information Officer, Charlie Most, to tell me about the role played by his agency in the Rare and Endangered Species program. Charlie's response follows:

The Bureau is actively involved in management of raptor habitat on public lands throughout the West. The Snake River Birds of Prey Area near Boise, a raptor area of national significance, is perhaps our best example of this involvement.

We are involved in the so-called 'foster parent' program, a coordinated effort with various States, the Fish and Wildlife Service, and Cornell University. The idea behind this program is that prairie falcons cannot tell peregrine eggs from their own (who can?); so peregrine eggs are placed in prairie falcon nests to be hatched and reared. The plan, of course, is to reestablish peregrine falcons in historical peregrine habitats. The idea has been used in the Snake River area we administer and in a couple of others, I believe. Cornell provides the eggs from their Colorado facility called 'Peregrine West.'

Also, millions of acres are being inventoried to identify essential raptor habitats and to come up with methods for mitigating impacts of energy development as well as any other action that might jeopardize raptors of their habitat.

Along these lines (no pun intended), we use right-of-way agreements to require energy companies to modify their transmission towers so eagles and other large birds that like to perch on them will not be electrocuted.

For specific facts and figures about Bureau of Land Management work on rare and endangered species, Charlie then turned me over to Dick Vernimen who is the Endangered Species Liaison Officer for BLM. Dick added the following information:

BLM administers 448 million acres of land within the eleven western states and Alaska (1976, BLM statistics). In addition, we are responsible for BLM-allowed actions taking place on the Outer Continental Shelf and Federally-owned subsurface minerals (i.e., coal, oil and gas, etc.). Hereinafter all of the above lands will be referred to as BLM-administered lands.

Within these vast acreages and areas of responsibility we must take into consideration the welfare of forty-eight threatened and endangered (T/E) animals (BLM Annual Wildlife Stat. Report 1977). The T/E animals occurring on the subsurface and Outer Continental Shelf (OCS) must also be considered if BLM-initiated actions affect a T/E species or its habitat (i.e. oil and gas impacts on marine mammals). A third category of species we must take into account are state T/E species. Our 1977 statistical report listed 138 species.

With the recent passage of the 1978 amendments to the Endangered Species Act of 1973 (ESA), proposed species must also be considered for formal consultation. A number of animals fell into this category.

Land Use

All actions that we allow on BLM-administered lands must be considered for impacts on threatened and endangered (i.e. oil and gas leases, land exchanges, grazing permits, pipelines, etc.).

The following figures were used for our fiscal year 1979 and 1980 budget that show actions requiring Section 7 consultation as per ESA of 1973.

—Energy—2500 leases (oil/gas, coal, geothermal)
—Timber—Sale of 1.25 billion board feet
—Grazing—Issuance of 24,000 use authorizations
—Wilderness—Completion of 55 studies
—State Selections—502,900 acres (excluding Alaska)
—Rights-of-way—1700 applications
—Mineral Leasing (Other)—63 million acres private, 290 million acres other Federal lands
—Other Land Actions—8,000 cases

The above are cases or actions readily identifiable. Each day we encounter new actions that require review.

Legislation and Authority

Authority—Sources:
A. Endangered Species Act of 1973 (16 USC 1531 et seq.) as amended.
B. Sikes Act, Title II (16 USC 670 et seq.).
C. National Environmental Policy Act (42 USC 4321 et seq.) as amended.
D. The Federal Land Policy and Management Act of October 21, 1976 (P.L. 94-579)
E. Departmental Manual 235.1.1.A., General Program Delegation Director, Bureau of Land Management.

The above Acts are our basis for developing and carrying out an endangered species program. The major thrust of our program is Section 7, compliance and inventory of habitat.

Section 7 of the ESA of 1973 directs all Federal agencies on how to comply with the Act. Procedures for this cooperation and consultation can be found in 50 CFR 402 or in the Federal Register, volume 43, pages 869-876, January 4, 1978.

The major contact on consultation for BLM is the Fish and Wildlife Service (FWS), but with our administrative responsibilities on the Outer Continental Shelf (OCS) we also consult with the National Marine Fisheries Service of the Department of Commerce. Since many of these OCS cases involve the high seas or foreign countries, we must also contact the State Department. As you can see, the Section 7 process can become highly involved and time consuming.

Because of the mandate placed upon us by Section 7 of the ESA of 1973, major emphasis in workload has been shifted to meet it. Budget increases were added to meet the need. This is a start, but we are working under pressure to meet the demand because of other priorities placed upon us such as the nation's energy needs.

Critical Habitat Inventory

The President's Environmental Message of May, 1978, requires the identification and determination of 'Critical Habitats' for endangered species to be accelerated.

The Secretary of the Interior is directing agencies to complete inventories and analyses for the determinations of 'Critical Habitats' for species on their lands by January 1, 1980.

We have thirty-two of the known species of animals officially listed on public lands. We have been given increased funds to complete this job. Inventories for some species are fairly simple since their respective habitats are small and centralized. The work begins when we look at species such as the bald eagle or the American peregrine falcon. Habitats of these species are broad and expansive, requiring many man-hours to complete inventories. Our participation on recovery teams has helped to cut this workload down.

Present Capabilities To Comply With The ESA of 1973

As of November 11, 1978, the BLM has 249 fisheries and wildlife biologists on board. The breakdown by numbers and areas is as follows:

Washington, D.C.	6	Nevada	22
Denver Service Center	5	New Mexico	15
Alaska	9	Oregon	35
Arizona	18	Utah	22
California	23	Wyoming	18
Colorado	22	Outer Continental	
Eastern States	3	Shelf	3
Idaho	22		
Montana	26	Total	249

Within the total of 249 biologists only two could be listed as working totally endangered species and that is stretching it. We all have other duties as assigned. I myself function as the lead in Washington on non-game species as well as endangered species liaison officer. Mr. Ken Walker, Endangered Plant Coordinator will cover the number of botanists we have working on plants.

Summary

Intensified public concern for our environment and the flora and fauna within it has created a demand for all levels of government to engage in active and positive programs to stem the tide of wildlife extinction. We have embarked on an ambitious program to protect and benefit endangered wildlife. Many of our avenues to success are clouded by complex, competitive demands on endangered species habitat by other resource uses and the nation's need for energy. Unraveling ecological complexities to isolate and solve habitat related problems is not a simple task. Funding and manpower are not available to meet all needs. Despite these difficulties and constraints, we are devoting our best efforts and energy in trying to insure that no additional plant or animal becomes either endangered or extinct on public lands.

46

The Role of Zoos

About 1959 or 1960, the U.S. Fish and Wildlife Service sent me to the San Antonio (Texas) zoo to help with a problem of controlling commensal rodents, primarily the roof rat, whose hungry hordes consumed about half of the food put out for birds and animals exhibited in the zoo.

I was appalled at the size of the rat population and suggested to Fred Stark, the head man, that he use zinc phosphide treated baits to knock the population down to a manageable size; then use anticoagulants in permanent stations to keep the population down.

Mr. Stark looked at me with a quizzical expression and asked, "What effect will zinc phosphide have on that big white bird over there?" The big white bird was a whooping crane! I had to admit that I had no idea (nor did anyone else) what effect zinc phosphide would have on a whooping crane. Mr. Stark added, "And we don't dare find out, do we?"

Screening out and "building out" the rats was tried to the utmost in San Antonio's zoo, but with little success. We didn't dare use any chemical agents, and without chemical controls it is almost impossible to control rodents in a zoo environment.

Let's look at the contributions made by zoo people in the field of captive propagation of some of the world's rarest species. Hoofed animals from Asia and Africa have long been successfully propagated in zoos in Europe and America. In a few cases, progeny from these zoo animals have been reintroduced into the wild with good results. There are a few species which would have been extinct if it had not been for the pen-reared individuals which augmented their depleted ranks.

When the plight of the Trumpeter swan first aroused national interest, there were many debates over the question of whether or not to give mated pairs of swans to the zoos in the hope that they could be propagated in captivity. The signal success enjoyed by the zoo people with the trumpeters is well-known. Injured and flightless birds cannot migrate up and down the migration paths, but they can reproduce their own kind and the young **can** fly!

The fact that a female condor in the National Zoo in Washington, D.C. laid many eggs lent credence to the suggestion that we rear condors in captivity. Experimentation with the similar Andean condor has proved that artificial propagation of California condors is their best hope for survival. Nene geese raised in captivity in England provided stock for reintroduction into native habitats in Hawaii; thus saving the genes in captivity for use in the wild.

On the other hand, we had a whooper in San Antonio and another in the New Orleans zoo. McNulty's excellent book on whooping cranes details the trials and tribulations standing in the way of a romance for these birds. Also, consider the inability of the pandas in the National Zoo to procreate.

Captive propagation is a means to an end in the fight for endangered species, never an end in itself. But our cause owes much to the hard-won experience and the careful attention to detail which has been exhibited by zoo people. Lessons learned in cages have proved applicable to the wider field of free-flying and free-ranging species.

We have wildlife species whose habitat has been so severely altered that there is, literally, no place for them in the wild. These species can survive in zoos or in wildlife sanctuaries of greater size. In some cases these are the only places where they can survive! Thus, the zoo serves as a repository for the genes which would be in peril of extermination outside of the zoo's protective mesh. Perhaps the day will come when those genes can be "turned loose" again to play their part in experimentation along the multi-faceted pathways of evolutionary development.

The knowledge gained in zoos is helping us to propagate the Texas red wolf, the Puerto Rican parrot, the Trumpeter swan, the Aleutian goose, the masked bobwhite quail and many other species.

Trumpeter Swans

47

Confrontation Tactics

The needs of endangered species and of man often meet in head-on collision. Human beings have put their lives on the line in defense of endangered species with a fervor and zeal often associated with religions. We have seen people operate a flimsy rubber inflatable boat out on the high seas, deliberately courting martyrdom by interposing their own defenseless craft between the whaling boat and the endangered whale. They risked being run over and drowned on the high seas where there is very little police protection, and they knew that their slayers would probably go unpunished because no court would claim jurisdiction.

We have seen other friends of the whales deliberately ram their ship into the side of a whale-processing ship, stopping it from its murderous task by brute force—in defiance of all civil and criminal laws.

Much more often the confrontation takes the form of a shouting match between opposing viewpoints at a public hearing concerning plans affecting the endangered species. Sometimes this is an argument between people who own land that awaits development and people who fear that such development will sound the death knell for a wild species. Where your sympathies lie depends almost entirely upon whose ox is being gored.

If you stand to reap a profit from the development, you are apt to refer to your opponents as "little old ladies in tennis shoes" or as "dicky bird lovers" who oppose PROGRESS. If you are siding with the endangered species, you are apt to refer to your opponents as "robber barons" or callous money worshipers who advocate DESTRUCTION of the wild. In most of these discussions, we generate more heat than light. Even if the parties to the discussion are calm, cool and reasonable scientists, there is still room for diametrically opposing views to surface. They usually do.

Picture a classic confrontation forty-five miles south of our nation's capitol. On one side are those who have the interests of the bald eagle at heart; people who feel that the preservation of our national bird is of over-riding importance. Obviously, these are outdoorsy people, sincere people, altruistic people.

Their opponents are those who want to build a park in the preferred habitat of the bald eagle. This park will be a learning laboratory where the values of wildlife preservation are taught. These people want to preserve a bit of the wild country which still remains in pristine state. Obviously, these are outdoorsy people, sincere people, altruistic people.

The park proponents point out that there is only one pair of nesting eagles now using the 2,500 acre tract donated by philanthropist Ann Smoot. That's true. The park opponents point out that as many as forty-five eagles winter there. That's true, too.

The Bald Eagle Recovery Team includes officials of the Fish and Wildlife Service, a part of the Department of the Interior. They fear that the army of picnickers resulting from creation of the park would frighten away the largest gathering of bald eagles on the east coast. And that's true, too!

The park developers seek a grant from the Heritage Conservation people, who are part of the Department of the Interior. They point out that development of a swimming pool, hiking trails and the preservation of the virgin forest are assuredly worthwhile projects for the expenditure of Interior's Heritage Conservation funds. Says Virginia's Ronald Sutton, "We want to preserve the virgin hardwood forest, and we want to let people come and walk in that forest." His words ring true. Then he adds, "The needs of eagles and people are directly opposite. The eagle needs solitude." And those words also ring true.

The moral of this dilemma in Virginia's King George County is that we cannot have a concentration of wintering eagles and a concentration of people in the same area. Must we choose between two deserving objectives? Can we find another place for the park? Will the eagles find another place if we push them away by development? What's your opinion?

One would think that every American would be in favor of the reintroduction of the whooping crane into its former range. Once that was true. Now, not everyone is in favor of increasing the range of the whooper. The State Game and Fish Department of New Mexico, which has worked hard for the whooping crane, is now worrying that it might have made a bad decision. You see, when the whoopers begin to spread their wintering range from the present miniscule spot on and near the Bosque del Apache National Wildlife Refuge, a large part of the state might be closed to activities such as waterfowl hunting that might imperil the endangered whoopers.

Is the state justified in curtailing a vast recreational opportunity for its citizens in order to propagate a bird which has no economic value to wildlife and which is never likely to be of sport or commercial importance?

Several states in the Rocky Mountain region (and elsewhere) are having second thoughts about the reintroduction of endangered species of fish. Based upon the Endangered Species and the Critical Habitat legislation, there may be more federal regulations governing sport fishing which adversely affect the state's ability to produce good wholesome outdoor recreation on state waterways. Does this mean that the endangered species can only be saved to exhibit in small areas or to keep in zoos? Just exactly that attitude may result. Perhaps the maxim "You can't go home again!" is correct.

Confrontation tactics seldom result in progress on either front. There are no winners in these environmental confrontations, only varying degrees of defeat. Far better the compromise which gains something for the species concerned than the direct confrontation which hardens the positions of both sides and leads to further wars and further degrees of defeat. When there is a possibility of finding a middle ground, that is the way to go.

48

Endangered Species Organizations

There are literally hundreds of organizations which have impact upon endangered species wildlife programs in North America. Some are composed of professionals in the field of wildlife management whose sole purpose may be the preservation of one species, or the simple furtherance of research into that species' problems. Others are composed of militant laymen who support their cause with a devotion bordering on fanaticism.

Some are publicly spirited and are composed of devoted conservationists. Some—very few—are interested in self-glorification, or are organized to guarantee the salary of their leaders.

Some are known for their long history of accomplishment, such as the Audubon Society, the National Wildlife Federation, the Wildlife Management Institute and the Izaak Walton League. These were fighting for endangered species, directly or indirectly, long before the fight became popular. Others are Johnny-come-latelies who have arrived on the scene to fill a particular niche in the newly aroused public awareness of the plight of the endangered.

Some emphasize fund-raising, for all organizations need funds; some merely want to guarantee the salaries of their leaders. Others emphasize political action and letter-writing campaigns to exert pressure on our lawmakers for or against a particular piece of legislation. Some are ultra-conservative and careful to have the facts to back up their statements; others are emotional and prone to shooting from the hip without adequate data to back up their claims to further the enactment of their proposals.

If you wish to enter the fight for endangered species, study the matter carefully before making your decision as to whether or not to join a particular crusade. Look for a record of accomplishment, not for an emotional approach. Beware of the organization whose sole function seems to be fundraising, and always study the record of how they spend their funds.

Talk to others who share your interests; see what their opinion of the organization is before you decide to join. Study the reports of congressional hearings on matters of import to endangered species. See if the organization provided testimony before those committees. The biggest, most influential, most respectable organizations are very active in this arena. It pays big dividends to wildlife.

Look before you leap onto the membership rolls. To help you in your search, here is a partial listing of organizations:

AMERICAN FISHERIES SOCIETY

5410 Grosvenor Lane
Bethesda, Maryland 20014   Telephone: 301-897-8616

The American Fisheries Society has been representing North American fisheries scientists for 110 years. Their 8,000 professional members include a special Endangered Species Committee dedicated to the identification, range determination, protection and better public understanding of rare, threatened and endangered species of North American finfish. In 1979, the Society published the first-ever comprehensive, illustrated report on rare, threatened and endangered freshwater species of Canada and the United States. This publication is still the best of its kind available to students of endangered species of fish.

AMERICAN SOCIETY OF ICHTHYOLOGISTS AND HERPETOLOGISTS

Department of Biological Sciences
Florida Atlantic University
Boca Raton, Florida 33431

The American Society of Ichthyologists and Herpetologists is dedicated to the study and conservation of fishes, amphibians, and reptiles. Several members of this society are conducting active research on rare and endangered species. Moreover, our Environmental Quality Committee has been very active in providing written supportive commentary to agencies on proposals dealing with rare and endangered species and the listing of Critical Habitat. This committee has also been active in opposing proposals that would weaken the Endangered Species Act of 1973.

AMERICAN SOCIETY OF MAMMALOGISTS

c/o Daniel F. Williams
California State College, Stanislaus
Turlock, CA 95380

The American Society of Mammalogists is a professional, non-profit organization with a membership of more than 4,000 scientists. The principal objective of the Society is to promote the sciences of mammalogy. This is accomplished by: (1) publication of information on mammals—original research in the Journal of Mammalogy, longer research or review papers in Special Publications and summaries of the biology of mammals in Mammalian Species; (2) holding an annual meeting where the results of research on mammals is presented, and where persons interested in mammals meet; and (3) aiding research through the award of small grants and honoraria, and through a great variety of other activities. The society is dedicated to the conservation of all wildlife species, and serves as a source of information and an impartial counselor on issues pertaining to conservation of mammals through its committees on conservation of land mammals and on marine mammals. Official stands on conservation issues are articulated through resolutions adopted by the society. The society promotes research and disseminates knowledge of all mammal species, and gives special consideration to publication of accounts of rare and endangered species in *Mammalian Species*.

AUDUBON SOCIETY

8940 Jones Mill Road   (also the national & state chapters)
Washington, D.C. 20015   301-652-9188

The Audubon Naturalist Society of the Central Atlantic States, founded in 1897, is one of the original independent Audubon societies. Throughout its history, the society has engaged in activities to protect birds and other wildlife and to increase public awareness of environmental problems. Recognizing that changes in bird populations indicate environmental changes, the society for many years has sponsored annual bald eagle surveys, Christmas bird counts, and nesting bird surveys to monitor threatened and endangered species in this area. The society also supported Lawrence Zeleny's censusing and restoration efforts for the threatened Eastern Bluebird and sponsored publication of his well-known book, *The Bluebird*. The monthly *Audubon Naturalist News*, free public seminars, and environmental education courses for people of all ages aim to heighten public awareness of habitat destruction and its effects upon wildlife. This past year, the society's conservation committee spoke out on park development plans that would have negative ecological impact; monitored threats to bald eagle nests along the Potomac River and Chesapeake Bay; and contacted Maryland, Virginia, and Delaware congressmen to urge their vote for reauthorization of the Endangered Species Act.

CHIHUAHUAN DESERT RESEARCH INSTITUTE

P.O. Box 1334
Alpine, TX 79830

The Chihuahuan Desert Research Institute has been actively seeking out data relating to the peregrine falcon in West Texas, New Mexico and Mexico since 1974. Research in this area has focused on nesting, courtship, behavior and migration. CDRI is also documenting the status and life histories of the Thick-billed and Maroon-fronted parrots in Mexico. In addition, preliminary studies are in process on the status of twenty-six potentially endangered plants in the West Texas region.

CONSERVATION AND RESEARCH FOUNDATION

7615 Cabin Road
Bethesda, Maryland 20034

The Conservation and Research Foundation has been attempting to deploy its modest resources, which have averaged about $15,000 per year over the last seven years, in as catalytic a way as possible toward the preservation of the environment. Habitat preservation has been a high priority. Operating grants have been made to the Nature Conservancy during its formative years and, more recently, to the Vermont Natural Areas Program and the Latin American Natural Areas Program. A book on the legal aspects of the preservation of open land has been published, and specific natural area projects in California, Connecticut, New York, Pennsylvania, Rhode Island, and Costa Rica have been supported. A grant was made to the New York Botanical Garden to underwrite the development of a tissue culture laboratory for the propagation of rare and endangered plants—especially orchids. In an even more fundamental way, the Foundation has been attempting to help modify human attitudes and destructive attitudes which create the endangered species problem. Grants have been made to the Institute for Ecology, which addresses basic ecological problems at the regional and global levels and to the Council on Economic Priorities. At the international level, research leading to the publication of Lynton K. Caldwell's *In Defense of Earth,* written for the United Nations Stockholm Conference on the Human Environment, was funded, as was the computer processing of information regarding the world's non-governmental organizations supporting the United Nations Environment Programme.

DEFENDERS OF WILDLIFE

1244 Nineteenth Street N.W.
Washington, D.C. 20036   202-659-9510

The Defenders of Wildlife maintains a strong interest in the field of endangered wildlife. To this end, it seeks to strengthen and support the government's program to implement the Endangered Species Act of 1973. This includes encouraging restoration of species, enforcement programs, habitat acquisition and protection, and consultation (pursuant to Section 7 of the Endangered Species Act) to ensure that federal activities do not jeopardize the existence of endangered species or neither destroy nor modify critical habitat. It researches and drafts petitions for the listing of wildlife species believed to be endangered or threatened. In addition, it has been actively involved in supporting the reauthorization of the Endangered Species Act in Congress and opposing weakening amendments to this law. Finally, it has sent delegates to the meeting of the Convention on International Trade in Endangered Species including the original convention to draft the treaty, and has taken an active role in supporting the concepts embodied in this document.

DESERT FISHES COUNCIL

407 West Line Street
Bishop, CA 93514

This organization, dedicated to the preservation of America's desert fishes, and established in 1970, was the outgrowth of deep concern by a group of laymen, biologists, scientists and administrators over the serious threat to the native fishes of the Death Valley region, California-Nevada. Of primary interest then were the pupfishes of the genus *Cyprinodon*, especially the unique Devils Hole Pupfish, an endangered species. The basic purpose of the Council is to provide for the exchange and transmittal of information on the status, protection and management of the desert fishes and their habitat.

ELSA WILD ANIMAL APPEAL

5000 Lankershim Boulevard, Suite 10
North Hollywood, CA 91601   213-769-8388

The Elsa Wild Animal Appeal works to protect rare and endangered North American wildlife through a massive nationwide educational program, the Elsa Clubs of America, involving thousands of school-age young people in learning about and working to help our wildlife to survive. EWAA also purchases vital wildlife habitat for threatened species, works with state, local, national and international agencies on behalf of wildlife and natural habitat, and acts in close cooperation with other organizations to protect our world's wildlife from extinction. EWAA supports worthwhile research and educational programs to benefit our national environment and wildlife, and works to prevent inhumane and cruel treatment of wild animals. EWAA claims to have rendered assistance to the following endangered species of wildlife in the recent past: Tule elk, bald eagle, peregrine falcon, Florida key deer, sea otter, whales, brown pelican, timber wolf, red wolf, manatee and northern fur seal.

EWAA also lists aid to native wildlife species such as the coyote, cougar, porpoises, herons, wading birds and the common loon.

ENVIRONMENTAL DEFENSE FUND

475 Park Avenue South
New York, N.Y. 10016   212-686-4191

Water resource legal cases brought by EDF opposing projects to drain wetlands or dam and channel rivers have helped preserve habitats, including some essential to endangered species.

Efforts to prevent use of pesticides such as mirex, DDT, aldrin, dieldrin, heptachlor, chlordane and endrin have reduced their damage to birds, fish and other non-target species. EDF has also confronted threats to particular species, with emphasis on the protection of marine mammals, including activity in defense of whales on the international scene. EDF seeks to assure that ecologically sound principles govern wildlife management programs, and emphasizes the need to protect non-game as well as game species.

ENVIRONMENTAL FUND

1302 Eighteenth Street N.W.
Washington, D.C. 20036   202-293-2548

President Justin Blackwelder gave me the following statement with regard to the Environmental Fund: "The danger to 'endangered' species is man and his numbers. If the human population continues to double every thirty-five years, many species of life face almost immediate extinction. Of course, many, from the mastodon to the carrier pigeon, are already gone. That is our message."

FRIENDS OF ANIMALS, INC.

11 West 60th Street
New York, N.Y. 10023   212-247-8120

Friends of Animals approaches the rare and endangered species issue as an integral part of the overall wilderness policy of the United States. Because of this, FOA has gone to court to fight habitat manipulation under the Pittman-Robertson Act which manipulates wilderness to artificially stimulate hunted species that cause commensurate loss to other species, including those considered rare. Friends of Animals has also been appointed, and participated in, the Convention on International Trade in Endangered Species (CITES).

INTERNATIONAL CRANE FOUNDATION

City View Road
Baraboo, Wisconsin 53913   608-356-9462

The ICF, located in Baraboo, Wisconsin, is the world center for the study and preservation of cranes. Here a worldwide effort is coordinated to meet the following goals: research, habitat preservation, captive propagation, restocking and public education. Both sandhill and whooping cranes, the only two crane species native in North America, are to be found. Particular attention is being given to propagation of the whooping crane. Photoperiodicity, the courtship dance ritual, imprinting implications and special diet are some of the factors considered in the research on whooping crane breeding. The "foster parent" program between sandhill and whooping cranes in Idaho will serve as a model for a similar program to be tried in the Soviet Union. Public education concerning the birds and their habitats is a major part of the ICF program, with tours given by appointment only to more than 6,000 people each year.

INTERNATIONAL WILD WATERFOWL ASSOCIATION, INC.

Box 1075
Jamestown, North Dakota 58401

Founded in September of 1958, their official history says that the organization was formed by a group of farsighted aviculturists, conservationists and ornithologists. Their first president was Jean Delacour, one of the most famed of all ornithologists. Famed waterfowl artist Peter Scott of England became a vice president. In the first years of this organization, it became actively involved in efforts to save the whooping crane and the Trumpeter swan. It was through the efforts of aviculturists that the captive propagation of Trumpeter swans was so successful. This organization pushed for captive propagation of Nene geese, and can claim some credit for that successful program at the Wildfowl Trust in Slimbridge, England. They have continued to assist in programs for the Aleutian goose, the New Mexican duck and other species which can be propagated in captivity.

IZAAK WALTON LEAGUE OF AMERICA, INC.

1800 North Kent Street, Suite 806
Arlington, Virginia 22209   703-528-1818

The IWLA is a non-profit conservation organization of more than 50,000 members dedicated to the conservation of our natural resources. The League promotes endangered species protection through its continuing support for a strong federal Endangered Species Act and for ample funding and aggressive implementation of the endangered species program. The League fought for years to protect the endangered snail darter in the Little Tennessee River by attempting to permanently halt construction of the Tellico Dam. The League also campaigns for many other programs that contribute to protection of endangered species habitat, such as full funding for the Land and Water Conservation Fund, which is used to acquire habitat under the Endangered Species Act; expansion and the successful operation of the national wildlife refuge system; and establishment of a National Heritage program that would identify endangered species and their habitat throughout the nation. The League educates its membership and the public to the needs of endangered species protection in its bi-monthly magazine, *Outdoor America*, and the newsletter, *Izaak Walton News*.

NATIONAL WILDLIFE FEDERATION

1412 16th Street N.W.
Washington, D.C.   202-797-6800

The National Wildlife Federation's involvement with threatened or endangered species covers a wide range of activities from broad educational programs to specific habitat acquisition. The Federation has produced and distributed numerous publications about endangered species, including booklets, wildlife notes and feature articles in NWF's three magazines. For example, in 1974, an entire issue of National Wildlife was devoted to endangered species, and the NWF established the Raptor Information Center, providing many services to professionals involved with protecting birds of prey, some of which are endangered. NWF now is in the process of establishing a comparable Feline Information Center, which will prove equally valuable for wildlife professionals who manage the world's cats. For the bald eagle alone, NWF has produced (1) a feature film, "We Can Save the Eagle", (2) acquired four refuges totaling 2,275 acres of prime eagle roosting habitat, (3) coordinated a national population survey, and (4) provided $500 rewards (eleven to date) for information leading to the conviction of persons having killed bald eagles. Staff members of the Federation have maintained close liaison with federal and state wildlife agencies regarding endangered species issues and management decisions. NWF has also lobbied vigorously to protect the Endangered Species Act, and participated in international affairs (such as the International Whaling Commission meetings and the CITES meetings). NWF attorneys have been involved in litigation to protect the habitat of endangered species, and pioneered a new method of resolving endangered species conflicts through mediation. This involved the timber management of a small section of the Francis Marion National Forest, believed to be the habitat of the elusive Bachman's warbler. In addition, every year the National Wildlife Federation awards research fellowships to postgraduate students for their work with threatened or endangered species.

NATURE CONSERVANCY

1800 North Kent Street
Arlington, VA 22209   703-841-5300

The Nature Conservancy is a national, non-profit, membership conservation organization. Over 1.5 million acres throughout the United States have been preserved through the efforts of the Conservancy since its founding in 1950.

The Conservancy takes immediate action to preserve land and wildlife, sometimes stepping in and buying irreplaceable lands to save them from commercial development and then turning over management of those lands to private or public entities best suited to further the work of protecting the natural values. Funded by membership dues, individual contributions and foundation grants, the Conservancy provides a revolving fund available for emergency action to be repaid by local fundraising. Because the Conservancy can act more quickly than can a governmental agency, the Conservancy has been able to step in and buy land in advance of governmental needs—often with considerable savings to the taxpayer.

OCEANIC SOCIETY

Fort Mason
San Francisco, CA 94123   415-441-1104

The Oceanic Society is a 65,000 member non-profit environmental organization dedicated to wise management of the world's oceans and the organisms which inhabit those oceans.

Some of the Society's activities relative to education and protection of cetaceans and pinnipeds include whale watching trips through which it has introduced more than ten thousand people to the wonders of the migrating gray whale. In addition it has sponsored or supported research on whale and dolphin behavior in a number of the world's oceans. Through the pages of its magazine, *Oceans,* it endeavors to make people aware of the plight of the world's whales. Practically every issue of the magazine carries some information relative to the protection of the whales or the status of the various species of whales.

PROJECT JONAH

Box 40280
San Francisco, CA 94140

Project Jonah is a non-profit, tax exempt international society devoted to the protection and understanding of all species of Cetacea: whales, dolphins and porpoises. "We will continue to encourage and conduct live observational research with wild, free-living whales and dolphins, and to work diligently for the establishment of marine sanctuaries for them throughout the world."

RARE ANIMAL RELIEF EFFORT, INC.

National Audubon Society
950 Third Avenue
New York, N.Y. 10022   212-832-3200

This was developed to aid programs carried out for the protection of endangered species and habitat, especially in tropical America, the oceans, and developing countries. Supported by contributions from the general public, this tax-exempt organization is run almost entirely by volunteers.

SIERRA CLUB

530 Bush Street
San Francisco, CA 94108

The Sierra Club believes that the key to wildlife conservation is the continued existence of diverse, non-degraded ecosystems. The club is committed to maintaining the world's remaining natural ecosystems and to restoring to a natural condition those ecosystems which are presently degraded. Wildlife is an essential component of these ecosystems, as well as a barometer of the well-being of the total biosphere. The better wildlife can be maintained in all its abundance and diversity, the better the habitat for all life on earth and the greater our ecological choices for the future. No species should be allowed to become extinct due to man's influence if it is within the power of man to prevent it. Every effort must be made to prevent any species from becoming threatened, and to restore to optimum populations those species that are currently threatened, endangered, or in unnatural decline.

SOCIETY OF TYMPANUCHUS CUPIDO PINNATUS, LTD.

Box 737
Milwaukee, Wisconsin 53201

This society has been in existence almost 20 years and is comprised of people throughout the country who are interested in trying to save the prairie chicken from extinction. Through the efforts and contributions of some 1200 members, it has recovered more than 10,000 acres of land in Wisconsin, which is managed by the Wisconsin Department of Natural Resources for that purpose. It is happy to report that the project is proving successful and hopes that in time it will find its flock growing ever larger.

SPORT FISHING INSTITUTE

608 Thirteenth Street N.W. Suite 801
Washington, D.C. 20005   202-737-0668

Many years ago the Sport Fishing Institute gave a pioneering grant to Dr. James Deacon, University of Nevada at Las Vegas, to study the status of pupfish and to develop the concept of natural refugia in the desert area. This led directly to the Bureau of Land Management pupfish conservation program. Since that time the Sport Fishing Institute has cooperated with the Endangered Species committee of the American Fisheries Society.

URBAN WILDLIFE RESEARCH CENTER, INC.

4500 Sheppard Lane
Ellicott City, Maryland 21043   301-596-9111

The Urban Wildlife Research Center conducts research and develops planning methodologies that will help urban residents, planners, land developers, and managers to provide and maintain optimal conditions for wildlife in urban and suburban areas. Its research program is concerned with wildlife in a broad sense, and includes aquatic and terrestrial animals and the habitats in which they live. Any rare and endangered animal found to occur in urban, suburban and urbanizing environments would receive its primary attention. In addition to urban development, the Center is interested in the effects of other types of development on wildlife—highways, mining, the channelization of streams, construction of reservoirs and power plants—all of which might affect endangered species as well as the more common forms of wildlife.

WHALE CENTER

3929 Piedmont Avenue
Oakland, CA 94611   415-654-4892

Responding to the need for a resource and action headquarters directly involved in international and domestic cetacean affairs, the Whale Center provides a focus for whale conservation, education and research activities. Its participation in whale policy formation both in the United States and abroad is strengthened by affiliation with the Whale Protection Fund of Washington, D.C. and by qualification for observer status with the International Whaling Commission. The outlook is global, the tone positive.

WILDLIFE SOCIETY

7101 Wisconsin Avenue N.W. Suite 611
Washington, D.C. 20014   301-986-8700

Founded in 1937, the Wildlife Society is a professional, non-profit organization dedicated to the wise management and conservation of the wildlife resources of the world. Ecology is the primary scientific discipline of the wildlife profession. The interests of the Society, therefore, embrace the interactions of all organisms with their natural environment.

The principal objectives of the Society are: to develop and promote sound stewardship of wildlife resources and of the environments upon which wildlife and man depend; to undertake an active role in preventing man-induced environmental degradation; to increase awareness and appreciation of wildlife values, and to seek the highest standards in all activities of the wildlife profession.

The Society's membership of nearly 10,000 is comprised of research scientists, educators, communications specialists, law enforcement officers, resource managers and administrators from more than seventy countries of the world.

WILD CANID SURVIVAL AND RESEARCH CENTER

P.O. Box 20528
St. Louis, Missouri 63139   314-645-4488

A non-profit organization which functions as an informational clearinghouse and educational facility to promote the preservation of all North American threatened and endangered species with emphasis on the wolf. Membership, 1,000.

WILDERNESS WATCH

Box 3184
Green Bay, Wisconsin 54303   414-499-9131

Wilderness Watch has monitored the U.S. Forest Service management of the breeding areas of the Bald Eagle in national forests of Wisconsin and the Upper Peninsula of Michigan. Wilderness Watch has offered management advice and has resorted to court action to protect this species.

WORLD WILDLIFE FUND

1601 Connecticut Avenue N.W.
Washington, D.C. 20009   202-387-0800

World Wildlife Fund is a private non-profit international conservation organization dedicated to preserving endangered and threatened species and their habitats throughout the world and to protect the biological resources upon which human well-being depends. Within this global framework, World Wildlife Fund-U.S. focuses on endangered and threatened animals and plants and on the land and sea environments upon which they depend, particularly in the Western hemisphere. Current conservation activities in North America might include offering support to the Alaska Coalition, conducting or supporting projects related to the Endangered Species Act, study of the effects of toxic substances on certain habitats and species, protection of whales and the development of cetacean sanctuaries, captive breeding and release into the wild of peregrine falcons, protection of migratory birds, sea turtles, the California condor and the California sea otter, among others. Ongoing is the active support of the Convention on International Trade in Endangered Species (CITES). This year WWF-US established TRAFFIC-USA to monitor import and export of endangered species and of species potentially endangered by trade, and to lend its support to strengthening the regulatory efforts of U.S. agencies in this regard.

In the past the World Wildlife Fund was among those instrumental in the development of the international polar bear treaty. WWF-US also helped initiate studies of the Florida manatee and the Florida cougar; responsibility for these projects was later assumed by state and federal agencies.

Acknowledgements

It is impossible for any one man, in one lifetime, to amass a thorough and complete book on endangered species. One man's efforts could never encompass this variegated field; rather, the task must be to distill data from thousands of researchers and managers into one volume.

My greatest concern in writing this book was the development of an ethic concerning the future of animal species other than man. This ethic development necessarily preceded the collection of information. For this writer, developing that ethic has been a lifelong process, aided and influenced and guided by hundreds of devoted wildlifers, none of whom ever intended to be my teacher.

To acknowledge the help of all those whose lore I have profited from would require a separate book even larger than this volume. But I must single out for special thanks a few people who had much to do with this book, even though some of them never even knew such a book was in the making.

First, I must acknowledge the unquestioning support and understanding I have always received from Elida, my wife of nearly four decades and my partner for life. Then I must thank my daughter Mrs. Marie Hodges, who is so much more than a typist for me. She has always been an alter ego, a person who knows what I mean when I fail to make it clear. She is the person who puts in commas when I forget, and who takes out apostrophes when I throw them, willy-nilly, into the manuscript. My editors thank her, for she has produced the copy upon which they began.

In my salad days, I was taught a deep-seated admiration for wildlife by three old time Game Management Agents. All three would scoff at the idea that they had inculcated value standards, but they did just that. Harry A. Jensen was my first contact with the field of professional wildlife management, and thus influenced me more than any other. Steve Creech and Harry Maltby, also Game Management Agents, were not very far behind.

There were many other professional wildlifers who helped me. Naming some must slight others, but I must mention John Gatlin, Regional Director for more years than any other Fish and Wildlife Service employee. John taught me while he gave me the run of a huge region, stretching from Yellowstone Park to Port Arthur, Texas, and from Yuma, Arizona to Tulsa, Oklahoma.

Keith Schreiner, whom I worked with in the North Dakota State Game and

Fish Department in the early 1950's and who went on to rise through the federal ranks to head the office of Endangered Species; and Ray Buller, a tough-minded completely honest professional waterfowl man—these were my closest hunting and fishing partners for some years. I lost many arguments to Keith, and Ray probably added more common sense to those campfire discussions than the other two of us put together. Ray sticks up for his principles, and his peers account him a good wildlifer who is intellectually honest.

Jack Hemphill, who taught me more about fisheries management than I could have learned in a university, was an innovative thinker back in the days when fisheries management on Indian lands was in its infancy. Using imaginative techniques in fisheries work and in raising money for fisheries projects, Jack accomplished much for several species of endangered fishes.

Of all who deal with endangered wildlife, perhaps the most important are the managers of the national wildlife refuges. Without these inviolate sanctuaries, many endangered species would have long gone through the pale.

There have been hundreds of wildlife managers who have helped me and taught me, more often by example than by words. I'd like to thank a special few: Marcus Nelson, Jim Harmon, Julian Howard, Earl Benham, Don Redfearn, Lynn Greenwalt (now Director of the Fish and Wildlife Service) and Wayne Gueswel. To them, and to all the men and women of the Division of Wildlife Refuges, and to all the members of the Recovery Teams who have helped me so much, I extend my sincere thanks.

And lastly, I want to thank four school teachers who kept on telling me that a book such as this would help them to teach the plight of endangered wildlife. Without their urging, I would not have started, much less completed, this book.

Index

ALSO BY CHUCK CADIEUX—

GOOSE HUNTING

Lively, personal stories of goose hunting from Quebec to Mexico are interwoven with an encyclopedia of facts about good management and good goose watching. Types of geese, migration paths, banding, kinds of decoys, goose calling, and controversial short stopping are all discussed with warmth and humor. "Anyone else thinking about writing on the subject ought to look at Cadieux's book before starting."—Washington Post.
208 pgs., fully illustrated, clothbound. $18.95 postpaid

AND FOR THE ENVIRONMENTALIST—

BACKWOODS ETHICS:
Environmental Concerns for Hikers and Campers

by Laura and Guy Waterman. "...undeniably important. They argue that hikers and backpackers must protect natural resources and maintain the 'spirit of wildness' of our country's backwoods...they describe a new code of backwoods ethics they feel is necessary to accommodate the increasing number of hikers in the wilds."—*Publishers Weekly*. Positive and up-beat, this book documents progress while appealing to a raised natural consciousness.
192 pgs., paperback. $8.95 postpaid

If these titles are unavailable through your bookstore, please send us your check or money order along with your printed name, mailing address and ZIP. Ask for our brochure of other outdoor books. Thank you!

STONE WALL PRESS, INC.
1241 30th Street, N.W., Washington, D.C. 20007